THE EGYPTIAN SOCIAL CONTRACT

For my mother, Yuta Shechter

THE EGYPTIAN SOCIAL CONTRACT

A History of State–Middle Class Relations

Relli Shechter

EDINBURGH
University Press

Edinburgh University Press is one of the leading university presses in the UK. We publish academic books and journals in our selected subject areas across the humanities and social sciences, combining cutting-edge scholarship with high editorial and production values to produce academic works of lasting importance. For more information visit our website: edinburghuniversitypress.com

© Relli Shechter, 2023

Edinburgh University Press Ltd
The Tun – Holyrood Road
12 (2f) Jackson's Entry
Edinburgh EH8 8PJ

Typeset in 11/15 Adobe Garamond by
IDSUK (DataConnection) Ltd

A CIP record for this book is available from the British Library

ISBN 978 1 3995 1030 1 (hardback)
ISBN 978 1 3995 1033 2 (webready PDF)
ISBN 978 1 3995 1032 5 (epub)

The right of Relli Shechter to be identified as author of this work has been asserted in accordance with the Copyright, Designs and Patents Act 1988 and the Copyright and Related Rights Regulations 2003 (SI No. 2498).

CONTENTS

Preface	vii
Introduction: The Social Contract as History	1

PART ONE   FROM SOCIAL REFORM TO SOCIAL JUSTICE, 1922–52

1 A Liberal Social Contract	25
2 The Making of an Effendi Social Contract	51

PART TWO   THE SOCIAL CONTRACT IN NASSER'S EFFENDI STATE, 1952–70

3 Old Regime, New Regime	91
4 Old Society, New Society	119

PART THREE   THE TORTUOUS SEARCH FOR A NEW SOCIAL CONTRACT, 1970–2011

5 The Social Contract Broken Twice	145
6 Planning a New Social Contract	175
7 The Problem with the New Social Contract	208

Conclusion: Old Social Contract, New Social Contract   245

Bibliography   258
Index   277

PREFACE

The 2011 Uprising in Egypt was a momentous event in Egyptian history and historiography, and one that changed the direction of my research. I was educated professionally to push against an overwhelming presence of politics in the analysis of the Middle East and to focus instead on the culture, economy and society of the region. Moreover, as an economic historian by training, and though I have been teaching the political economy of the Middle East for many years, changes in the 'substructure' often took priority over the political 'superstructure' in my research. Prior to 2011, I had studied the consumption and production of tobacco in Egyptian markets. I had also engaged with research on how the oil-boom of the 1970s and the early 1980s transformed Egypt's consumer society. The 2011 Uprising caught me and most researchers in the field by surprise, and led me to change course. In what turned out to be my next book, *The Rise of the Egyptian Middle Class: Socio-Economic Mobility and Public Discontent from Nasser to Sadat*, I turned to politics, class politics in particular, in studying the impact that the oil-boom, intertwined with President Sadat's liberal Open Door policy, had on Egyptian society. It was in this book that I also began to explore the class history of the Egyptian social contract.

The present book is in some respects a sequel to *The Rise of the Egyptian Middle Class*. The book expands the scope of analysis of the Egyptian social contract and its timeframe, from the period since semi-independence under a newly established liberal monarchy (1922) until the 2011 Uprising. As such, it picks up from an earlier point in time than most previous studies of the social contract in Egypt and it emphasises persistence over time, where past analysis often saw ruptures or new beginnings. *The Egyptian Social Contract* sets a broad framework for the study of the 2011 Uprising as a protest against both the breakup of the old Nasserite social contract – the effendi (local middle class) social contract discussed in this book – and the failure to bring a new social contract to Egypt.

The book reconnects a mostly lost thread in Egyptian socio-political history in that it explores why and how state–middle class relations shaped politics and society in the long run. For reasons discussed in the book, previous analysis of the so-called 'populist-authoritarian' social contract often downplayed the centrality of this class in shaping the social contract. The book offers this class-based analysis of the social contract through the study of two key and sometimes contradictory terms and causes for action – 'social reform' and 'social justice' – and how they shaped the social contract. The purpose of the first was to alleviate poverty, ignorance and disease among the lower classes – or the poor, mostly peasants and workers – in Egypt. The aim of the second was to secure equity and equality of opportunity for a growing middle class of mostly urban, educated and often state-employed Egyptians. Both terms were at the core of shifting state–society relations and Egypt's course of socio-economic development, and were therefore at the centre of the formulation, and later change, of Egypt's social contract.

The Egyptian Social Contract traces the establishment of a liberal social contract and its conservative tenets of social reform under the monarchy. It follows the transition from social reform to social justice in the period between the mid-1930s and the 1952 Free Officers revolution, a transition that was both explicitly and implicitly lobbied for by an expanding middle class. The book later investigates the social contract in Nasser's effendi state, when social justice, including mobility into the middle class and this class's social reproduction, took centre stage. The last part of the book discusses Egypt's economic liberalisation under President Sadat and its neoliberalisation under President Mubarak, focusing on the tortuous search for a new social contract that would bring social reform back to the poor at the expense of social justice to the large, struggling middle class.

The book discusses changing ideas and ideologies embodied in the Egyptian social contract, as expressed in political pronouncements, constitutions and development plans. It follows state legislation and budgeting and the history of state institutions responsible for implementing the welfare state in Egypt and for forming its politics, and hence, the political economy of the social contract. The book further focuses on how public discourse – often a discourse led by middle-class intellectuals – shaped and reshaped this social contract over time. It pays less attention to the lived social contract – how it was manifested in the quotidian lives of middle-class Egyptians and, indeed, of other social classes. Future detailed social histories of the Egyptian social contract are still required.

An Israel Science Foundation grant (No. 404/17) sponsored the research and writing stages that led to this book. I have benefited much from taking on board the five reviews received.

The three reviewers of the manuscript for Edinburgh University Press made important comments that helped me refine the manuscript, as did the press's selection committee. My graduate students, Atar David, Kaitlin Regina Wachsberger, Kassim Alsraiha and Shir Baruch, helped me formulate the ideas expressed in this book as I was advising them on their own research projects; they also helped me assemble sources for the project. Students in the seminars 'Middle Class in the Middle East: Past, Present, Future(?)' and 'Towards a New Social Contract? State–society Relations in the Middle East, Past and Present' further enabled me to think this project through. I warmly thank Ben Zarhi and Oded Marck for commenting on the manuscript at various stages.

This book gained much from the archival work previously undertaken at the Egyptian National Library and Archives, the American University in Cairo Library, the Netherlands-Flemish Institute in Cairo (NVIC) and the Centre d'études et de documentation économiques, juridiques et sociales (CEDEJ). I augmented the research for this book at the Moshe Dayan Center for Middle Eastern and African Studies (MDC) Library, and the MDC Arabic Press Archives, both at Tel-Aviv University; at the Roberta and Stanley Bogen Library and Documentation Center, the Harry S. Truman Research Institute for the Advancement of Peace at the Hebrew University; the National Library of Israel; and the Zalman Aranne Central Library at the Ben-Gurion University of the Negev, especially its Elie Kedourie Collection. The core writing of the manuscript took place while I was on sabbatical at the Middle East Centre in St Antony's College, the University of Oxford – my academic home away from home. The Middle East Centre Library at St Antony's College and the Oriental Institute Library in Oxford were very useful resources for this research. Under the influence of COVID-19, but also the spread of digitisation, significant amounts of research for the book took place online. The CEDEJ archive of digitised Egyptian press turned out to be an invaluable source for qualitative but also quantitative analysis of the press. The Bibliotheca Alexandrina offered me ample digital entry into relevant documents. Interlibrary loan services at my university and abroad were very useful in facilitating access to sources from around the globe.

I presented various parts of this project at seminars and in lectures in Israel at the Ben-Gurion University of the Negev and The Van Leer Jerusalem Institute; in the UK, at the University of Oxford, the University of Cambridge, the University of Edinburgh and the School of Oriental and African Studies (SOAS, University of London); in France, at L'École des hautes études en sciences sociales; and in the Netherlands at Radboud University. I also presented my work at various Middle East Studies Association (MESA) meetings, the British Society for Middle Eastern Studies (BRISMES) meeting, and at meetings of the Middle East and Islamic Studies Association of Israel (MEISAI). In all these places, I benefited from the comments made by discussants and audience members.

While engaged in research and writing, I acquired much intellectual debt to many. Here, I acknowledge the various contributors in alphabetical order: Walter Armbrust, On Barak, Nathan Brown, Anthony Gorman, Israel Gershoni, Khaled Fahmy, Roel Meijer, Yoram Meital, David Parker, Elie Podeh, Haggai Ram, Eugene Rogan, Avi Rubin, Cyrus Schayegh and Robert Springborg. Roel Meijer sponsored an Erasmus+ training grant to Radboud University, where I had the pleasure of presenting my work in progress to his students. Many talks with him then and since were very fruitful in formulating my thoughts on citizenship and the social contract in Egypt. To many on this list, I will not be able to reciprocate their generosity and good advice. I will attempt similar academic generosity by extending it to others.

Emma House, the commissioning editor at Edinburgh University Press, made very useful suggestions for the book's proposal that later found their way into the book. The Edinburgh University Press team – Eddie Clark, Louise Hutton, Isobel Birks – and their cover co-ordinator, Stephanie Derbyshire, were a pleasure to work with. Yonatan Mendel was indispensable in offering solutions regarding translation and transliteration of Arabic to English. I am much indebted to Deborah Schwartz, my editor, for her meticulous and timely service and her precision in choosing wordings and formulations that better reflected my thoughts. Many thanks to the copy-editor of the book, George MacBeth, and to the indexer, Angela Hall.

I have used a simplified *International Journal of Middle East Studies* (IJMES) system for the transliteration of Arabic words, and the IJMES Word List of commonly used words, in which all diacritical marks were omitted except for *ayn* and *hamza*. I have deferred to commonly used English spellings of Arabic places, names and titles. I have also deferred to the self-spelling of first and last names. I have kept the letter *jim* in standard Arabic titles and names transliterated from written sources.

INTRODUCTION
THE SOCIAL CONTRACT AS HISTORY

In the aftermath of the 1977 Food Uprising – which had shocked Egyptian politicians and the public – an official call for a new social contract, a new agreement between citizens and their state, emerged. First appearing in Egypt's Development Plan for the years 1978–82, this new social contract (*'aqd ijtima'i*), if implemented, would set Egypt on a new intertwined economic and political course. It would also partly liberalise the economy and, in tandem, democratise politics. In 2008, some four decades later, the newly established Social Contract Advisory, Monitoring and Coordination Centre was a joint project between the Egyptian government and the United Nations Development Programme (UNDP), whose purpose was, yet again, to promote this new social contract. During the intervening years, there was a broad consensus in Egypt that the old social contract had been broken, and various state economic and political reforms that were to replace it were put in place. As the 2011 Egyptian Uprising clearly demonstrated, the new social contract had barely materialised, and the reforms associated with it hardly constituted a wilful agreement between citizens and their state.

The Egyptian Social Contract sets out to explore the intricacies of the making, partial breaking and persistence of the old social contract, from the time that the semi-independent state was established (1922) until the 2011 Egyptian Uprising. It offers a history of the social contract that centres on analysis of state–middle class relations in Egypt and how these relations have shaped the social contract and Egyptian society over time. In particular the book probes the circumstances in which these relations brought about the intertwining of socio-economic development and governance in this contract. In this political economy, state-led socio-economic development took precedence over the political participation of citizens, or democracy. Later, economic and political reforms scarcely unfolded as planned, because Egypt's ruling elite, but equally its middle-class society, did not consider a new social contract desirable – each for their own reasons. The book therefore attempts a more nuanced analysis of the 'authoritarian bargain', as it is often portrayed in the literature on authoritarianism in Egypt and the Middle East. Such analysis sheds light on a central conundrum that preoccupies many regarding Egypt and the region today: how to promote a just and sustainable social contract in the region. Considering the pervasiveness of Middle Eastern authoritarianism, the book argues that the key for change lies with Egyptian and regional societies and, therefore, with their socio-economic transformation.

The social contract discussed here engages with similar, basic questions that preoccupied European scholars of the Enlightenment.[1] This book studies state–citizen relations, including the legitimacy of the ruler's sovereignty and citizens' economic and political rights, and provides a discussion on how and why the social contract came into being and under what conditions it can be dissolved. However, while I take my lead from that earlier scholarship, and while Egyptians have read and discussed such texts since at least the Arab Renaissance (*al-nahda*) that took place between the second half of the nineteenth century and the early twentieth century, my research is not committed to a close engagement with past analysis of the social contract as a political theory.[2] Instead, the book offers a political economy – a practice-based analysis of the social contract – through the study of relevant state legislation, state budget allocation and political discourse, to actively engage with the making and trajectory of the vertical social contract between the state and its citizens.[3] Moreover, I insert class analysis into the study of the Egyptian social contract and examine how this contract catered to the interests of different social classes in Egypt. Such a horizontal analysis of the social contract disaggregates 'society' and the agreement between state and society to more specific relations between the state and the middle class; the making and trajectory of the Egyptian social contract closely interacted with those of this class. A horizontal analysis of the social contract further denotes how a social contract with the middle class shaped social relations and socio-economic mobility in Egypt – this supposed agreement among citizens was shaped, to a large extent, by middle class vision and interests. As will be clear throughout the book, the vertical and horizontal social contracts are analytical tools, not distinct realities, and they continuously co-constituted each other.

The book first explores the liberal social contract of semi-independent Egypt, a contract based on nineteenth-century liberalism that offered conservative social reform (*islah ijtima'i*) under the newly established constitutional monarchy. Beginning in the mid-1930s, effendi critiques from within and without the parliamentary system increasingly challenged this social contract. The effendi middle class then called upon the state to do more to facilitate social justice (*'adala ijtima'iyya*) in tandem with an effendi vision of progress and with effendi (local middle class) interests in mind. In the aftermath of World War II, a new, effendi social contract emerged in Egypt and was partially implemented. Importantly, an upsurge in public exacerbation over the slow pace of implementing that contract launched the 1952 Free Officers' revolution, and there was a broad coalition of support for such action.

The explicit use of 'social contract' in the political discourse in Egypt dates to the mid-1970s, especially to the aftermath of the 1977 Food Uprising. Indeed, this use came to define what the state by then regarded as a seemingly defunct or unsustainable Nasserite social contract, as part of an attempt to replace it with a new social contract. Under Nasser, and during a period that many in Egypt would come to consider the heyday of the social contract, this concept found limited traction in the political discourse, and Nasser did not mention it in his speeches.[4] For much of the period under discussion here, I use 'social contract' as an analytical tool, not as a term used in Egyptian politics. And yet, while not often part of the Egyptian political vocabulary of the time, I argue that political life and the implementation of post-revolutionary socio-economic policy in Egypt carried both explicit and implicit contractual aspects of social and state–middle class reciprocity.

Post-revolutionary Egypt was for the most part an effendi state, and Nasser's authoritarian regime largely realised an existing effendi social contract. This social contract, I argue, was not particularly populist, in the sense of catering to the needs of ordinary Egyptians. Indeed, the majority of Egyptians, who at the time were peasants and workers, benefited from the social contract less than the effendi middle class did. The effendi social contract significantly influenced social stratification and the shape of post-revolutionary Egyptian society, an influence that has frequently been lost in the prevailing political analysis. Moreover, this social contract channelled socio-economic mobility and determined the making of middle-class society in Nasserite Egypt. During the late 1960s, Nasser's effendi social contract came into question because it was economically unsustainable. After the 1970s, Egypt's search for a new social contract was arduous because neither an alternative socio-economic model of development nor real change in governance came into being.

Egypt's long, tortuous and largely unsuccessful attempt to bring about a genuinely new social contract – as opposed to one that simply rehashed the broken effendi social contract – paved the road for the 2011 Uprising. Unlike the old effendi social contract, this new social contract found little support, whether among Egypt's ruling elite, who resisted political reform, or with middle-class society, which resented economic reform. For over four decades Egypt was caught in a trap in which any advancement toward economic or political reform would be through attrition or a reluctant give-and-take between the two sides, rather than by following a new agreement within society and between society and the state. Because of this trap, economic and political informality – from crony capitalism to rigged elections – became widespread and normative. Given this trap, and under an entrenched authoritarian regime, I propose that only wide social transformation that uncouples Egypt's middle-class society from state provision will allow the much-needed political change.

Beyond the authoritarian pact

In the analysis of the Egyptian social contract, I differ from the conceptual frames of 'authoritarian pact' or 'bargain' through which scholars have often studied Egypt's political system since Nasser, and politics in the Middle East more broadly.[5] The authoritarian pact has invariably been discussed as a top-down, unilateral carrot-and-stick system based on state provision of services and employment (economic rights) in exchange for citizens' exclusion from political participation (political rights). This analysis presents the state – with its oversight of the national budget, and the army and security forces – as the all-powerful factor in determining both state–society relations and politics, and it credits citizens with little real say in government or freedom to organize politically. This emphasis on a top-down pact left limited place in Egypt and elsewhere in the Middle East for either bargaining between citizens and the state based on the existing 'articles' of the authoritarian pact, or for a demand that the state fulfil its end of the bargain. Moreover, analysis of the authoritarian pact downplayed the study of reciprocity or exchange between different classes in society and the state.

I challenge various aspects of the framework discussed above and offer a broader, more nuanced analytical approach. I refute the zero-hour narrative of the authoritarian pact in Egypt – its seeming emergence after the 1952 revolution, especially under Nasser – and with it some of the central aspects of such analysis. I argue that we need to consider this pact more closely in the context of an earlier, liberal social contract in Egypt – as a reaction to this liberal social contract but also as a marker of continuity between the liberal and authoritarian social contracts in Egypt.

That this authoritarian social contract was a response to the failure of the liberal monarchy to bring about comprehensive socio-economic development, as well as full independence for Egypt, is one, less surprising, conclusion of research that would close the gap between the old and new regimes. However, this book goes further by demonstrating that Nasser's social contract had been gradually coming into place even before the 1952 Free Officers' revolution. It argues that there was already a broad consensus in Egypt, particularly among the effendiyya, that the country required a more comprehensive developmentalist state, and therefore a stronger state.

I investigate the making of this consensus by studying the transition in Egypt from a conservative-liberal economic perspective on social reform – alleviating poverty, ignorance and disease through means of self-help for the poor – to an effendi-centred call for social justice. According to this social justice stance, the state was to take charge of facilitating equity and equality of opportunity for all Egyptians, and in practice, for the effendi middle class. In return the state would take greater charge over society, also to the benefit of this class. The Free Officers largely acted upon such a consensus, as opposed to formulating a new socio-economic and political agenda. Indeed, it was the failure of the liberal monarchy's political elite to fully act on this social contract that triggered much support for the revolution.

Arguably, the most surprising conclusion arising from partially phasing out the gap between the constitutional monarchy and the post-revolutionary regime is that this so-called authoritarian social contract was based on a similar conditionality from pre-revolutionary, monarchic Egypt. During the last years of the liberal monarchy, this conditionality wove a state commitment to promote social justice through socio-economic development together with a centralised political power – which Nasser's regime accepted. As a result, during the heyday of Arab socialism in Egypt, the country's command economy and the expansion of social services were closely bound up with limiting citizens' participation in politics – officially, at least, for the sake of expediting socio-economic progress.

Also beginning in pre-revolutionary Egypt and intensifying under Nasser's regime was a moral economy – or social expectations from the state based on the effendi social contract – a moral economy that was closely intertwined with the principle of social justice.[6] Such public expectations that the state fulfil its end of the promised bargain became ever more visible under Presidents Sadat and Mubarak in the face of the state attempt to move away from the by then old social contract to a new (if ill-defined) social contract. The use of the term 'moral economy' here requires two clarifications. First, while originally employed to study and give voice to the crowd, or subalterns, in any society, the moral economy to which I refer was mostly articulated by the effendi social contract. This is not to say that other social groups such as workers and peasants did not take part in social protests that were to uphold social expectations from the state, for example, during the 1977 Food Uprising. Rather, at the core of the moral economy, the state paid closer attention to its own constituency than to other social classes. Therefore the state was much more sensitive to the expectations of the state-educated and state-employed middle class, to whom it did its utmost to cater, as opposed to the lower classes, for whom it often reserved repression. Second, the concurrent use of 'social contract' and 'moral economy' may seem confusing because the first term often refers to the formal – legislated and budgeted – state obligations towards its citizens, while the second outlines social expectations from the state, often put in moral/ethical terms. I suggest that the two terms are in fact intertwined – being two sides of the proverbial coin – in which state legislating and budgeting and, no less so, official state pronouncements outlined this state moral responsibility, which the Egyptian public embraced when opposing the state.[7]

After the early 1970s, attempts to reform Egypt's state-centred socio-economic model of development also came to include an official state commitment to increasing citizen participation in political decision making, resulting in democratisation. Thereafter, and using a reversal of the same past logic, the Egyptian state conceded that reform in developmentalism required reform in politics because the two were intertwined – a change in the first required a change in the second. I argue that this, and a move back from comprehensive social justice to limited social reform, strongly exposed the inverse logic of a pre-revolutionary liberal social contract within the authoritarian social contract. To the extent that the latter social contract was built upon citizens relinquishing political power for the sake of a more comprehensive socio-economic advancement of their state, a partial reversal required the state to cede political power back to the citizenry.

I do not argue that this reversal of exchange between citizens' economic and political rights indeed took place. However, the Egyptian regime and public commentators invariably raised this exchange, or conditionality. Since the late 1970s, this conditionality has also been publicly present in calls for a new social contract for Egypt, or a new intertwining between economic reform that would facilitate a market economy and political reform that would potentially enhance citizens' political participation. Such a conditionality, which was further underwritten by the persistence of the moral economy, mounted the greatest obstacle to both reforms. Indeed, the survival or upgrading of Egypt's authoritarian regime, and the only-partial-success of Egypt's economic reform and structural adjustment (ERSA) programme since the 1990s, clearly testifies to the trap that this conditionality created. Without this conditionality, Egypt could arguably go through a more determined top-down economic transformation. Alternatively, Egypt could experience faster political reform. Under such conditionality, however, and for the last forty years or so, Egypt has found itself between partial and simultaneous attempts to implement both.

The social origins of the social contract

Former scholarly analysis of the authoritarian pact, while admitting social agency in resisting changes to an existing social contract, mostly precluded the study of citizens' agency in the formulation of the social contract. True, in much of the existing literature the robustness of authoritarian regimes was rightly attributed to their relative success in avoiding parts of the existing social contract. Nevertheless, previous works have downplayed the fact that though the authoritarian state was successful in eroding, diluting and delaying benefits to citizens, it did not succeed in omitting such benefits altogether, which testifies to such social agency.[8]

This book foregrounds the social origins of the social contract in Egypt, as well as the reciprocity (or social agency) between citizens and the state in its making, rather than presenting it as a mostly top-down authoritarian social pact. I examine the historical, pre-revolutionary context under which various articles of the social contract – most notably, state-sponsored higher education and state employment – became formalised, and why.

A central argument here is that the social contract in Egypt was a de facto contract between the effendi middle class and the state. Increasingly dominant in parliamentary and extra-parliamentary politics during the liberal monarchy, Egypt's social contract reflected, to a considerable degree, the *effendiyya*'s broad vision and interests. This process had been evident since semi-independence, especially since the mid-1930s, and finally culminated in the full implementation of an effendi social contract under Nasser. This social contract determined the legal, institutional and economic means that largely guided socio-economic mobility into the middle class, and this class's social reproduction – its making and remaking in Egypt ever since.

The effendi middle class discussed here – an educated and often state-employed middle class – emerged during the early nineteenth century under the auspices of the modernising Egyptian state. The *effendiyya* developed in conjunction with the state's growing demand for bureaucrats, technocrats and military personnel. Muhammad 'Ali, an Ottoman military commander and the founder of modern Egypt, introduced a series of economic and military reforms that required newly trained employees to fill civilian and military posts. Even when his state-building project was partially halted under foreign pressure (from the 1838 Balta-Liman treaty), the *effendiyya* that had emerged under him did not disappear. This state-driven class continued to expand throughout the nineteenth century under his successors, owing to the expansion of modern, professional education and the enlargement of the modern state apparatus in Egypt. While a middle class – as a stratum positioned between the Ottoman ruling elite and the rest of the Ottoman subjects – already existed, scholarship on the *effendiyya* has rightly identified them as being the antecedent of a new social stratum having much more influence on Egypt's future culture and politics.

In *The Egyptian Social Contract*, I have chosen to employ the term 'effendi middle class' over '*effendiyya*' to allow a structural discussion of this male-dominated social group, while keeping the discussion closely engaged with changing Egyptian contexts. I use 'effendi middle class' somewhat anachronistically in later chapters, to emphasise a structural class continuity over time. 'Effendi middle class' denotes four positions of this class in relation to its place in the economy, society, culture, and politics. First, economically, the effendi middle class discussed here was foremost a state, as opposed to a market, creation. This class originated as part of a state-building process that took place in what was, nominally, Ottoman Egypt. The effendi middle class acquired its professional status through state initiatives – from sending students to study abroad, to the establishment of new state educational institutions in Egypt. The emerging, modern state later served as the main employer of this social group.

The state was central to creating the effendi middle class in Egypt and, more broadly, the Ottoman Empire, because the forced economic liberalisation of Egypt and the empire left only limited space for the rise of a middle class through market initiatives, as had happened with the bourgeoisie of western Europe. Beginning with the Treaty of Balta-Liman, and ending with European economic control over the empire's finances (1876) and direct British economic and political control over Egypt (1882), the introduction of a free market spelled European economic-turned-political dominance in these regions. In Egypt, under the newly established colonial capitalism, an existing system of capitulations was transformed into one that ensured significant economic, commercial and legal advantages to Europeans and their local protégés, who often came from foreign and local minority groups. The effendi middle class, therefore, often found its relative economic advantage through state employment as opposed to employment in the free market.

Second, socially, the effendi middle class was positioned between several other social groups. It was located below Egypt's social elite – the extended ruling family and Ottoman Egyptian notables, mostly landlords with large holdings – and above the vast majority of Egyptians. Direct British occupation of Egypt meant another layer of socio-political elites was added to the Egyptian elite of the past, and the same was true for economic migrants from the Ottoman Empire and Europe who made their fortune when Egypt was integrated into the European-led world economy during the closing decades of the nineteenth century. In this context, the effendi middle class strove for a more equal footing with Egypt's socio-political elites. The effendi middle class competed for state positions, including in the military, with elements of the established Ottoman elite. The call for the Egyptianisation of state employment was already marked in the 'Urabi Revolt (1879–82), which demanded the nativisation of the Egyptian state that was dominated by the Ottoman elite.[9] Under British rule, this call regained momentum when a British-induced state retrenchment led to a squeeze on state employment, while the available, top-ranking positions often went to Britons and Europeans.

Third, politically, and for the reasons suggested above, between the time of the British occupation and 1952, a dual class animosity guided the effendi leadership of the national movement: (a) mounting resentment of the British, which led members of the effendi middle class to form the leadership of the national movement, and (b) discontent with the Egyptian ruling elite of the liberal monarchy. This discontent intensified over time, especially as the effendi middle class expanded down the social ladder. Effendi members of political parties in the parliament, as well as those leading extra-parliamentary parties and organisations across the political spectrum and the secular/religious divide, concurred over the need to gain full independence from the British. They also came to agree that the then-current political system, being unstable and far from resolving Egyptian socio-economic hardships (and therefore effendi hardship), should be replaced by a more state-centred political management in which the effendi middle class was destined to play a greater role. In both political struggles – against the British and against what after the 1952 revolution would become known as the 'old ruling elite' – the effendi political leadership drafted other effendis into the national struggle. Furthermore, it sought to enlist the support of other social groups further down the social ladder, though as much to control peasants and, more so, workers, as to secure their help.

Fourth, culturally, the effendi middle class dominated the Egyptian intelligentsia, and therefore cultural production and dissemination, mostly through a fast-developing print culture. Here, the term 'middle' in middle class also stood for the positionality of this social group between the global (at times read Western) conventions that guided Egyptian socio-economic life and politics and the search for authentic expression of such practices in Egypt. While the title 'effendi' stood, above all, for a combination of an educated person and often a state employee, this term came to represent a search for an authentic, modern Egyptian society and nation. From the late nineteenth century until 1952, an effendi-dominated public discourse meant that this effendi vision of modernisation and progress dominated the media. Moreover, so did immediate effendi interests – from a demand for more inclusive and free-of-charge higher education to a call for the state to better compensate state employees and to improve living conditions in the cities, where the majority of effendis lived.

The discussion above risks two overgeneralisations of the role that the effendi middle class played in shaping Egyptian sociocultural spheres and politics. Class delineation in Egyptian society, as much as in any other society, was never as clear cut as may be inferred from the above analysis. Class lines were less rigid and more permeable between the effendi middle class and Egypt's local and foreign elites. Effendis shared a desire for modernisation and progress with these cosmopolitan elites; they also shared a fear that swift change could lead to rapid change in the social structure, with social upheaval as a result. Increasingly over time, socio-economic mobility into the effendi middle class changed this social group from within – for example, in placing significance on the role of religion within the state, as the Muslim Brotherhood did. The effendi middle class further came to represent, in its own eyes, the 'average' Egyptian, as opposed to an exclusive social group, as it had in the past. In addition, the socio-economic plight of peasants and workers, as well as popular protests, no doubt brought genuine effendi sympathy and attempts at reform that went beyond class interests or fear of social unrest or that attempted to contain them through the making of a more organic society.

The above analysis of structural class interests further risks understating inner class tensions and disagreements, of which there were plenty within the effendi middle class. Political life and public discourse under the liberal monarchy were rife, with all types of effendi-led and effendi-supported political parties and organisations – left, right and religious – and they were far from in agreement as to how to improve Egyptian society. Political rivalry and contending visions of socio-economic and cultural development further disrupted an image of inner class cohesion, as did the geographical variations between those living in large cities and those in regional towns. Research is increasingly attentive to the need to carry historical social analysis beyond Cairo and, to a lesser degree, Alexandria, and therefore to allowing a more nuanced study of the lived experience of the middle class beyond large cities.[10] And yet, and this is a central argument in my emphasis on effendi agency in formulating the social contract and maintaining it over time, the tenets of the social contract carried distinctive effendi attributes and represented the shared, core interests of this social group beyond the differences mentioned here.

Considering the socio-political and cultural centrality of the effendi middle class up until the 1952 revolution, there remains an ongoing puzzle in Egyptian historiography regarding the whereabouts of that class since. In the events that followed the revolution, this class seems to have disappeared as a player. Furthermore, research on Nasser and his generation invariably located the Free Officers' background within the lower and middle ranks of this social group, only to later downplay its persistence in socio-politics from the period of the liberal monarchy to Nasserite Egypt.[11] Likewise, recent Egyptian historical and sociological analysis has argued that under the revolution, Egypt's middle class grew quickly and reached its heyday.[12] In this analysis too there remains a gap between the new middle class of the 1950s and especially the 1960s, and the *effendiyya* of the past.

The puzzle above is perhaps not entirely surprising. New generations of effendis had – since the late nineteenth century – invariably felt alienated from their biological and, more so, 'social' fathers (the generation that preceded them), and they sought new ways to reform their society and themselves.[13] Since the 1930s, the expansion of this stratum had further deepened generational gaps in a period that had experienced growing activity of extra-parliamentary, effendi social movements and parties throughout the political right and left and, significantly, the Muslim Brotherhood. Yet, effendis – past and present – continued to share a common vision of national progress, at the centre of which was the effendi middle class itself. New generations of effendis strove for reform and progress, with little acknowledgement of past attempts, much like the Free Officers upon their ascendance to power. Thus, the so-called new middle class that emerged under Nasser was different in name but not in essence from the pre-revolutionary class of old.

A central argument in this book is that the effendi middle class did not disappear with the Free Officers' revolution. Rather, under Nasser, Egypt turned into an effendi state. If '*effendiyya*' disappeared from the vernacular of the revolutionary regime, it was because its worldview, interests and modes of action now became congruent with that of the nation through the expansion of an effendi social contract. Moreover, other social groups from above and below were channeled to follow this social contract, which educated, disciplined and managed peasants and workers through state policies on education and welfare. During the first years following the revolution, there was a significant political scramble over power, including among former effendi allies from within the left and the Muslim Brotherhood, but not over the implementation of an effendi social contract in Egypt.

In his book *The Wretched of the Earth*, Frantz Fanon, a profound critic of colonialism, pronounces deep disappointment with the national middle classes that had come to dominate new nation states.[14] According to Fanon, the political dominance of such national middle classes created a gap between national liberation and the liberation of those most in need within the nation. In an aptly titled chapter, 'The Pitfalls of National Consciousness', he discusses how this middle class followed its own self-interest rather than that of the masses. My analysis of the Egyptian social contract since the revolution echoes Fanon's. I study how a self-centred effendi vision and practice of socio-economic development shaped that of the nation, and how an effendi social contract guided socio-economic development in Egypt over time. Politically, the vertical effendi social contract stood at the core of authoritarianism in Egypt, and it largely impinged on the horizontal production of a new social coalition that would successfully struggle to alter it. Thus, Fanon's argument that national independence mostly benefited the national middle class finds strong resonance in the narrative that follows.

I discuss the centrality of the effendi middle class in the making and partial breaking of the social contract in Egypt, with less reference to other classes – the Egyptian upper and lower classes. My research here diverges from the recent emphasis placed on both in the analysis of the long-term events that led to the 2011 Uprising.[15] I argue that the Egyptian upper class by and large excluded itself from the social contract because it had a more direct venue to secure its interests through exerting influence on politics and immediate participation in it. Egypt's lower class – peasants and workers – mostly remained subaltern in the political discourse over the social contract and was marginalised in benefiting from it, despite often being the official object of socio-economic development in Egypt. Moreover, the effendi social contract that offered some socio-economic mobility from the lower into the middle class invariably meant that it was unlikely to be challenged by the more dynamic members of lower-class Egypt. Last, in the 2011 Uprising, it was the middle class that took a central role in the protest over the erosion of the social contract in Egypt.[16] I foreground the analysis of the role that this social class played in shaping and reshaping the social contract over time, and suggest that the history of the effendi middle class and an effendi social contract in Egypt have long been intertwined. Any search for a new social contract will have to take this intertwining into consideration.

The Egyptian social contract could have been further disaggregated into a religious social contract based on the infusion of this concept with Islamic belief and religious practices, a kin social contract in which the family and not the individual is the basic participant, or a closely interacted gendered, patriarchal social contract, to which men have, in practice, been the 'signatories'.[17] All these approaches in discussing a disaggregated social contract are valid, and my decision to focus on class analysis of the social contract does them some injustice. Nevertheless, I argue that for many of the tenets that have become associated with the social contract, effendi middle class vision and interests preceded all others. Moreover, a male effendi middle class social contract embodied clear references to religion, gender, and kin social contracts. My discussion of the effendi middle class social contract, therefore, potentially sacrifices a more nuanced analysis of the social contract for a broader statement on state–middle class relations in Egypt.

Global best practices Egyptianised

The Egyptian Social Contract investigates how, since its establishment, the social contract in Egypt – a horizontal contract within society and a vertical contract between citizens and society – was envisioned, debated, implemented and later, criticised and changed in tandem with contemporary global best practices of governance and economic management. A standard, dictionary definition of 'best practice' would suggest 'a procedure that has been shown by research and experience to produce optimal results and that is established or proposed as a standard suitable for widespread adoption'.[18] My analysis of global best practices in the making and remaking of the Egyptian social contract questions that definition, eschewing the universality of global best practices and their supposed inherent superiority in delivering better governance and economic management to society as a whole. Instead, I investigate how changing global best practices interacted with the Egyptian social contract in various ways that served a specifically middle-class worldview and interests. Furthermore, I study the adoption and adaption of global best practices as a class venue to project itself onto contemporary international settings. Therefore, I explore gaps between such global standardised practices and their implementation in Egypt over time.

According to the Google Books Ngram Viewer, the term 'best practices' emerged in the late 1980s, and its use rapidly increased during the 1990s.[19] 'Global best practices' as pertaining to governance and economic management also appeared during the same period. An era of rapid globalisation, coupled with the end of the Cold War, resulted in a new, neoliberal hegemony that guided such best practices, because these practices had often been backed by dominant (read Western) political powers and supported by international financial institutions worldwide.

In my study I further project the analysis of global best practices back to Egypt's liberal social contract after semi-independence from Britain. In an earlier era of globalisation, the making of Egypt's liberal economy also interacted with the global, liberal, political and economic conventions of the late nineteenth century. Since the mid-1930s, and particularly in the aftermath of World War II, changing global conventional wisdom on the role of the state in socio-economic development has been closely related to the emergence of a new, effendi social contract in Egypt. I refer to such conventional wisdom, somewhat anachronistically, as 'best practices', to emphasise continuous trends in local-global ('glocal') socio-economic policy and political formulations throughout the book. The history of the social contract in Egypt, I argue, cannot be read without reference to these changing, broader contexts. From this perspective as well, the Egyptian social contract has been one site in which to investigate global best practices in a specific setting, or how such conventional wisdom was installed in a specific place.

Methodology and sources

In this book I examine the formal aspects of Egypt's social contract(s) through an analysis of state legislation, especially Egyptian constitutions. Since semi-independence, Egypt has had a long tradition of putting forward new constitutions when transitions in local governance and/or socio-economic development took place.[20] In addition I discuss related, seminal documents such as President Nasser's National Charter and President Sadat's October Working Paper. I take Egyptian constitutions and these seminal policy papers to represent official state intentions regarding the social contract, even if posthumously, as often was the case. President Mubarak's insistence on keeping the 1971 constitution long after Egypt went through a neoliberal economic reform would suggest the same in reverse – an insistence on keeping an ambiguous official social contract as opposed to admitting that it had, de facto, already gone through significant transformation.

My analysis of constitutions and, when available, the deliberations of constitutional committees and the political discourse and politics leading to the decree of constitutions, refers to the socio-economic rights of citizens. The book examines such rights in constitutional articles related to education, health, provision of food and housing and employment. I further study citizens' economic duties, most notably through articles related to taxation. I particularly focus on how various constitutional articles related to citizens' economic rights and duties in fact reiterated a broad public consensus over such matters and were not simply an authoritarian dictate. A central attempt here is to expose an effendi middle class bias in such constitutionalised rights and duties.

I follow the analysis of the formal social contracts with the study of their actual implementation in Egypt through an examination of the changing state institutional capacity to provision citizens. The book studies the creation and expansion of relevant state ministries and analyse the quantity and quality of services, including employment, that they provided over time. Significant here is the analysis of the state budget for and relative expenditures on various articles of the social contract. I juxtapose the study of how the social contract has been implemented over time with research into the trajectory of the effendi middle class itself – how it has expanded and transformed. Moreover, I examine how the social contract has increasingly channelled Egyptians to search for socio-economic mobility through professional effendication: a quest for higher education leading to state employment.

Throughout the discussion, I put the study of constitution making and the implementation of the social contract in the context of the lively political discourse in Egypt, which was well reflected in the press. Through detailed textual analysis, this book traces both explicit and implicit public criticism of perceived state breaches of the social contract, protests and demonstrations against such breaches, and state responses to such critiques and threats. This political discourse was itself dominated by effendi middle class commentators, and therefore by their worldview and interests. I further examine how shifting global conventions regarding best practices in socio-economic development and governance interacted with the making and breaking of the liberal and the effendi social contracts, and with attempts to bring about a new social contract in Egypt – the latter being examined through a particularly close analysis of the Egypt Human Development Report project.

A keyword search in the digitised press (see the list of sources in the Bibliography) for terms such as 'middle class' and 'social contract' eased locating relevant press references – dailies and magazines. I also used timelines – the frequency of appearance of such terms in the press – to document the upturn in public and political interest in these terms. Timelines constituted an important quantitative layer of evidence in narrating histories of social contracts in Egypt. Google Books Ngram Viewer offered the analysis of changing buzzwords (in English), and hence changing trends in the literature on global socio-economic development. In using these search engines, I am aware of human choice in the selection of what is included in press compilations, and the pitfalls of Ngram analysis.[21] I used both *alongside*, not instead of, a detailed qualitative analysis of the sources. Digitisation further allowed for a quantitative analysis of official political pronouncements such as, for example, President Nasser's speeches.

Recent developments in digital indexing and archiving facilitated my research into primary sources, the more efficient use of such sources, and new ways of utilising information. The Bibliotheca Alexandrina offered me ample digital entry into relevant documents; institutional archives in Egyptian universities, commercial archives such as KotobArabia for multidisciplinary books, and ALMANHAL for books, journal articles and dissertations from the Arab world, including Egypt, were also of great help. No less useful were the online archives of Egyptian public authorities and ministries and of international development institutions such as the United Nations Development Program and the World Bank.

Better indexing and digitisation of secondary sources from a variety of disciplines were also of great assistance. A broad survey of the secondary literature from various disciplines – including anthropology, economics, education, public health, political science, public administration, sociology and urban studies – allowed me to account for the actual implementation of the different articles of the social contract, showing which social class was officially targeted, and who actually benefited from it. The secondary literature from a variety of disciplines was very helpful in putting together an inclusive overview of the informal political economy in Egypt, a political economy that has become ever more significant with the erosion of the formal social contract in recent decades. WorldCat and interlibrary loan services have enabled astounding access to library materials, including primary documents from around the world.

Finally, at the risk of repeating a Google Scholar cliché, this research indeed stands on the shoulders of giants in delving into past, often forgotten social science research on Egypt in a new narrative of the history of that country's social contract. Moreover, I put such analysis in the context of changing trends in socio-economic development, in which international and especially local economists, sociologists, and political scientists not only commented upon state policy and its implementation but actively shaped it. Therefore, I refer to their work as primary documents as well as accounts of the unfolding events – and as evidence to the effendication of the Egyptian social contract over time.

The three parts of this book investigate the Egyptian social contract chronologically. Part One, 'From Social Reform to Social Justice, 1922–52', examines the transformation from the liberal social contract that emerged under Egypt's constitutional monarchy to an effendi social contract that started to take shape after the mid-1930s. The liberal social contract mostly promised social reform through the alleviation of poverty by advancing means of self-help to the poor. An emerging effendi social contract now pledged social justice for an expanding middle class. Part Two, 'The Social Contract in Nasser's Effendi State, 1952–70', offers three significant revisions of our current understanding of Nasser's social contract. First, it demonstrates that Nasser's social contract in fact crystallised in Egypt between 1945 and 1952. Second, it shows that peasants and workers – the majority of average Egyptians – benefited from the social contract less than the middle class did. Third, Nasser's social contract was not a simple, top-down exchange of political for economic rights, as is often suggested in the literature on the authoritarian bargain in the Middle East. Rather, Nasser's effendi state well reflected past calls for statism – often associated with socialism in Egypt – and effendi goals in socio-economic development. Part Three of the book, 'The Tortuous Search for a New Social Contract, 1970–2011' narrates the seeming breaking down, yet great persistence of, the effendi social contract, from the time of President Sadat's Open Door Policy until the 2011 Uprising. It explores, through a comparison with the past establishment of the effendi social contract, the failure of attempts to bring a new social contract to Egypt.

Notes

1. For instance, see Thomas Hobbes, *Leviathan*, ed. Noel Malcolm (Oxford: Clarendon Press, 2014); John Locke, *Second Treatise of Government* and *A Letter Concerning Toleration*, ed. Mark Goldie (Oxford: Oxford University Press, 2016); and Jean-Jacques Rousseau, *Rousseau: The Social Contract and Other Later Political Writings*, 2nd ed. (Cambridge: Cambridge University Press, 2018).
2. Albert Hourani, *Arabic Thought in the Liberal Age, 1798–1939* (London: Oxford University Press, 1967); Peter Hill, *Utopia and Civilisation in the Arab Nahda* (Cambridge: Cambridge University Press, 2020); Wael Abu-'Uksa, *Freedom in the Arab World: Concepts and Ideologies in Arabic Thought in the Nineteenth Century* (Cambridge: Cambridge University Press, 2016).
3. The terms 'vertical' and 'horizontal' social contract are taken from Markus Loewe, Tina Zintl and Annabelle Houdret, 'The Social Contract as a Tool of Analysis: Introduction to the Special Issue on 'Framing the Evolution of New Social Contracts in Middle Eastern and North African Countries', *World Development* 145 (2020), https://doi.org/10.1016/j.worlddev.2020.104982.
4. I concluded this based on a keyword search in the electronic compilation of President Nasser's speeches. See Huda Jamal 'Abd al-Nasir, comp., *al-Majmu'*

al-Kamila li-Khutub wa-Tasrihat al-Ra'is Jamal 'Abd al-Nasir, 1954–1970 (Cairo: Academic Bookshop, 2005–9). The compilation and search engine are found online, ALMANHAL, accessed 12 April 2020, https://platform.almanhal.com/Search/Result?q=&sf_31_0_3=Reign+of+Jamal+Abdul+Nasser+1954+-+1970&opsf_31_0=1 (Arabic).

5. Among the vast literature on the authoritarian pact, these are often cited: Steven Heydemann, 'Social Pacts and the Persistence of Authoritarianism in the Middle East', in *Debating Arab Authoritarianism: Dynamics and Durability in Nondemocratic Regimes*, ed. Oliver Schlumberger (Stanford, CA: Stanford University Press, 2007); and Mehran Kamrava, 'The Rise and Fall of Ruling Bargains in the Middle East', in *Beyond the Arab Spring: The Evolving Ruling Bargain in the Middle East*, ed. Mehran Kamrava (New York: Oxford University Press, 2014). For a typology and analysis of various approaches to the authoritarian bargain, see Roel Meijer, 'Citizenship, Social Pacts, Authoritarian Bargains, and the Arab Uprisings', in *The Crisis of Citizenship in the Arab World*, ed. Roel Meijer and Nils Butenschøn (Leiden: Brill, 2017), 79–82.

6. For the employment of 'moral economy' in labour history in Egypt, see Marsha Pripstein Posusney, 'Irrational Workers: The Moral Economy of Labor Protest in Egypt', *World Politics* 46, no. 1 (1993): 83–120, https://doi.org/10.2307/2950667. I thank Cyrus Schayegh for drawing my attention to the importance of moral economy in the study of effendi middle class opposition to the state in his critique of my earlier work.

7. My use of moral economy dovetails, in some respects, with Sara Salem's analysis of a hegemonic Nasserist project. This hegemonic project became the standard for successful governance that would haunt any future attempt at an alternative such project. The establishment of a successful effendi social contract and its underlying moral economy indeed did so in Egypt. See Salem's *Anticolonial Afterlives in Egypt: The Politics of Hegemony* (Cambridge: Cambridge University Press, 2020).

8. See exceptions in Diane Singerman, *Avenues of Participation: Family, Politics, and Networks in Urban Quarters of Cairo* (Princeton, NJ: Princeton University Press, 1995); and Cilja Harders, 'The Informal Social Pact: The State and the Urban Poor in Cairo', in *Politics from Above, Politics from Below: The Middle East in the Age of Economic Reform*, ed. Eberhard Kienle (London: Al-Saqi Publications, 2003).

9. Alexander Schölch, *Egypt for the Egyptians! The Socio-political Crisis in Egypt, 1878–1882* (London: Ithaca Press, 1981); and Juan. R. Cole, *Colonialism and Revolution in the Middle East: Social and Cultural Origins of Egypt's 'Urabi Movement* (Cairo: AUC Press, 1999).

10. Peter Gran, 'Asyut in Modern Times: The Problem of Invisibility', *International Journal of Middle East Studies* 53, no. 1 (2021): 113–17, https://doi.org/10.1017/S0020743821000106; Hanan Hammad, 'Daily Encounters That Make History: History from Below and Archival Collaboration', ibid., 139–43, doi:10.1017/S0020743821000076.
11. P. J. Vatikiotis, *Nasser and His Generation* (New York: St. Martin's Press, 1978), 23–46.
12. See Mushira al-'Ashri, *al-Tabaqa al-Wusta: Min Marhalat al-Izdihar ila Siyasat al-Ifqar* (Cairo: Misr al-'Arabiyya li-l-Nashr wa-l-Tawzi', 2014) for the term 'heyday' and an analysis of the Egyptian middle class during the 1952 revolution. See also the detailed discussion of a surge in interest in the middle class in Egyptian academic writing and public discourse, which accounts for such Egyptian historiography of the period.
13. Lucie Ryzova, *The Age of the Efendiyya: Passages to Modernity in National-Colonial Egypt* (Oxford: Oxford University Press, 2014).
14. Frantz Fanon, 'The Pitfalls of National Consciousness', in *The Wretched of the Earth* (New York: Grove Press, 1968).
15. Angela Joya, *The Roots of Revolt: A Political Economy of Egypt from Nasser to Mubarak* (Cambridge: Cambridge University Press, 2020); and Salem, *Anticolonial Afterlives*.
16. For the centrality of the middle class in the 2011 Uprising, see Hazem Kandil, 'Why Did the Egyptian Middle Class March to Tahrir Square?', *Mediterranean Politics* 17 (2012); Ishac Diwan, 'Understanding Revolution in the Middle East: The Central Role of the Middle Class', *Middle East Development Journal* 5, no. 1 (2013), https://dx.doi.org/10.1142/S1793812013500041; and S. Devarajan and E. Ianchovichina, 'A Broken Social Contract, Not High Inequality, Led to the Arab Spring', *Review of Income and Wealth* 64 (2018), https://doi.org/10.1111/roiw.12288.
17. Shahrough Akhavi, 'Sunni Modernist Theories of Social Contract in Contemporary Egypt', *International Journal of Middle East Studies* 35 (2003); Mervat Hatem, 'The Nineteenth Century Discursive Roots of the Continuing Debate on the Social-Sexual Contract in Today's Egypt', *Hawwa* 2 (2004); Suad Joseph, 'The Kin Contract and Citizenship in the Middle East', in *Women and Citizenship*, ed. Marilyn Friedman (Oxford: Oxford University Press, 2005). Lucie Ryzova, *Age of the Efendiyya*, argues that the term 'effendi' referred to male Egyptians only.
18. *Merriam-Webster*, s.v. 'best practices', accessed 16 April 2020, https://www.merriam-webster.com/dictionary/best%20practice.

19. Google Books Ngram Viewer, accessed 29 April 2020, https://books.google.com/ngrams/graph?content=%22best+practices%22&year_start=1900&year_end=2008&corpus=15&smoothing=3&share=&direct_url=t1%3B%2C%22%20best%20practices%20%22%3B%2Cc0. In a keyword search I used smoothing 3. 'Global best practices' did not appear in the search.
20. Egypt endorsed a new constitution in 1923, upon achieving semi-independence. It experienced constitutional changes in the following years: 1930, 1935 (restoration of the 1923 constitution), 1956, 1958, 1964 (interim constitution) and 1971. As I discuss in Chapter 7, President Mubarak's insistence on not changing the constitution, despite significant economic reform, was an exception.
21. Sarah Zhang, 'The Pitfalls of Using Google Ngram to Study Language', *Wired*, 18 December 2015, accessed 29 April 2020, https://www.wired.com/2015/10/pitfalls-of-studying-language-with-google-ngram/.

PART ONE

FROM SOCIAL REFORM TO SOCIAL JUSTICE, 1922–52

The following two chapters narrate the making and remaking of the Egyptian social contract between 1922 and 1952. Chapter one discusses how a liberal social contract inspired by global best practices, one that had gradually taken shape since the late nineteenth century, found its formal expression in the 1923 Egyptian constitution. Chapter two explains why, from the mid-1930s, and particularly between 1945 and 1952, a new, statist social contract emerged, again in close interaction with changing global conventional wisdom on politics and socio-economic policies of development. At the core of my analysis is a significant yet little-studied change in the Egyptian social contract: the move from an emphasis on social reform to an insistence on social justice. The expanding effendi middle class was both the main reason for and the main advocate of this change in a period of gradual decolonialisation.

Readers may wonder over the absence of a broader reference to politics in the analysis of a new social contract under the liberal monarchy. Indeed, while contemporary politics serves as an important context regarding the formulation and implementation of the social contract, Part One refrains from closely following both the familiar upheavals of Egyptian democratic life during this period and the constant rivalry and shifting alliances between the Wafd Party, the palace and the British. It also refrains from delving into the study of extra-parliamentary politics in Egypt. I intentionally put aside the study of immediate politics under the liberal monarchy for the sake of close engagement with a broader, infrastructural or paradigmatic transformation of what formulated the political itself. Hence, Part One foregrounds the debate over what an emerging Egyptian nation required, who should provide it, and how this should be accomplished.

1

A LIBERAL SOCIAL CONTRACT

This chapter investigates how nineteenth-century concepts of liberalism in Egypt shaped that country's political economy under the liberal monarchy after semi-independence. It first focuses on social reform in Egypt – a central call of the emerging national movement – and why it remained mostly a private, philanthropic initiative to introduce tools for self-improvement to alleviate poverty, ignorance and disease, primarily through education. Such self-help schemes left little room for the state provision of services, especially those related to health, or for redistribution that would reduce economic inequality, in the form of state transferal of resources between social classes. The chapter later studies the relevant articles of the 1923 constitution, including the deliberations of the constitutional commission that first drafted and later debated these articles. I discuss articles in the constitution related to mass education because schooling was to be the only social service inscribed in this formal manifestation of the liberal social contract. In addition, I discuss what was not included in the constitution – higher education – despite its seminal centrality in national politics, and why. Similarly, the chapter examines the demand for state employment, a central demand of the emerging Egyptian national movement, and how it became legislated in the constitution. In both cases, selective and higher education leading to state employment stalled the spread of the social reform that it was meant to promote: the class interests of the effendi middle class blocked those of other social groups further down the social ladder.

Productivist welfare

From the 1870s onward, the call for social reform became an integral part of an emerging national movement in Egypt, and it was central to an effendi – personal and social – mission to bring positive change to society. Effendi intellectuals, at that time part of the socio-economic and political elite of Egypt, found common ground as agents of change: a self-conscious mission to set the conditions that would create a new society based on an enlightened civilization. They sought to create a modern, progressive society under the guise of a national society – as well as to free it from foreign occupation through the creation of an independent nation-state.[1] This personal-turned-national effendi reform was also well integrated with a contemporary religious revival in which a progressive new civility would facilitate the creation of true religious knowledge that would guide pious and virtuous Muslim life. It was to liberate Muslim society from its backwardness, but also prevent it from 'blindly imitating' European social mores and customs.[2]

The reform that emerged during this period and that was established under the constitutional monarchy was, to no small extent, a patriarchal social reform, with charities allowing a more significant role for women in social action.[3] As Michael Gasper suggests, this emerging effendi ethos of reform and renewal was embedded in a new type of 'honorable, virtuous, and civilized masculine subject that dominated so much of the discussion'.[4] A new kind of man was to strive to improve the state of the *umma* (both religious community and society). The early primacy of both an all-encompassing reform and charity – the two, in fact, often intertwined – in the making of effendi male subjectivity and the striving for national action established a robust sociocultural legacy in Egypt. Lisa Pollard emphasises the centrality of 'nurturing the nation', or hospitality and charity, as part of the national, effendi discourse.[5] Still, such gendered action was taken under male tutelage. As Lucie Ryzova demonstrates, well into the first half of the twentieth century this tradition of modernity in Egypt played a dominant role in the making of new generations of male effendis, their words and their actions.[6]

Central to social reform was the need to resolve 'the peasant question'. This question of how to address the all-encompassing challenge of improving the harsh living conditions and the productivity of most Egyptians was hardly new. It appeared periodically throughout the nineteenth century in the context of the commercialisation of agricultural production. Who was to resolve the harsh realities of peasant life and improve agricultural production was a source of economic and political contention between Egypt's ruling household and the landed elite who dominated politics, as well as within this landed elite.[7] Increasingly, 'the peasant question' came to play a role in international politics as an example of socio-economic mismanagement, and it therefore became a call for foreign interference in Egyptian affairs. 'The peasant question' was doubly significant for an emerging elitist- and effendi-led national movement. First, the socio-economic reform of the peasantry would galvanize it into a nation. Second, reformers envisioned social reform as a national goal that would be carried out by Egyptians for Egyptians, particularly because the British occupied the country and managed its internal affairs. Over time, economic growth and new economic opportunities in cities created a significant pull for rural migration. 'The peasant question', though intimately entangled with misery in rural regions, was brought into cities, where effendis lived. The public effendi call for social reform to resolve it was, significantly, the result of escalating social unrest in rural and urban regions, not only of benevolence. Social reform that would ease socio-economic pressure was both in the interest of the British and the Egyptian landed elite and an effendi call for socio-national rejuvenation.

Public awareness of deteriorating morality and a surge in crime in the cities further enhanced the demand for reform. In response to this, there was a proliferation of philanthropic organisations. Such organisations, part of a broader milieu of what Pollard terms (after Robert Putnam) 'bonding societies', comprised multinational and multiethnic and religious groups. British and Egyptians, Muslims and Copts, and members of minority and international communities who were all intent on alleviating poverty, ignorance and disease.[8] These organisations served just as much as gathering places and social clubs, social-spatial sites in which to negotiate social prestige and exert patronage over Egyptian society. Importantly, they mitigated a changing socio-economic reality that had seen the gradual erosion of past institutions of benevolence provision, such as waqfs and guilds.

Despite the centrality of 'the peasant question', philanthropic organisations mostly centred their activities on the urban poor. Some, no doubt, simply despaired over the extent of the reform required in rural regions, which was well beyond the capacity of such private initiatives. Conservative landlords wanted to avoid disruption in agricultural production that might result from, for example, an increase in education at the expense of child labour. Moreover, rising economic inequality and social despair in expanding cities drew attention to poverty closer to home. Labourers – as opposed to peasants – became the objects of benevolence. Rising public awareness of the need for socio-economic reform further emphasised reforms that would benefit women and, especially, children. This public awareness developed in a period that saw a worsening of their plight under growing economic pressure and a deterioration of the urban social fabric.

Under the British, the conservative-liberal economic policy geared toward reforming agriculture and paying back public debt limited the potential development of official state-based welfare to resolve the peasant question. Moreover, private philanthropy well-suited this liberal economy that seemingly left markets to their own devices, despite unequal, largely ethnicity-based access to markets under colonial capitalism, for example, through the system of capitulations. The British encouraged private philanthropic organisations as an alternative to direct state help, although such organisations received state transfers and the state regulated their activities. Philanthropic associations were often chaired by British and Egyptian politicians or state officials and the Egyptian ruling family.

This was by no means a straightforward process. Older institutions of benevolence – for example, soup kitchens – lingered alongside new institutions of learning and vocational training. Social and religious conservatives expressed reservations regarding various aspects of education, especially the education of girls and women. While the call for social reform was an integral part of an emerging, elitist- and effendi-led national movement, many within this movement believed that national independence should come first because achieving such independence required unity of effort. Closely connected was the argument that without national independence, socio-economic transformation would not take place.[9] Nevertheless, this vision of welfare provision spread down the social ladder alongside the proliferation of associational life in Egypt. It became dominant despite the growing segmentation of welfare provision along ethnic and religious lines (offering welfare services to the same community and coreligionists), which had taken place since the turn of the century, especially during and in the aftermath of World War I.

Productivist welfare gradually became the dominant form of welfare in Egypt.[10] Deeply ingrained in the conservative economic liberalism of the period, private philanthropy attempted to introduce tools for self-improvement to alleviate poverty, ignorance and disease. In this form of thought, once such tools were provided to those in need, primarily through education, the poor would themselves improve their socio-economic condition. Such self-help schemes left little room for state involvement in provision of services, or in redistribution in the form of state transferal of resources between social classes that would reduce economic inequality.

In bringing socio-economic reform to Egypt, philanthropic organisations focused on individuals and on delivery through self-help. Mine Ener describes it thus: 'A move away from indiscriminate charitable giving and toward the creation of vocational and educational opportunities for the poor was central to the activities of associations founded in Egypt during this period'.[11] This new, liberal-utilitarian approach was about helping those in need to help themselves. In this context education would become a remedy to cure all hardship. For effendi social reformers and the emerging national movement of which they were a part, education was the central vehicle for alleviating ignorance, poverty, and disease.

Education was assigned many tasks: from providing basic academic skills and vocational training that would improve the economic state of the poor, to leading toward preventive medicine through, for example, better hygiene and food consumption, which would alleviate malnutrition and disease. Education would also resolve social malaise and moral ills. Finally, education would change traditional social relations, and, centrally, gender relations, by providing education to women. This latter aspect was, in turn, at the core of family renewal through the modern upbringing of children and the modernisation of household conduct. It would help to establish the 'new woman', the 'new family' and therefore the 'new nation'.[12] In short, the effendis envisioned education as leading to the self-transformation – under the effendi's guidance – of children, women, peasants and workers. Such a vision of education was part of a contemporary global best practice, which carried with it an exciting twist. This strong belief in the transformative character of education further meant that for the British, education, particularly higher education, should also be politically controlled so as to avoid local socio-political unrest that would encourage protest against their rule. Indeed, the emerging, elitist- and effendi-led national movement made the development of higher education in Egypt a central demand, coupled with a contained system of mass education for the majority of Egyptians.

Hoda Youssef's study of petitions by students and their families for state help in sponsoring their education well illustrates the increasing public demand for such education between the 1820s and the 1920s.[13] This demand was cast as an act of safeguarding the future of both Egyptians and the nation. Through such petitions, Youssef reads the making of the modern education system not simply as a top-bottom act, but as developing reciprocal relations between the Egyptian state and its citizenry, and therefore as central to the emerging liberal social contract discussed here.

In employing productivist welfare, philanthropic organisations by and large sought to relieve poverty and advance society, with little intention of changing the social structure or promoting economic redistribution. Taxation that could have financed more state welfare was limited and mostly indirect, and therefore regressive. Philanthropic organisations concerned themselves with containing the negative impact of contemporary economic change and its social dislocations. Egypt's poor were long the reason for British and European accusations that the country was unable to manage its own affairs, and that therefore external interference in Egypt was needed. This further motivated the emerging national movement to take steps toward social reform.

Entangling education and state employment

While education was a primary tool for social reform, and more so under rising public demand, the Egyptian system of education had long been acknowledged as needing reform. Most Egyptians received a basic, religious education that entailed memorising the Qur'an in *kuttab* schools.[14] In the early nineteenth century, Muhammad Ali, the Ottoman ruler commonly regarded as the founder of modern Egypt, also established a new system of selective education – primary, secondary and professional public schools – to educate state cadres.[15] Even before the British occupation, the need for the improvement of both mass and selective education was clear, and Ismail, the last effective ruler of Egypt before the occupation, took steps toward producing this reform.[16] In 1882, when the British occupied Egypt, they encountered a dual system of public education already in place. Thus, the British inherited both this system and a growing call for its transformation.[17] The British also brought their own, imperial, considerations to bear on such reform.

The trajectory of Egyptian education up until semi-independence took shape in a political setting that birthed opposites: on the one hand, it saw broad agreement over the centrality of education in bringing social reform; on the other hand, it gave rise to a strong disagreement between the British and the emerging national movement over educational reform. Often associated with Lord Cromer (born Evelyn Baring), who in his official capacity as British consul general (1883–1907) dominated Egyptian politics from the early days of the occupation until his departure from Egypt, official British policy on education was that it should facilitate economic recovery under tight budgetary discipline. The British occupied and stayed in Egypt under the official pretext of putting the country's financial disarray in order. Conservative views on economic management prioritised investment in economic infrastructure, especially in agriculture, over human progress through education.

Under such constrictions and policies of occupation, reform of education was limited. Furthermore, elitist education was restricted by the carrying capacity of the Egyptian civil service and the economy. In addition to their belief in economic liberal orthodoxy, Cromer and other British officials believed that, as in British-ruled India, the introduction of elaborate modern education would result in the creation of a new political elite – a leadership for nationalist agitation that would be critical of British rule. Cromer's disposition against both public spending and the risk that education would bring incitement against the colonial rulers meant that between the years 1882 and 1902 less than 1 per cent of the state budget went to education.[18]

Under Cromer, the British undertook two educational-reform initiatives. In 1898 they introduced a limited reform attempting to centralise and standardise mass, if yet not compulsory, education in Egypt.[19] In a return to state subventions, elementary, *kuttab* schools joined the reform and were put under state regulation. The reform included improvement in the quality of teaching, a 'modernised' or 'secular' curriculum, and new vocational training, which trained children for more efficient participation in economic life and society. Under this system, reformed *kuttab* schools taught in Arabic only, unlike in selective state schools, where studying a foreign language was a central requirement. In both the subjects taught and the lack of a language requirement, the reformed system of elementary education meant that such schools gave up their position as potential feeding schools for secondary education, where higher academic achievement and a foreign language were mandatory. This reform, therefore, while not creating the dual system of education in Egypt, certainly exacerbated it by channelling the majority of Egyptian school children into a dead-end education, as opposed to allowing for socio-economic mobility.

British administrative reforms carried out under Cromer supplemented the formalising of a past nexus between education and state employment. In 1892, based on existing practice, the British formalised a two-tiered system of state employment – an upper division that required a secondary school certificate and a lower division that mandated a primary school degree.[20] After this reform, official education guaranteed state employment in Egypt.[21] However, a few years later, as part of the 1898 educational reform, the state initiated tuition for primary, selective public schools, which had previously been free. Cromer argued that the Egyptian elite whose sons frequented such schools should pay for education, rather than be subsidised by the state.[22] Over time, the state further consolidated the selective state schooling system and reduced the number of students.

After the turn of the twentieth century, the emerging Egyptian national movement increasingly demanded educational reform, now also contrasted with the 1898 British reform. The effendi spokespersons of this movement asked for a better system of mass education and called for reducing fees and enlarging the enrolment in elitist state schools.[23] The latter plea was especially strong because elitist education would help re-Egyptianise state employment. Moreover, such education would make the effendis advocating this change better able to serve the nation. Importantly, in the national demand for educational reform, as in the 1898 British reform, the dual nature of Egypt's system of education was not challenged. If anything, it was enhanced by the previous, British-led educational reform, as well as by the national movement's demand for better higher education, which constituted an economic and administrative alternative to investing in the mass education system. This approach further supports the argument made above regarding the nature of an overall effendi reform that would stabilize a national community as opposed to improve broad social mobility.

Following Cromer's departure, and no doubt as part of a growing British realisation that the national movement should be accommodated and contained, a gradual policy shift toward reforming Egypt's system of education occurred. Between 1907 and 1912, state expenditures on education as part of the state budget more than tripled, from a minuscule 1 per cent under Cromer to a still hardly sufficient 3.4 per cent.[24] Such resources were particularly insufficient in the face of the rising demand to concurrently reform both mass and elitist education in Egypt. Some two decades after the 1898 reform, the vast majority of children still studied in private *kuttab*s not regulated by the state, as opposed to publicly administered schools (*maktab*, singular). To actually implement such reform, according to the Elementary Education Commission, the number of *maktab*s would have had to be increased from 663 to 10,000, which would have meant building new schools rather than simply taking over existing *kuttab*s. What is more, the quality of education in both kinds of schools was often poor. In addition to reforming elementary, mass education, there was a continuing public/national demand to make improvements in and reduce tuition for elitist, primary and secondary state schools, and a call to establish a national university. Regardless of the huge financial effort that the spread of mass education would entail, spending on higher education as part of the educational budget was disproportionately large.[25] A clear, if implicit, emphasis on selective and higher education in Egypt, and hence, a clear preference for effendi interests over those of the majority of Egyptians, was apparent then and has remained so ever since, because such education was a prerequisite for state employment.

Somewhat paradoxically, a period of rapid liberalisation of the economy under the British saw an increased demand for state employment. Competition over state employment was central to the emergence of the Egyptian national movement and national politics because a British-induced state retrenchment led to a squeeze on state employment, while the available, top-ranking positions often went to Britons and Europeans.[26] Concurrently, the liberalisation of the Egyptian economy under the British – the rapid integration of Egypt into the European-led world economy – provided only a partial alternative for the employment of skilled/educated Egyptians. Under colonial capitalism, the free market was restricted for the vast majority of Egyptians by an already established discriminatory system of capitulations, coupled with a European system of 'mixed courts', the inception of which predated the occupation by a few years (1876). Europeans and non-Muslim communities in Egypt and a small, elite group of Egyptian landowners dominated the expanding economy. The double bind of restricted state- and market-based employment turned into a central cause for agitation in the emerging national movement.

By World War I, the British had established a dominant position in the Egyptian civil service and the military, despite their self-proclaimed aim of preparing Egypt for self-rule.[27] The war and the establishment of the British Protectorate in Egypt (1914) further exacerbated this process. In 1921 the Milner report summarised the work of a British fact-finding mission to Egypt in the aftermath of the 1919 Revolution.[28] The report exposed existing inequalities in the Egyptian civil service and, based on the 1919/20 state budget, it identified two brackets of state employment. The lower bracket, or 'lower posts', was almost entirely (98.5%) occupied by Egyptians. Likewise, Egyptians held the vast majority (86%) of 'upper posts'. Still, the gap between Egyptians and non-Egyptians in high civil service positions was clear from a discrepancy in wages within this category – Britons in high official positions earned more than their Egyptian counterparts in similar positions.[29] Gaps between the salaries of Egyptians and the others were even more pronounced when lower and upper posts were disaggregated to expose huge discrepancies in earnings between these categories.

Between 1905 and 1920, the total percentage of Egyptian employees increased slightly. This rise was in lower posts, while in upper posts the percentage of Egyptians slightly decreased, and that of Britons significantly increased. The Egyptian civil service was thus twice ethnically stratified: (a) between the majority of Egyptians occupying low positions and paid relatively low wages and Britons and others who dominated higher positions, and (b) within the upper echelons of the civil service, where Britons clearly occupied higher positions and were better compensated than Egyptians.

In evaluating the overall situation, the Milner report states:

> Egyptians generally no doubt think, and they are right in thinking, that the importation of British officials has sometimes, especially of late years, been overdone. They hold firmly to the principle that no Englishman or other foreigner should be appointed to any post for which a reasonably competent man of their own race can be found. They look forward to the time when the whole or almost the whole of the public service will be staffed by their fellow-countrymen. They feel that progress in that direction has been unduly slow and would like to see it sensibly accelerated.[30]

Implicit in the evaluation above of what 'Egyptians generally no doubt think' was an effendi agenda of Egyptianising the public service, now internalised within the Milner report and soon, in the 1923 Egyptian constitution.

Constitutionalising the social contract

In November 1914, mere months after the onset of World War 1, Britain ended Egypt's nominal suzerainty to the Ottoman Empire by unilaterally placing Egypt under a British protectorate. In doing so, the British promised that Egyptians would not have to go to war against the Ottoman Empire and their coreligionists, and also would not suffer the consequences of war, which Britain would face alone. The British took immediate steps toward fulfilling this latter promise to safeguard civilian life in Egypt, by putting together a system of food provision and rationing. These measures came hand in hand with a British policy of rent control in cities. Both were meant to safeguard against shortages and were mostly concerned with securing the standard of living of urbanites. The British also put together four commissions to discuss significant reforms in public health (the Commission on the Reorganisation of the Public Health Services), the economy (the Commission on the Expansion of Commerce and Industry, also known in Egyptian historiography as the Sidqi Commission) and education (the Elementary Education Commission and a commission for the establishment of a national university).[31] These commissions were the British response to Egyptian public pressure during the war, and were a promise for change after the war.

The 1919 Revolution that would bring partial Egyptian independence was to a significant extent a protest against war-induced distress, which came despite the above measures and in clear violation of the earlier British promise to the Egyptians.[32] It is worth asking to what extent the 1923 constitution that formalised the social contract of the future liberal monarchy indeed responded to such misery and to the ongoing call for social reform.

The short answer is that the constitution and the liberal monarchy brought much of the liberal socio-economic approach of the late nineteenth century into the newly established nation-state. They were not the outcome of the immediate hardships that were at the root of the 1919 Revolution and semi-independence, but of the liberal age that preceded it.[33] In the wake of the reforms of the Edict of Gulhane (1839), the Ottoman Empire, including Egypt, experienced a quest for more power sharing between the ruler and the ruling elite, as well as within the ruling elite and between old and new socio-economic forces. Imperialism further introduced global (read European) best practices that supported such transformation as a measure for bringing political stability and furthering regional imperial interests.[34] Emerging national movements, including the 1879 'Urabi Revolt in Egypt, had embraced constitutionalism as part of a growing national call for political independence. Thus, the 1923 constitution carried traces of all the above, which has made analysis of what it stood for rather fuzzy and open to interpretation. One thing was clear though: it was not going to quickly remedy the misery of those most in need among lower-class Egyptians.

The constitution established a new political system in Egypt, but one that allowed the continuation of British presence to safeguard British and international interests in the country, as well as those of local minorities. It also curtailed the power of the king by limiting his legal authority.[35] It further limited the power of the national movement represented by the Wafd (the dominant political party during this period), by allowing some among the Egyptian elite who were closer to the British a greater say in the constitutional process, or so Saad Zaghlul, who led the Wafd and boycotted the constitutional commission, felt.[36] Ultimately, the constitution created an often-contested power-sharing balance between the king and parliamentary politics dominated by the landed elite, and therefore, often between the palace and the Wafd.

The short 'preamble' to the 1923 constitution is quite telling regarding the constitution's civilising goals:

> Having, since mounting the throne of our ancestors and vowing to keep safe the trust which God Almighty has entrusted to us, always done our utmost to pursue the good of our nation, and pursue the path which we know will lead to its welfare and advancement and to deriving the enjoyments of free and civilized nations;

> And since such end cannot be properly attained unless in a constitutional system similar to the most advanced constitutional systems in the world, under which our nation can happily and satisfactorily live and pursue the path of an absolutely free life, and which ensures active participation in running state affairs and overseeing the drafting and enforcement of laws, and brings a

sense of comfort and assurance about our nation's present and future, while maintaining the national qualities and distinctions which constitute the great historical heritage thereof;

And as the fulfilment of such end has constantly been our desire and one of the greatest endeavours we are determined to seek so as to help our People's rise to the highest of standards which the People is readily qualified and capable of meeting, which befit the ancient historical greatness of our People, and which enable our People to attain the appropriate status among peoples of civilised nations;[37]

The 'Preamble' well exposes contemporary, liberal conventional wisdom. It outlines the promotion of welfare and progress as basic motivations for the constitution and establishes the constitutional system as the best global practice of the time, and therefore also its suitability for Egypt, which would join the civilised and progressive nations club.

These were not simply empty words. The constitutionalists who deliberated over the document took ample account of other, mostly European constitutions. The 1923 constitution was not, as Abdeslam Maghraoui argues, European cultural implantation that, under the guise of liberalism, forced Egyptians to give up on their Arab-Islamic identity and heritage.[38] It did represent an elitist, Egyptian vision for the political, economic and social future of Egypt that was in tandem with such a global vision. The liberal monarchy that the constitution established later alienated many, not because it was perceived as foreign or inauthentic but because under the prevailing socio-economic conditions and continuing foreign domination, politics could not entirely deliver on local aspirations, particularly those of an expanding effendi middle class. It was the multitasking ingrained in the constitution that hampered its stability. Moreover, it was an implementation of a national vision that only partly accounted for the rising economic needs of the effendi middle class and those of most Egyptians.

The newly established social contract under the liberal monarchy disappointed many from early on. First, Egypt's political independence from the British was only partial, and Britain continued to play a central role in Egyptian politics throughout this period. A capitulation system still in place was another aspect of the imperial intervention, and was an actual barrier to change in local economic policy, especially taxation. Such conditions existed until the mid-1930s, when they started to change with the signing of the Anglo-Egyptian Treaty of Alliance (1936) and the subsequent abrogation of the capitulations. Egyptian fiscal policy, and therefore its social policy, was limited owing to foreign intervention. As long as the two lasted, Egypt had to run a conservative state budget.[39]

Second, the palace and the national party (the Wafd), were far from in agreement on the source of the constitution (its origins), and therefore over the nature of the social contract embodied in the liberal monarchy. In this debate the royalists supported a formalist argument that enshrined the central role of the king in granting the constitution to citizens through a royal decree. According to this argument, the constitution was a one-sided, royal grant to the nation.[40] The Wafd, at the other end, and despite the fact that it was dominated by the landed elite, emphasised the nation as the source of all power and authority, based on article 23 of the constitution. It depicted the constitution as a contract between members of the nation, and the Wafd itself as representing the citizenry when negotiating with the king. The above debate between royalists and Wafdists was by no means theoretical only. It underscored a real power struggle during the liberal monarchy period between the two sides of Egypt's political elite, with the British remaining a third contender in the contemporary triangle of power.

The third argument in local public debate against the constitution as the embodiment of the social contract was related to the issue of who, exactly, within Egyptian society was represented in this contract. The liberal monarchy was socially outdated from its inception. The parliament represented the partial triumph of an existing, mostly landed, Egyptian elite over the British and the king, in wrenching political power from both. The liberal monarchy and its political system were less attentive to rising social forces, labour and especially the effendi middle class in cities, while also inadequately catering to the majority of peasants. During the 1930s, the emergence of extra-parliamentary forces among workers, particularly among the expanding effendi middle class, clearly demonstrated this. The contested social contract upon which the liberal monarchy was established eroded not long after its 'signing'.

Often less noticed in the analysis of the liberal, political social contract during the late nineteenth and early twentieth centuries was the concurrent introduction of a conservative-liberal, free-market economy to the Ottoman Empire and Egypt. In 1838, a year before the Edict of Gulhane, the British–Ottoman Treaty of Balta-Liman that partially abolished trade barriers between the empire and Europe preceded the ushering in of the age of reform. Indeed, the age of reform itself was about economic no less than political reform – the establishment of the rule of law through the constitution was equally central to economic rights (property rights) and to political rights. An egalitarian system of taxation as mandated by the constitution complemented a request for popular participation in politics; the latter was predicated on the first (as in the maxim 'no taxation without representation').

The Treaty of Balta-Liman and subsequent economic legislation officially replaced the Ottoman command economy with a liberal economy. Essentially, the Ottoman state disengaged from markets. In Egypt in particular, liberal economic reform countered the more recent mercantilist management of the economy that Muhammad Ali had introduced at the beginning of the nineteenth century. While limiting state management of and participation in the economy, economic reform further limited 'market welfare' principles that had previously ensured economic stability and equity at the expense of economic growth.[41]

Before and after semi-independence, the conservative-liberal economic regime meant that there was limited state spending on social welfare. British influence still limited the liberal monarchy's economic discretion over spending. The lingering legacy of the Egyptian state bankruptcy that led to Egypt's occupation guided not only the British but also Egypt's political landed elite in keeping with an austere budget. Section 4 of the constitution, which discusses state finances, says in article 141 that Egypt would honour public debt before undertaking any other financial obligations. In doing so, this article imposed another barrier to augmenting public spending. As part of economic cautioning, and as a countercyclical measure against fluctuations in cotton prices, the state held on to large public funds, further limiting its discretion on state expenditures.

Taxation, to allow for more state services and greater equity through economic redistribution, was limited by the capitulations.[42] Any attempt at imposing an income tax, a more progressive form of taxation, was impossible as long as the capitulations were in place. The protectionist policies and practices granted under the capitulations also meant that any change in Egypt's taxation regime would not include residents of foreign communities in Egypt. Until 1930, Egypt relied on limited tariffs and certain excise duties. Two taxes on land and buildings (based on their rental values) were considered systematically underestimated, and therefore underpaid. When a change in taxation was being considered, it was thought doubtful that the Egyptian economic elite would readily accept an increase in taxation.

In his edited volume *War, Institutions and Social Change in the Middle East*, Steven Heydemann (and other contributors) highlight the centrality of wartime institutions for the making of nation-states in the Middle East in the aftermath of World War II. Yet, in the aftermath of World War I, state interference with provision and rationing of food was gradually phased out in Egypt.[43] The same was true of rent control. Despite strong outbursts of protest in rural regions among peasants and in urban regions among labourers, working conditions for the majority of Egyptians did not improve much, and social insurance barely existed.[44] Similarly, public health received little attention, despite the appalling public health conditions in Egypt. The call for greater state participation in economic regulation (the Sidqi Commission) largely remained dormant. In short, the presence of wartime institutions and planning commissions did not much change the staunch economic liberalism that was restored after the war, despite partial independence. Wartime institutions were supposed to alleviate temporary economic scarcity and wartime hardships, while the planning commissions mostly placated the public outcry for a larger role for the state in socio-economic affairs. There was much structural similarity between wartime management/regulation of the economy between the two world wars, with quite different consequences regarding such institutions in their aftermath. In the aftermath of World War I, state involvement in the economy remained limited; welfare remained mostly productivist and was based upon philanthropic associations. The only important exceptions to this conservative-liberal economic management, but quite in tandem with their pre-war centrality in the public (read effendi) discourse, were education and state employment.

Analysis of articles 17, 18, and 19 of the 1923 constitution demonstrates that these articles set the course for the future of education in Egypt in several ways.[45] First, in establishing the worthy principle of free-of-charge, compulsory, elementary education for boys and girls alike, article 19 set too high a standard; for many years to come, elementary education in Egypt would fall behind in efforts to meet it. Elementary education reform partially failed because it was based on upper-class aspirations that were too high and was not accompanied by a commitment to dedicate enough funds for its implementation.

Second, despite the centrality of elitist and higher education in the national cause, the constitution made no mention of it. Study of the deliberations of the Constitutional Commission that drafted and debated the constitution – the commission consisted of members of Egypt's socio-political elite – reveals that a suggestion to offer free-of-charge places to students based on availability in state schools was withdrawn from the original draft. A later suggestion for a progressive system of tuition in such schools – reduction in tuition for those unable to pay – was similarly rejected by the upper-class deliberators. In Egypt's dual system of education now under the liberal monarchy, mass education quickly expanded with little regard to the quality of the education provided. Elitist and higher education likewise quickly expanded, but also under a growing effendi middle class sense of injustice regarding economic inequality and a demand to reduce tuition to allow more egalitarian entry into such institutions of learning.

Third, article 17 of the constitution established the principle of 'free education' – education free from external social and political interference – based on the law. This article faced, and ultimately ignored, the reality of a complex system of education that included multi-religious schools – Muslim, Christian, and Jewish – local and foreign schools, state schools, and private schools, each with its own system and curriculum. Moreover, free education itself was challenged by a mounting national demand for the 'Egyptianisation' of education by the state, notably through the use of Arabic. Over time, a gap developed between free education as laid down in article 17 and the national cause that called for state regulation of educational content, a central call in both parliamentary and, increasingly, extra-parliamentary activities in Egypt.[46] Article 18, which implemented the rule of law in education in transferring decision making regarding educational policy to the newly established parliament, further politicised multiple, sometimes conflicting, sets of demands. The first was a demand to expand and improve mass education, and the second, to allow greater entry into elitist and higher education, while improving the quality of teaching. In Egypt, such a systems overload meant constant political discourse calling for reforms of already substantial reforms.

In the first years after the establishment of the liberal monarchy, state-sponsored elementary education grew quickly. The 1920s saw a revolution in the number of children entering elementary schools, as their number rose nearly elevenfold, from 23,345 in 1922 to 256,747 by 1930.[47] The same period also saw a rise in private (non-state supervised) school enrolment from 43,007 to 87,282.[48] Selective primary, secondary and higher education also rapidly expanded under the liberal monarchy from 24,539 students in 1922, to 60,422 in 1931.[49] Here too the overall number of students in higher education was presumably higher because some of these institutions were under the supervision of other ministries, and were therefore not counted in the ministry of education figures above.

While the overall expansion of Egypt's system of education had already begun before World War I, with the establishment of a semi-independent Egyptian state, a generation of Egyptians benefited from the new educational opportunities. The enrolment of students across this system increased well beyond demographic growth.[50] Despite a conservative-liberal economic policy in state management, by 1925/26 state expenditures on education increased to 6.4 per cent of the national budget, almost double the pre-war level, and further increased to 7.4 per cent by 1930/31, a clear testimony to the centrality of education in Egyptian politics.[51] This impressive rise aside, the ongoing public and professional debates over education continually exposed a conflict between 'quantity' and 'quality', or whether the education system should be allowed rapid numerical growth or be improved in terms of content and teaching first.[52] Importantly, during that period Egypt's system of education remained heavily biased toward boys and men, despite a constitutional promise of public elementary education for both boys and girls, and an effendi public discourse that emphasised education as a venue for the advancement of women's role in society. What is more, there was also a clear educational bias, and hence a class bias, in favour of higher education that catered to both the elite and, partially, an aspiring middle class, as opposed to the majority of Egyptians.[53]

In the final analysis, through the constitution, education in Egypt retained its dual purpose – to facilitate broad social reform, but also to provide cultural, economic and political leadership – in the transition to a semi-independent state. The legacy of the dual system of education remained intact, despite the increasing role of the state in education, the establishment of new educational institutions, and the modernisation of curricula. As the discussion on state employment below elaborates, while education in Egypt was regarded as a means to alleviate ignorance, poverty and disease for the majority of Egyptians, through measures of self-help, its expansion over time benefited mostly the effendi middle class, who seized on new opportunities for socio-economic mobility through education.

In the 1923 Egyptian constitution, under section 2 – the rights and duties of Egyptians – the second part of article 3 constitutionalised the above-mentioned view regarding the Egyptianisation of state employment: 'Egyptians shall solely be appointed in public positions whether civil or military. No foreigners may be appointed in such positions other than in exceptional conditions stated by law'. In the deliberations over the constitution, this part of article 3 was barely debated.[54] Similar to article 19, which promised free-of-charge, compulsory elementary education for all Egyptians, the call for greater Egyptian participation in state employment was, by then, widely established.

A closer reading of article 3, in the context of the statistics presented in the Milner report, suggests a somewhat different interpretation of this article than simply Egyptianising state employment. The article clearly establishes the principle of national/self-governance. Nevertheless, in practice, and since the vast majority of state employees in lower posts already were Egyptians, article 3 implicitly calls to Egyptianise the upper echelon of state employees. Considering that most of the constitutionalists came from within this socio-economic group, this is perhaps not surprising. Still, and as in education, the first years of semi-independence also saw the rapid expansion of state employment, as well as its Egyptianisation. Between 1915 and 1925 the number of permanent civil servants increased from 15,000 to 33,000, a 120 per cent increase.[55] For a generation of aspiring effendis, the establishment of the liberal monarchy brought an important economic boon.

In 1954, shortly after the overthrow of the liberal monarchy, sociologist Morroe Berger oversaw a first-of-its-kind survey of 249 middle- and low-ranking officials in four ministries: agriculture, education, finance and economy, and municipal and rural affairs.[56] This survey serves as a time capsule for quantifying the reasons that such employees joined the civil service, and the change over time in the reasons given for joining. Respondents were divided into two age groups: the first (who at the time of the interview were between 46 and 60) had joined the civil service primarily before 1930; the second (aged between 31 and 45) had joined the civil service during the 1930s and 1940s. In reply to the question, 'Why did you select the civil service instead of some other kind of work?', 30.2 per cent of all participants replied that they had joined because they had limited opportunities elsewhere. An additional 14.9 per cent offered inadequate funds to start their own business as an answer.[57] Thus, 45.1 per cent of those responding to the survey said that they had joined the civil service because they had no economic alternative. Another 22.6 per cent gave job security as their main reason, while 8.9 per cent of the respondents claimed that the civil service was the only place for an educated person.

An age group division exposes some variance in the reasons given above. Significantly, the older generation, who had joined the civil service before 1930, did so to improve their economic/material conditions (74.2%), while among the younger generation only about 50.8 per cent responded that they had done the same.[58] Furthermore, those who had joined earlier did so less because of a lack of economic opportunity elsewhere. Of the older age group, 5.6 per cent responded that they had joined the civil service because of a lack of funds to open their own business, in comparison with 24.2 per cent among the younger age group. Thus, the first generation of Egyptians joining the civil service clearly experienced the state employment benefits that the 1923 constitution and the liberal monarchy had ushered in.

While the civil service partly opened up to Egyptians, this employment opportunity was still very limited for Egypt's general working population of the time. Moreover, it was obviously biased in favour of the elite, as well as of the already existing effendi middle class and a minority of social climbers who joined it. This is well reflected in Berger's survey. The vast majority in both age groups of civil servants were males, with women found only at the ministry of education.[59] Of the respondents to this survey, 74.3 per cent were born in cities, with only a tiny minority (2.8%) living in rural areas until the age of 30, implying an earlier movement to urban areas for schooling.[60] Among the respondents, almost 38.4 per cent were sons of civil servants, suggesting the hereditary nature of state employment.[61] The sons of small merchants, independent professionals, army officers and white collar, non-civil service employees – hence, also middle class – constituted about 22 per cent. Among the rest, 23.6 per cent were sons of landlords, in comparison with 16.1 per cent who were sons of peasants. As suggested in the figures above, state employment hardly facilitated large-scale socio-economic mobility.

Under the liberal monarchy, state commitment to spending on education, notably on higher education, as well as on state employment, stifled the social reform of those most in need. Furthermore, while the question of social reform often intertwined with the 'peasant question' in Egypt, only a limited portion of state expenditures and state services centred on rural regions. In the period 1922–36, the allocation of the state budget to various urban development projects more than doubled, from 2.3 per cent of the budget before 1922 to 4.8 per cent.[62] These allocations were unequally distributed between large and small (provincial) towns, with Cairo being the main receiver. City planning and public works, in turn, further facilitated the expansion of other services such as education (construction of schools) and health (sanitation) in urban settings.

A central explanation for such paucity was the centrality of education as a panacea that would cure all ills.[63] In public discourse and private and state action, a central and rather simplistic solution for matters related to hygiene, sanitation, disease prevention, proper child rearing and birth control lay in the education of social dependents: peasants, the urban poor and women and children.[64] Under an austere budget, and the assumption that education was so central to social reform, the state took little action toward levelling the economic ground through the provision of services, notably those related to health, and redistribution through taxation or social insurance/benefits. With little state participation, education as a cure-all proved a source of self-help only to those who could afford it; for those in economic need, state help was barely available.

An elitist- and effendi-led national movement adamantly demanded the expansion of education, particularly higher education, and state employment, as well as their Egyptianisation. Under the liberal monarchy, the implementation of such demands soon constituted a central paradox or dilemma in a conservative-liberal economic setting. With few lucrative prospects in the economy, graduates of selective primary and higher education institutions clearly preferred to work for the state. The state, for its part, still offered little by way of socio-economic development initiatives that would justify large-scale state employment. Additionally, and in a somewhat paradoxical fashion, such employment itself was a significant state expenditure, hence it partly inhibited other state expenditures required for social or economic reform.

Progressively over time, the political system came under pressure to further open up the selective primary and higher education systems, and with them state employment. Both of these demands became central to public and political discourse in the press and the parliament during the 1930s and 1940s. Higher education trickled down the social ladder as being essential both to socio-economic mobility into the expanding effendi middle class and to that class's social reproduction, and it therefore became a demand that the state could not ignore. The same was true for state employment. The call for social reform for peasants, and especially for workers, women and children, remained central in public discourse, and it would become significantly politicised after the mid-1930s. Such demands were, however, slow to materialise into state action, considering the state's growing economic commitment to the effendi middle class's expectations.

Notes

1. Michael Ezekiel Gasper, *The Power of Representation: Publics, Peasants, and Islam in Egypt* (Stanford, CA: Stanford University Press, 2009).
2. Ibid., 40.
3. Mine Ener, *Managing Egypt's Poor and the Politics of Benevolence, 1800–1952* (Princeton, NJ: Princeton University Press, 2003), 99–133.
4. Gasper, *Power of Representation*, 40.
5. Lisa Pollard, *Nurturing the Nation: The Family Politics of Modernizing, Colonizing and Liberating Egypt, 1805–1923* (Berkeley: University of California Press, 2005), 166–204.
6. Ryzova, *Age of the Efendiyya*.
7. Kenneth M. Cuno, *The Pasha's Peasants: Land, Society, and Economy in Lower Egypt, 1740–1858* (Cambridge: Cambridge University Press, 1992).
8. Lisa Pollard, 'Egyptian by Association: Charitable States and Service Societies, Circa 1850–1945', *International Journal of Middle East Studies* 46, no. 2 (2014): 243–5.

9. Alain Roussillon, 'La modernité disputée: réforme sociale et politique en Égypte', in *Entre réforme sociale et mouvement national: identité et modernisation en Égypte, 1882–1962*, ed. Alain Roussillon (Cairo: CEDEJ, 1995), 14–16.
10. I have borrowed the notion 'productivist welfare' from Ian Holliday, 'Productivist Welfare Capitalism: Social Policy in East Asia', *Political Studies* 48, no. 4 (2000), https://doi.org/10.1111/1467-9248.00279.
11. Ener, *Managing Egypt's Poor*, 101.
12. Mona L. Russell, *Creating the New Egyptian Woman: Consumerism, Education, and National Identity, 1863–1922* (New York: Palgrave Macmillan, 2004). Pollard, *Nurturing the Nation*.
13. Hoda A. Yousef, 'Losing the Future? Constructing Educational Need in Egypt, 1820s to 1920s', *History of Education* 46, no. 5 (2017), https://doi.org/10.1080/0046760X.2017.1338361.
14. See James Heyworth-Dunne, *An Introduction to the History of Education in Modern Egypt* (London: Frank Cass, 1968), for a detailed analysis of Egypt's system of education prior to the British occupation.
15. Private schools, sponsored by individuals, benevolent associations, missionaries and members of ethnic and religious – Christian and Jewish – communities were also prevalent in Egypt. They have largely been omitted from the analysis of state education in this chapter, as they are less pertinent to the discussion. However, see the analysis of the impact of Egypt's convoluted education system on articles of the constitution in the second part of this chapter.
16. Heyworth-Dunne, *An Introduction*, 342–423.
17. Hoda A. Yousef, 'Seeking the Educational Cure: Egypt and European Education, 1805–1920s', *European Education* 44, no. 4 (2012), https://doi.org/10.2753/EUE1056-4934440403.
18. Robert L. Tignor, *Modernization and British Colonial Rule in Egypt, 1882–1914* (Princeton, NJ: Princeton University Press, 1966), 346.
19. Mona Russell, 'Competing, Overlapping, and Contradictory Agendas: Egyptian Education Under British Occupation, 1882–1922', *Comparative Studies of South Asia, Africa and the Middle East* 21, no. 1–2 (2001): 52; and Gregory Starrett, *Putting Islam to Work: Education, Politics, and Religious Transformation in Egypt* (Berkeley: University of California Press, 1998), 31–2.
20. Tignor, *Modernization*, 204–5.
21. Morroe Berger, *Bureaucracy and Society in Modern Egypt: A Study of the Higher Civil Service* (Princeton, NJ: Princeton University Press, 1957), 29.
22. Roger Owen, *Lord Cromer: Victorian Imperialist, Edwardian Proconsul* (Oxford: Oxford University Press, 2004), 314–16; and Donald M. Reid, *Cairo University and the Making of Modern Egypt* (Cairo: AUC Press, 1991), 17–19. See Russell,

'Competing, Overlapping', 51, for a different interpretation of the reform, according to which both the British ruling elite and the Egyptian upper class saw in raising tuition as an opportunity to improve on the 'moral standard' in government schools by excluding undesirable students from lower social backgrounds.

23. Russell, 'Competing, Overlapping', 53.
24. Tignor, *Modernization*, 346. According to the Ministry of Education, Egypt, *Report of the Elementary Education Commission and Draft Law to Make Better Provision for the Extension of Elementary Education* (Cairo: Govt. Press, 1921), 35, hereafter the *EEC Report*, such expenditures for the years 1909–13 were even lower – 2 per cent of the total budget.
25. It was further heavily biased toward elitist state-run public schools and higher education, which catered, according to the Elementary Education Commission 'to a small privileged class'. *EEC Report*, 37.
26. Tignor, *Modernisation*, 202–6.
27. Ibid., 181.
28. Great Britain, Special Mission to Egypt, and Alfred Milner Milner, *Report of the Special Mission to Egypt* (London: H. M. Stationery off., 1921).
29. Here, 86 per cent of Egyptian employees earned only 71 per cent of the combined total of these salaries, while British employees held 6 per cent of such posts yet earned 19 per cent of the salaries. 'Others' (non-Egyptians, non-British) held 8 per cent of posts and earned 10 per cent of the combined salaries. Ibid., 30.
30. Ibid., 29–30.
31. On the Sidqi Commission, see Robert Vitalis, *When Capitalists Collide: Business Conflict and the End of Empire in Egypt* (Berkeley: University of California Press, 1995), 42–4. For an analysis of the University Commission, see Haggai Erlich, *Students and University in 20th Century Egyptian Politics* (London: F. Cass, 1989), 46–50; and Reid, *Cairo University*, 76–7.
32. Ellis Goldberg, 'Peasants in Revolt – Egypt 1919', *International Journal of Middle East Studies* 24, no. 2 (1992).
33. I have borrowed the term 'liberal age' from Hourani, *Arabic Thought*.
34. See Elizabeth Thompson, *Justice Interrupted the Struggle for Constitutional Government in the Middle East* (Cambridge, MA: Harvard University Press, 2013), for analysis of what she terms 'the rise of a constitutional model of justice', 11–88.
35. Elie Kedourie, 'The Genesis of the Egyptian Constitution of 1923', in *Political and Social Change in Modern Egypt: Historical Studies from the Ottoman Conquest to the United Arab Republic*, ed. P. M. Holt (London: Oxford University Press, 1968).
36. Afaf Lutfi Sayyid-Marsot, *Egypt's Liberal Experiment, 1922–1936* (Berkeley: University of California Press, 1977), 64.

37. See the 1923 constitution online in *Bibliotheca Alexandrina*, accessed 17 April 2020, http://modernegypt.bibalex.org/NewDocumentViewer.aspx?DocumentID=DC_20256&keyword (Arabic). In translating articles from the 1923 constitution into English, I consulted 'Royal Decree No. 42 of 1923 on Building a Constitutional System for the Egyptian State', *Constitutionnet*, accessed 17 April 2020, http://constitutionnet.org/sites/default/files/1923_-_egyptian_constitution_english_1.pdf.
38. Abdeslam Maghraoui, *Liberalism without Democracy: Nationhood and Citizenship in Egypt, 1922–1936* (Durham, NC: Duke University Press, 2006), 39–51.
39. Bent Hansen, *Egypt and Turkey* (Oxford: Oxford University Press for the World Bank, 1991), 59–60.
40. Mervat F. Hatem, 'The Pitfalls of the Nationalist Discourses on Citizenship in Egypt', in *Gender and Citizenship in the Middle East*, ed. Suad Joseph (Syracuse, NY: Syracuse University Press, 2000), 38.
41. Relli Shechter, 'Market Welfare in the Early-Modern Ottoman Economy – A Historiographic Overview with Many Questions', *Journal of the Economic and Social History of the Orient* 48, no. 2 (2005).
42. See a summary of Egypt's system of taxation in Bent Hansen and G. A. Marzouk, *Development and Economic Policy in the UAR (Egypt)* (Amsterdam: North-Holland, 1965), 246–7.
43. David, 'Food, Food Subsidies'.
44. For the political constraints on achieving workers' rights, benefits, and protection, even for the better organised part of Egypt's working class, see Marius Deeb, 'Labour and Politics in Egypt, 1919–1939', *International Journal of Middle East Studies* 10, no. 2 (1979).
45. Significantly, these articles appeared in the second section of the constitution, which established the rights and duties of Egyptians. The argument above is fully developed in Relli Shechter, 'The 1923 Egyptian Constitution – Vision and Ambivalence in the Future of Education in Egypt', *History of Education* 48, no. 5 (2019).
46. For a study of public and political debates over reforming education, including elementary education in Egypt, see Misako Ikeda, 'Toward the Democratization of Public Education: The Debate in Late Parliamentary Egypt, 1943–52', in *Re-Envisioning Egypt 1919–1952*, ed. Arthur Goldschmidt and Amy J. Johnson (Cairo: AUC Press, 2005).
47. Amir Boktor, *School and Society in the Valley of the Nile* (Cairo: Elias' Modern Press, 1936), 122, table 10. This fast increase in numbers suggests the large-scale incorporation of existing private schools into the new state system alongside the actual enlargement of public schooling.

48. Ibid., 122, table 11.
49. Ibid., 134, table 18, based on a survey by the Ministry of Education. According to this survey, the surge in student numbers started earlier, but such numbers grew particularly fast in this period. The vast majority of students were boys.
50. See a significant upturn in enrollment ratios per thousand population as calculated in Reid, *Cairo University*, 112, table 11. This table further indicates that such an enrollment increased much faster than the demographic increase, and especially so in secondary and university education.
51. Ibid., 177, table 20.
52. Ikeda, 'Toward the Democratization'.
53. Such a critique appears in Boktor, *School and Society*. Charles Philip Issawi, *Egypt: An Economic and Social Analysis* (London: Oxford University Press, 1947), who cited Boktor, concurs with this analysis (see his critique on pp. 182–3). For a similar critique, see also Berger, *Bureaucracy and Society*, 69.
54. The deliberations of the 1923 constitution are found in Muhammad al-Sharif, *'Ala Hamish al-Dustur* (Cairo: Matba'at al-I'timad, 1938). In this lengthy compilation, Muhammad al-Sharif, secretary of the Commission for Constitutional Affairs in the Upper House (Majlis al-Shuyukh) of the Egyptian parliament, gathered relevant information and arranged it based on the different sections and articles of the constitution. For the deliberations over article 3, see ibid., 15–39.
55. Marius Deeb, *Party Politics in Egypt: The Wafd & Its Rivals, 1919–1939* (London: Ithaca Press, 1979), 316–17.
56. Berger, *Bureaucracy and Society*.
57. Ibid., 71, table 14. See further analysis of generational differences in the decision to enter the civil service on pp. 104–6.
58. Ibid., 73, table 15.
59. Ibid., 46n13.
60. Ibid., 42, table 4.
61. Ibid., 45, table 7.
62. Mercedes Volait, 'Town Planning Schemes for Cairo Conceived by Egyptian Planners in the Liberal Experiment Period', in *Middle Eastern Cities, 1900–1950: Public Places and Public Spheres in Transformation*, ed. Hans Chr. Korsholm Nielsen and Jakob Skovgaard-Petersen (Aarhus: Aarhus University Press, 2001), 88.
63. Yousef, 'Seeking the Educational Cure'.
64. Ener, *Managing Egypt's Poor*, 99–133; Omnia El Shakry, *The Great Social Laboratory: Subjects of Knowledge in Colonial and Postcolonial Egypt* (Stanford, CA: Stanford University Press, 2007).

2

THE MAKING OF AN EFFENDI SOCIAL CONTRACT

Linda Darling suggests that social justice in the Ottoman Empire emanated from an earlier 'circle of justice', a paradigm that dominated earlier political thinking, taking its final shape in the sixteenth century.[1] According to the circle of justice, a ruler having a divine blessing or appointment had the duty to protect the state from enemies both external and internal, for which he required a military force. To maintain that force, the ruler had to tax economic activity. To ensure high taxation, the ruler needed to secure basic economic infrastructure such as irrigation for agriculture, roads and markets, as well as to ensure legal justice, including protecting producers (peasants) from the elites. Islamic thinkers objected to the exaltation of the ruler but, nevertheless, accepted the circle of justice. According to this concept, if any part of the system malfunctioned, it threatened the entire system, and it therefore required close cooperation between ruler and ruled to maintain its equilibrium.

According to Darling, 'the new concepts of nationhood and citizenship did not replace, but were added to, older concepts of interdependency and justice between rulers and people'.[2] She further argues that while the use of the circle of justice disappeared from political discourse in the aftermath of the Ottoman Empire, some aspect of this concept remained embodied in modern Middle Eastern politics, namely 'the expectation that the state is responsible to provide the means of protection, prosperity, and social justice or to compensate for their lack'. Darling continues: 'In the modern monarchies and republics that developed after World War 1, condemnations of violations by indigenous elites or foreign rulers and demands for just rule from national governments echoed the Circle's definition of justice'. While the circle of justice might have had an implicit impact on a later notion of social justice, Darling's analysis does not account for social and economic changes and their impact on the de facto content of the latter term. Beyond the overall responsibility of rulers, the exact meaning of social justice in a fast-changing economy and society in Egypt and elsewhere in the Middle East is quite vague.

In contrast to Darling, Elizabeth Thompson envisions the collapse of the circle of justice during the nineteenth century as a political turning point in the history of the Ottoman Empire, and later the Middle East.[3] According to Thompson, after the nineteenth century, social justice emerged as part of the dynamic search for a new form of political arrangement – a constitutional model – in the Ottoman Empire, including in Egypt. She argues that between 1839 (the Edict of Gulhane) and 1920, the empire engaged in a quest for a constitutional model of justice, inspired by a similar global quest. This constitutional model involved the representation of subjects-turned-citizens in the political process and the accountability of the ruler to the citizens, based on the constitution. According to Thompson, the 'Urabi 'constitutional revolution' (1879–82) already embraced the liberal principles of popular sovereignty, representation and equality under the law.[4] It was a popular movement set against the background of the privilege of the non-Arabic-speaking/Ottoman elite and Europeans. Thompson suggests that this revolution planted the seeds for mass politics in Egypt, leading to the 1919 Revolution.[5] Despite this, the political justice that emanated from the implementation of the constitutional model in Egypt's liberal monarchy became ever more distanced from the notions of political and social justice that would emerge after the mid-1930s. During this period and after, the growing independence of the Egyptian state from external British and European interference and the concurrent expansion of the effendi middle class increasingly challenged the definitions of both.

This chapter focuses on the period between the end of World War II and the Free Officers' revolution in 1952 – a period in which the effendi, statist social contract became formulated in public/political discourse and state action. It investigates the transition from a dominant public call for social reform to a no-less central demand for social justice. The chapter seeks to explain this change in the search for the resolution of what contemporaries referred to as the 'social question', as opposed to the earlier 'peasant question'. Certainly, the many concerns associated with the need to alleviate poverty, ignorance and disease did not disappear. Nonetheless, the new call for greater equity and equality of opportunity suggested that the ways of resolving these concerns were not working, hence the call for a new model of state involvement in socio-economic development that would assert effendi interests.

Not unlike World War I, which led to semi-independence, wartime hardships and new expectations during World War II and in its aftermath made the period between 1945 and 1952 crucial in shaping demands for social justice and the statist political vision that would implement it. This new vision of the state and its duties toward its citizens was strongly supported by various global best practices (which is to say, contemporary conventional wisdom) – from the contemporary social democracy and socialism of Western Europe, notably Britain, to the Communism of the USSR and the emerging Eastern Bloc. A regional and global process of decolonialisation also intensified the call for participation of the nation-state in bringing about full independence concurrently with social justice. For local, regional and global reasons, the period between 1945 and 1952 was not simply one of ongoing socio-economic and political crises. It was also one of a reinvigorated search, stalled earlier by the war, for the resolution of such crises and the active making of an effendi social contract for Egypt.

The chapter first predates the notion of socialism in Egyptian public/political discourse to the aftermath of World War II. It demonstrates that 'socialism' as a call for state action and 'social justice' as a demand for equity and equality of opportunity were closely intertwined in the contemporary public expectation of fast socio-economic development. The chapter later examines the hierarchy of social hardships in Egyptian public discourse to explain what contemporary social justice stood for, and for whom. It concludes with the study of state actions taken to augment social justice in Egypt, and an analysis of the hierarchy of state actions aimed at implementing social justice and, therefore, who actually benefited from that implementation.

Between 'socialism' and 'social justice'

In 1946, Muhammad Fahmi Lahita, a professor at the Commerce College, Cairo University, published the third volume of his trilogy, *The Economic History of Fouad the First: Egypt on the Road to Complete Guidance*.[6] This volume,

Social Justice: Egypt and the Standards of Living of the Egyptians, was an homage to King Farouk and was dedicated to Ali Mahir, Farouk's crony and the authoritarian prime minister of Egypt before and after World War II. It narrates Farouk's economic achievements in having brought social justice to Egypt in ways that, at that time, were hotly debated. The topics in this book include agricultural reform and state improvement of the peasants' standard of living, state support for industrialisation, state support for the workers' standard of living, and steps taken toward the Egyptianisation of the economy. Many achievements in all these spheres had already been attributed to the guidance of King Fouad and his successor, King Farouk. Indeed, according to Lahita, it was Fouad's 'governmental socialism' that was at the root of these successes.

By 1952, when the Free Officers took to power, socialism, however broadly defined and with a number of variations, had already become a convention accepted by many political groups in defining the need for greater state involvement in the economy and society. This trend was shared with British politics, in which the Labour Party returned to power in the aftermath of World War II. A new British government nationalised central industries and expanded the welfare state, notably through the creation of the National Health Service. Socialism in Egypt was further adapted twice: it was Egyptianised, and it was soon to be Arabised in serving the unique requirements of the local economy and society. It harmonised the economic and social interests of various classes in Egyptian society for the sake of social solidarity and the nation. This was significant because social justice and socialism became closely intertwined during this period and afterward. This adaptation resembled the development of contemporary African socialism, which similarly searched for venues to adapt global socialism to African traditions and realities.

Lahita was clearly reading social justice and its implementation in Egypt backward. Fouad died before the signing of the Anglo-Egyptian agreement (1936) that allowed the state to start flexing its administrative, legal and economic muscles to bring about the broad changes that Lahita associated with him. Indeed, Lahita had no qualms about attributing governmental socialism to Muhammad Ali, the Ottoman ruler-turned-founder of modern Egypt, during the first half of the nineteenth century. According to Lahita's narrative, governmental socialism was gradually abandoned later by Muhammad Ali's successors – namely, the khedives (viceroys) Said and Tawfiq – under foreign influence. King Fouad returned to this form of state guidance of the economy and society, to the benefit of the Egyptians and Egyptian nationalism.

Lahita was quick to note that governmental socialism was different from socialism and communism, but also from what he calls individualism, capitalism and at times, individualistic capitalism. Lahita's argument was a forerunner to many later debates in Nasserite Egypt over 'our socialism', or Egypt's unique way of implementing Arab socialism as opposed to a purportedly universal socialism, during that period. Intentionally or not, this analysis echoes what Marxist theory terms 'state capitalism'. Indeed, Lahita's governmental socialism represented an amalgam of principles from all related ideologies seeking to benefit the Egyptian economy and society. Governmental socialism meant a model of socio-economic development led by the state, but in close cooperation with private entrepreneurship. Additionally, it promoted national interests – those of Egypt and its people – while avoiding class tensions. In governmental socialism, there was ostensibly no gap between the individual and the state. They were the same because the state was made of individuals and, similarly, their interests were the same: working for the benefit of the individual would also improve the socio-economic conditions of the state.

When Lahita published his book, socialism was all the rage in Egyptian public and political discourse.[7] This phenomenon has been attributed to a rising leftist – socialist, and communist – presence and influence in Egypt, where a drift to the left meant increased attention to questions of social justice.[8] However, the call for more state participation in economic and social development also arrived from the political right, notably the Young Egypt Party, and from the political centre, with the spread of state planning, direct involvement in economic management, and the further dissemination of the welfare state. Even the Muslim Brotherhood had its own socialist streak. Across this political spectrum, socialism and social justice became intertwined. All this was already made clear in Lahita's book. Arab socialism took much from an already existing economic and political toolbox and social contract; in many ways, it was the aggregation of both.

After the mid-1930s, and more so during and after World War II, public opinion called upon the state to take a greater role in socio-economic development – to face the challenges discussed above – and to bring independence from the de facto British imperial control that remained in place in Egypt's semi-independent state. The call upon the Egyptian state to develop the economy, implement social justice and promote full independence interacted with global changes and their presence in Egypt. Examples of such changes are the rise of Keynesian economics in the aftermath of the Great Depression, the centrality of planning and management institutions such as the Middle East Supply Centre (MESC) during World War II and after the war, the re-emergence of Western social democracy and the welfare state, the influence of socialist thought and action in Egypt, and a growing fear of international communism. However, statism also had significant effendi middle class roots that would explain why such influences gained traction in Egyptian public opinion and politics.

To fully understand statism in Egypt, it is important to differentiate between the call for a larger state role in society, the economy and national liberation, and authoritarianism in which those who manage the state limit the political freedom of other social players and citizens. Egypt has no doubt had its share of autocratic leadership since the 1930s. Nevertheless, in the mid-1930s the public outcry against the limitation on political freedom associated with the abrogation of the 1923 constitution and Ismail Sidqi's autocratic government clearly suggests a strong resistance to this antidemocratic step. In 1935 the return of the liberal constitution and a newly elected government were coupled with a growing effendi demand for greater state involvement in social and economic affairs. Simultaneously, and across the range of intellectual and political groups in Egypt, effendi public opinion increasingly considered the state – its civil service and state ministries – to be a central tool for socio-economic development, while the government was criticised for not doing enough to face the contemporary crisis.

During the second half of the 1930s, an earlier vision of social reform through productivist, often privately-provided welfare was increasingly replaced by a new vision of social reform, in which the state would take a greater role in modernising society through social engineering.[9] At the same time, there was a rising demand for state control of the economy – to protect it from foreign competition and to Egyptianise it. This intertwined call for the state to facilitate both social and economic development became the core of the future integrated model of development under Nasser.[10] Importantly, this call for state action on social and economic reform reflected a political consensus within the ruling landed elite. In 1935, and in its first National Congress, which broadened its social base, the Wafd Party added a state-led reform programme to its nationalist objectives.[11] Interestingly, the Wafd had few qualms about further adopting a similar policy of protecting local industry, as its arch-rival Ismail Sidqi had done a few years earlier. In 1936, under Ali Mahir, the royalist prime minister, the state established the Higher Council for Social Reform.[12] Suggestions for a greater role of the state in socio-economic development even came from liberal intellectuals within Egypt's landed elite, such as Mirrit Butrus-Ghali and his colleagues at the Society of the National Renaissance.[13] The rise of extra-parliamentary political activism from the right-wing Young Egypt, the socialist and communist left, and the Muslim Brotherhood further brought to light a rising demand that the state do more to advance socio-economic development. This broad consensus in calling upon the state to resolve socio-economic hardship and to bring full independence stood in some contrast to what seemed to many to be chronic political instability and frequent changes in government. Nevertheless, despite such instability there emerged a shared vision of how to fix society and the economy.

Gradually, statism – the call for state involvement in the economy and society – overlapped with socialism in Egypt. Like statism, socialism was employed throughout the political system, and it similarly referred to required state action in resolving socio-economic hardship. The call for socialism also overlapped with the contemporary demand for social justice, which gained much traction during this period. We need not confuse various calls for state action and socialism with a growing sympathy toward revolutionary socio-economic change. If anything, in a period of a mounting socio-economic unrest among Egypt's peasantry and the urbanite working class, statism and state socialism pre-empted a revolution – hence, the support they received from Egypt's upper and middle classes.

Less noticeable, but by no means less significant in formulating statism and socialism in Egypt, was the fact that the state employed an ever-increasing number of effendis. This happened in the aftermath of semi-independence (1922), during a period in which the state still strictly adhered to a conservative-liberal economic policy. The state was inadvertently creating a machinery whose members were central to public discourse and political activism. Importantly, since the 1930s the effendi middle class plight – and, at the same time, its social expectations – had become central to the local political agenda. Students, another important category in the unfolding politics, were often state employees in the making, while unemployment among graduates formed yet another major political concern for the state. From the perspective of state employment, the call for statism was about better, more effective utilisation of the state apparatus to improve not only society and the economy but also the state apparatus itself. From early on, state employment was infected with cronyism, political patronage, corruption and inefficiency, which the state found difficult to reform, despite broad awareness of the need for such reform.[14]

In a somewhat paradoxical fashion, therefore, a growing yearning for state command of economic and social affairs came in a period in which belief in the existing political system and in the landed elite were eroding. Extra-parliamentary political activism involving a wide range of political organisations pushed official politics into action. The politicisation of social reform and, after World War II, the rising demand for social justice further contributed to the demise of the existing political system in the public eye because the government was constantly seen as not doing enough. This was clear not only in the growing social unrest and public protest but in the significant surge in nonstate benevolence that was provided by religious (the Muslim Brotherhood) and political associations/parties.[15] Here too associational life, initially an elite initiative, increasingly became dominated by a broad-based effendi middle class activism. It was this gap – between the belief in state action and disbelief in those controlling the state – that brought about radicalisation in Egypt.

From the mid-1930s, and particularly with the signing of the 1936 Anglo-Egyptian treaty, which further enhanced independence, the Egyptian state was indeed flexing its muscles. In 1919, the Egyptian government included ten ministries, a figure that was retained until 1935. After that, a steep climb in the number of ministries indicated deepening state participation in socio-economic development. In 1935, the establishment of the ministry of commerce and industry was a clear response to growing financial independence, but also to an intensifying state effort at invigorating the economy, especially through industrialisation. In 1936, the ministry of public health was established. This was followed in 1939 by the ministry of social affairs, and in

1940 – after the outbreak of World War II – the state formed the ministry of supply, which continued operating after the war.[16] In 1950, the last Wafd government under Prime Minister Mustafa al-Nahhas added two new ministries – the ministry of village and rural affairs, and the ministry of national economy.[17] Between 1935 and 1950, then, the establishment of new ministries was closely related to main public concerns in Egypt, while the government increased its administrative capacity in an attempt to resolve such concerns and, no doubt, increase its power. Such capacity did not simply mean that the state had a greater ability to handle public concerns. Throughout this period and after, there was public apprehension over the administrative efficiency of this new state bureaucracy in providing the required services, and widespread alarm over nepotism and corruption in state services.

In the period under discussion, statism – as indicated above in the growth in state ministries – largely meant more state regulation to promote the economy and social justice. For example, a central venue through which the state augmented its role in social welfare was through regulation of philanthropic associations. Such associations had been encouraged earlier through the support and patronage of the political elite. Over time, their numbers increased and their membership spread down the social ladder. Associations became a political as well as a social means of change across the range of political organs and the secular-religious divide. In return, the state sought to tighten control over welfare provision. For some state officials, state regulation meant more professionalisation that boosted social reform. However, this regulation further centralised state power at the expense of civil society. It also served to curtail the opposition's attempts to bolster influence through service provision while shaming the government for not doing enough.

After 1945, a series of laws regulated associational life, progressively putting it under the supervision of the ministry of social affairs (MOSA). Law 49 of 1945 (which was further amended in 1952) required the registration of all associations and made the ministry of social affairs an overseer of their financial and organisational affairs, thus facilitating state control of them. To a large extent, MOSA became a regulatory body of welfare, rather than a service provider in its own right. Its responsibilities stretched over an array of actions, including a significant overlap with other ministries such as the ministry of education, the ministry of public health, and the ministry of waqfs.

MOSA became a supervisory body, with little budget of its own, but with a great array of responsibilities.

The Egyptian state's growing involvement in the economy was likewise in the form of regulation. Notable here was an ongoing attempt to Egyptianise the economy.[18] This demand for expanding Egyptians' share in the country's economy may be traced to the Sidqi Commission Report (1918). Already in 1923, the council of ministers had decided that at least one director in any newly established enterprise in Egypt had to be Egyptian, and that 25 per cent of the shares in the company had to be purchased in Egypt.[19] In 1924 the state made another legislative effort to force government representatives into important positions in foreign enterprises. In 1927, a ministerial decree stipulated that at least two members of each newly established joint-stock company had to be Egyptian.

During the 1930s, attempts at Egyptianisation intensified and received broad public support as a result of two concurrent changes in the Egyptian economy and politics: an economic crisis among the effendi middle class, particularly unemployment among the educated youth, and increasing state independence from foreign domination. In August 1936, in the aftermath of the Anglo-Egyptian agreement, Makram 'Ubayd, then the minister of finance, told the chamber of deputies that the government intended to revise the 1927 decree to state that 50 per cent of all enterprises' staff and 90 per cent of their workers had to be Egyptian. In 1938, with the end of the capitulations (after the Montreux Convention, 1937), another attempt at such legislation took place.[20] By 1947, when the joint-stock Company Law passed in parliament, Egyptianisation had become a widely accepted, state-based solution to the effendi middle class's market-based inequality of opportunity.[21]

Between 1945 and 1952, political radicalisation resulted from not only economic hardship but also rising political promises and mounting effendi public expectations in this sphere, with which the state only partly complied. The same was true for promises and expectations regarding full independence for Egypt. While state institutions offered more solutions to the contemporary crisis, there was rising mistrust in the existing political system. In the effendi-dominated press, the parliament, political parties and political societies ranked much lower than the state as vehicles for bringing about change.[22] Thus, whereas the state was the tool with which to resolve the social and economic crises, the socio-economic elite in charge of the state were not perceived by the Egyptian public as doing their jobs. Political instability and frequent changes in the government added to the above. Moreover, throughout a significant part of the 1940s, during but also after the war, Egypt was governed by martial law, which kept social unrest at bay, though it surely also decreased public trust in a seemingly democratic system of governance maintained by martial law.

After 1950, the last governments of the Wafd promised much, and brought some change, which nevertheless in the face of huge public expectations seemed too little, too late. Although many were taken by surprise by the January 1952 Cairo fire, also known as Black Saturday, that preceded the revolution by a few months, these events were the culmination of past, escalating social unrest. In 1952, Nasser's 'blessed movement' was well received because it offered both an end to street radicalism and intensive state action to fix the economy and society. The 1952 revolution was a popular revolution because it promised fast delivery of social justice and economic growth, and carried a strong effendi belief in the state together with decisive state action that promised change.

The discussion above suggests that in an evolving effendi social contract, this emerging agreement between the state and society, socialism and statism became largely conflated. This contract supported a larger state role in socio-economic development, if not a full-fledged authoritarian regime. In this emerging social contract, there was a synergy between the intensification of public (read effendi) expectation that the state become more involved in bringing about social justice, and the readiness of the Egyptian political elite to take over such responsibilities and increase their power in the process. The next sections discuss this effendi social contract as an implicit agreement among citizens, in which effendi interests dominated those of other social groups in Egypt.

A hierarchy of social justice

Najwa Husayn Khalil conducted a quantitative analysis of the Egyptian press's use of the phrases 'social question' and 'social crisis' between the years 1945 and 1952. For this research she sampled responses from across the political spectrum, to concerns associated with socio-economic hardship, and arranged them based on their frequency of appearance in the press.[23] In Khalil's typology of various social problems, and based on 416 articles and opinion columns, 'lack of equality between the people's classes and social justice' was by far the largest category with which press articles and opinion columns engaged (532 appearances). Furthermore, commentators suggested that while these were Egypt's greatest concerns, they were nonetheless also potential solutions – since bringing more equality and social justice to Egyptians would go a long way toward resolving their socio-economic hardship.

Khalil's finding is commensurate with a broad agreement in scholarship that the post–World War II period was indeed one in which equity and equality of opportunity, or social justice, became the centre of public/political interest.[24] Khalil's analysis further allows for insight into a hierarchy of social justice – the urgency or intensity with which commentators in the press dealt with different categories of social justice. In the press, the following categories appeared (in descending order of frequency): 'the question of education' (336), 'the question of food supply and increase in prices and inflation' (332), 'social pathology' (296), 'the place and role of women' (278), 'the health and nutritional problem' (229) and 'the workers' problem' (215). 'The housing problem' (76) and 'the problem of population increases' (12) were by far of considerably less interest to writers in the press.[25]

All such topics were closely related. As suggested by their frequency of appearance in the press, they were often discussed in tandem. (The total number of appearances is larger than the overall number of press articles discussed in Khalil's research). Interesting in the list above is the relative lack of immediate attention in the press to the problem of population increase, a central concern before the war.[26] Similarly conspicuous by its absence is 'the peasant question' (how to alleviate rural social and economic conditions through social reform), another central target of past public concern. These aspects of the social crisis might have been partially absorbed into more immediate concerns regarding rural regions, particularly the health and nutrition problem and social pathology. What is more, such a change in the public agenda indicates a change in focus, as suggested by the centrality of 'the workers' problem'.

The hierarchy in social problems based on their frequency of appearance in texts is telling because it exposes a bias in public commentary in which the effendi agenda dominated the social concerns of other social groups, notably workers and peasants. This was so despite the fact that in such commentary the 'middle class' was the least-mentioned category among other social categories in the analysis.[27] The press – the quintessential medium of mass communication in Egypt – was dominated by effendi writers and readers, whose writing seemingly lacked self-awareness; their agenda was dominant, though they did not acknowledge that. As we shall see, the centrality of effendi demands for social justice did not completely turn aside earlier demands for the alleviation of poverty, ignorance, and disease. All these remained, no doubt, central in the collective conscience. Moreover, 'social justice' emphasised social solidarity in the face of the plight of labourers and the urban poor, but mounting anxiety over social tension/malaise and a fear of political unrest made the call for social solidarity paramount. Class denial – the fact that the middle class did not appear in public commentary – should not be confused with the ample and various middle-class interests as they appeared in the Egyptian public discourse.[28]

Importantly, the state's minor contribution to welfare in rural regions in many respects mirrored the overwhelmingly effendi social movements' and parties' relative lack of interest in rural affairs, despite their pretences to represent/ help society as a whole. In 1939, the Muslim Brotherhood hailed the establishment of MOSA.[29] The leader of the Muslim Brotherhood, Hasan al-Banna, suggested that the reorganisation of rural life and education were central to the socio-economic development of peasants, and the Muslim Brotherhood's daily papers took a keen interest in issues related to the state's village reform.[30] Still, the Muslim Brotherhood was never deeply involved in such reform. This bias was not particular to the Muslim Brotherhood; rather, it was shared across the political spectrum, including the Egyptian left. While reform was for a long time part of an effendi, performative self-making subjectivity, in reality, both the personal and social trajectory of generations of effendis in Egypt involved leaving the village, never to return. Indeed, a central structural problem of present and future reform in rural regions was that of filling the very positions that were to execute this reform: effendi bureaucrats, teachers and health providers refused to go where their services were most needed. The sheer size of the reform project no doubt caused some to despair. What many considered the depth of the countryside's traditionalism, stagnation and backwardness made for pessimism regarding the possibility of reform. Indeed, Egypt's political elite exacerbated a sense of national crisis by promising much more than it could deliver. This was especially true of the last Wafd governments before the Free Officers' revolution.

In what follows, this section delves deeper into the categories of contemporary social problems as outlined in the list above. It positions each category in the more immediate context of the unfolding events, to discuss how such events drove a growing public interest in what the effendi middle class perceived to be social justice. I have deliberately omitted two categories: the problem of population increase, and the place and role of women. The first is not discussed because it occupied less immediate public attention in the press at the time. The second category, though no doubt still significant, found little direct expression in the rising demand for social justice under the implied assumption that state provision of welfare would include women. Moreover, under the patriarchy, or what Suad Joseph terms an 'extended kin contract', equity and equality of opportunity among men was supposed to provide social justice for their families as well.[31] Despite the centrality of the debate over the place and role of women in Egyptian society, it was relatively marginal with regard to the demand for social justice.

It is important to remember that the public call in the press for greater state implementation of social justice was not simply a barometer of the mounting public alarm. It was also the outcome of relative freedom of the press in the aftermath of World War II, with the rollback of wartime censorship, and periods of relative freedom of the press between 1945 and 1952.[32] The press played an active part in the call for social justice not only by increasing public expectations that the state would resolve the crises but also because it was allowed to do so. This surge in public expectation contributed to a dynamic in which, despite significant steps toward greater state involvement in society and the economy, there was an outcry against a political system that, from the effendi middle class's perspective, did not do enough to allow for social justice, rapid economic development and full independence.

In the press, and throughout the political system, public concern over education took on a central place. Education remained the cure for all social ills and was in dire need of reform. In particular, there was a constant public demand for the reduction of tuition in the selective, state primary schools. Access to selective education became a central element of the effendi public quest for social justice.

In 1943, Nagib al-Hilali, minister of education under a new Wafd government, abolished primary school fees. Al-Hilali based his decision on the need to avoid a social schism that would result from the inability of poor parents to pay these fees.[33] However, this change in tuition was universal. It promised free tuition to all, as opposed to free tuition for those most in need. Then and later, most families sending their children to the still selective primary schools did not come from the lower class, but from an aspiring effendi middle class. Abolishing tuition, as well as other state-measures to counter the war-induced rise in the cost of living, significantly benefited this social group.

In addition, al-Hilali called for a future, complete overhaul of mass elementary education, in the name of social justice and democratic principles. However, he forewent integrating mass elementary education with primary education. This, he and other deputies in the parliament dominated by the landed elite argued, would potentially have a negative effect on agricultural production, with more hours spent on education as opposed to labour, and too many graduates of the system leaving agricultural labour. Education thus raised both hopes and fears because, from this perspective, it could lead to socio-economic upheaval in the countryside and might result in an onslaught of migration to the cities. Unspoken yet important here was a further worry that an increase in student numbers would endanger the position of the more established members of society by raising competition for entry into higher education and, later, state employment. Egyptian educational policy moved between a strong effendi belief in education as the cure for all ills and the motivation to create a glass ceiling through education – to cap socio-economic mobility through education, thereby avoiding wide-scale social change.

In 1945, ʿAbd al-Razzaq al-Sanhuri, the new minister of education, promised another change in policy, in which the state would expand the primary system of education and improve the elementary system. Al-Sanhuri further promised to integrate the two systems, but this was a less urgent priority.[34] Increasing social justice in education was clearly a priority here, but one that took an evolutionary course as opposed to proceeding at a revolutionary pace. In 1951, under a Wafd government formally committed to facilitating social justice, Minister of Education Taha Hussein – a central voice in the call to expand selective and higher education in Egypt – finally unified primary and elementary education.[35]

Important here, and in other measures geared toward social justice discussed below, was an escalation in social unrest. Peasant revolts, workers' strikes and student demonstrations, in addition to more extra-parliamentary political activism, played a role in pushing the government to adopt measures to mitigate class tensions and facilitate social and national solidarity. Integrating Egypt's dual system of education was meant to accommodate one such public pressure. Another central reason for the Egyptian state to become more involved in reforming the education system was the growing public demand to Egyptianise education. Effendi public commentators of all political persuasions agreed on the necessity for such reform in a convoluted education system that included private schools, minority schools, and missionary education (the latter in particular came under the scrutiny of the Muslim Brotherhood).[36] As in the past, many argued that education would cure all ills. Many further argued that education in Egypt should emphasise national/patriotic and Islamic themes. The state therefore had to better regulate/nationalise educational content.

In Khalil's analysis, second to education in terms of its frequency of appearance in the press was the question of food supply and the increase in prices and inflation, the result of the war, which had led to pressure on local resources. During the war, the MESC and the Egyptian state intervened in the economy through planning, management, and regulation, in order to mitigate this pressure and the price increases. In June 1940, the establishment of the ministry of supply secured the adequate provision of food to citizens under wartime conditions.[37] In 1944, another such order set maximum prices based on a price level dated to 1941. In the aftermath of World War II, unlike after World War I, wartime state involvement in the economy lingered. This state action was now called upon as part of a growing quest for social justice. In March 1946, the ministry of supply was abolished, and the state transferred its responsibilities to the ministry of commerce and industry. The state's continued rationing and subsidising of foodstuffs thus became an antecedent of another such policy during the post-1952 era.[38] Centred on cities, food provision, subsidies and similar universal state initiatives benefited effendi middle class city-dwellers more than other social groups in Egypt, notably lower-class Egyptians in rural regions.

The housing problem appeared less frequently in the press, in comparison to the question of food supply and inflation. I discuss it here because it was also the result of wartime pressure on resources – a combination of shortages of building materials and a rise in demand for housing in urban areas. This pattern expanded, owing to rural-to-urban migrants in search of employment with the Allied Forces, rapidly expanding local industry, and urban population growth. In 1941, along with other measures to forestall price increases, the state enacted rent control to prevent owners of real estate properties from evicting their tenants and thereby taking advantage of the inflation in housing costs by rerenting at higher prices. In 1947 the state again legislated a rent freeze based on rent indices dated to 1941.[39] As in the case of provision basic commodities, wartime rent control became a peacetime means to secure the local standard of living. While such measures were abolished in the post–World War I era, in the aftermath of World War II, with greater independence and a different political mood in Egypt toward statism, such measures remained.

Implicit in the press commentary for the period between 1945 and 1952 were complaints about price increases and inflation. These were presented as a public call for the state to protect its employees through wage increases and other means, such as price regulation, subsidies for food, and rent control, to counter economic upheaval. In addition to direct compensation and, no less important, job security, and starting as early as World War I, there had been a long-term legacy of the state sheltering its employees in times of economic crisis. An underlying theme in public discourse in the press was the call for the state to protect state employees through state employment of graduates. Likewise, maintaining the standard of living of state employees was a long-term concern of the state. As discussed in Chapter One, Egyptianising state employment was at the core of the national struggle for independence. Political patronage of state employment was central to the party politics of the liberal monarchy. Furthermore, protecting the standard of living of state employees was a major political concern because political patronage of state employees was central to Egyptian politics. Moreover, the plight of state employees was a constant source of complaints from extra-parliamentary organisations and parties whose membership often came from among the effendi middle class. Various suggestions – from within and without the

Egyptian government – on how to reform the civil service by making it more transparent and efficient were of little avail.

The health and nutritional problems discussed in the press were largely the outcome of wartime conditions that exacerbated severe epidemics in Egypt. Between 1942 and 1944, a devastating malaria epidemic was central in bringing health and nutritional problems to public attention, and to the rapid politicisation of these issues as political rivals both inside and outside the parliament called upon the state to resolve the matter.[40] By the end of the 1940s, public health 'had become an indispensable component of the national political agenda'.[41] Public discourse called for state participation in the provision of health services, including by effendi physicians and health professionals with close political ties.[42] Relapsing fever in 1946 and cholera in 1947 further drew public fear and attention to the state of public health. Despite a mounting public outcry and the politicisation of public health during and after World War II, and a call to improve health conditions in rural regions, state health services largely remained confined to cities. Moreover, the analysis below of state allocations to health services in relation to other state expenditures (their relative share of the national budget) suggests a gap between the politicisation of public health and actual state readiness to change priorities in public expenditures in the face of competing public demands.

Much like the mounting public/political outcry and the politicisation of public health, the workers' problem that had received much attention since World War II was the result of the wartime, and especially post-war, crisis, not unlike what had happened in the aftermath of World War I.[43] Both wars brought on a spurt of industrialisation – the result of a demand for commodities and services to supply the war effort – coupled with rural-to-urban migration in response to economic opportunities in cities and increased hardship in rural regions. In the wake of the two wars, a decrease in such demands, and hence a rise in unemployment, which was further coupled with a continuing rise in living expenses, brought about a surge in labour movement activism and demonstrations. After World War I, the workers' plight quickly became politicised because in an economy still dominated by foreigners and local minorities, the workers' struggle to improve wages and working conditions went in tandem with the national cause of liberation from British dominance. Moreover, significant for both its political implication and proximity to minds and hearts, the growing centrality of industry in cities, notably in Cairo and Alexandria, intensified effendi public interest in labour affairs. During the interwar era, both the palace and the Wafd extended patronage to workers, as did extra-parliamentary organisations.[44]

In the aftermath of World War II, the public consensus demanding relief for workers and peasants was not simply an act of social and state benevolence. It came in periods that saw growing misery among rural and urban lower classes, a rise in protests against such conditions, and an appeal for government help. For the Egyptian middle and upper classes, welfare for the poor was not simply social solidarity – it was meant to resolve the social malaise and rise in crime by reducing mass migration to the cities. Furthermore, poverty dashed hopes of developing local industry through an import substitute industrialisation (ISI) model, which was based on local purchasing power. It was also harmful to middle class professionals, as lower-class Egyptians could not afford the health, legal and other professional services they offered. Equity was an economic precondition for both economic growth and social development.

Increasingly during this period, the plight of labour again received much attention in political discourse and action. However, beginning in the 1930s, and particularly during the war, local industrialisation brought an upsurge in labour tensions between Egyptian workers and their employers. Labour regulation and legislation benefited mostly the aristocracy of labour employed in large factories, often under some form of foreign management or ownership, leaving the vast majority of workers with little regulatory or legal protection, and no social security benefits when unemployed. A conflict would later emerge within the elitist- and effendi-led national movement, since labour rights and benefits stood in contrast to their economic interest and a national call for industrialisation. In 1947 the huge strike in al-Mahalla al-Kubra tipped the balance between effendi support for workers' demands and effendi self-interest. This strike explicitly prioritised the interests of Egyptian ownership and management of this large textile production centre over that of Egyptian workers, setting a precedent for future state–worker relations during the 1952 revolution.

The hierarchy of social problems based on their frequency of appearance in the press tellingly exposes an effendi middle class bias, despite little acknowledgement of this fact in the press. This bias was multifaceted: it revealed concern over deteriorating middle-class standards of living relative to that of other social groups; it also exposed a concern for the socio-economic reproduction of this class over others, notably, through education. In the unfolding hierarchy of social justice in Egypt, state provision of urban regions was greater than in rural regions. Urban workers received more public (read effendi) attention than peasants; their plight was closer to home, and it presumably raised greater concern over social pathology or crime associated with the lack of social solidarity. Peasants, on the other hand, were marginalised because they were less immediately visible from an urban, middle-class perspective. Often, peasants were either 'authenticated' as the sons of the country or presumed too backward to be reformed, which further marginalised their plight. Despite some initiative, land reform was forestalled because it came into direct confrontation with the interests of the landed elite, as well as with effendi economic interests. In short, the effendi social contract represented an agreement among citizens that was clearly biased in favour of this social group.

Justice implemented

During and after World War II, and in response to social unrest and critical public opinion, Egyptian governments did much to cater to a rising demand for social justice in Egypt. This point has oftentimes been downplayed in the narrative of the 'old regime' as later portrayed by the Free Officers and echoed in academic analysis. The following study of state action in response to the rising demand for social justice demonstrates this point, while also showing a lasting bias in state involvement, in favour of the effendi middle class.

The period under discussion saw a continuing, rapid expansion of higher education. Between 1940/41 and 1951/52, university enrolment (per thousand) tripled, and the number of students in secondary education more than doubled.[45] In 1951–2, university students accounted for about 1.6 per thousand of the overall population, or 34,842 of 21,200,000 Egyptians.[46] The number of students in secondary education was larger – by a multiple of 5.5 (192,454) – but still exclusive. In 1951–2, and despite improvement over time, the ratio of about 1:6 between secondary and primary students would suggest that only a few could advance in their education beyond the first level, and the same was true for advancement from secondary schools to university education. The numbers above suggest a concurrent, rapid increase in enrolment at institutions of higher education, but there was still much demand for entry into secondary and especially university education, which were necessary for securing future gainful employment, a demand yet to be fully addressed by the state.

In addition to rapid demographic growth, the pressure to expand higher, and particularly university, education was the result of the law of supply and demand, in which the increase in the number of students contributed to rising competition for lucrative jobs, primarily in state employment. During the 1930s and 1940s, a BA as opposed to a secondary school degree was required to obtain lucrative employment in the Egyptian bureaucracy and to advance within its ranks. In 1954, according to Berger's survey of civil service officials, the vast majority (77.1%) of those who joined this service during this period had a BA or equivalent, 10.9 per cent held higher degrees than BAs, and only 11.6 per cent held a secondary school degree.[47] The civil servants interviewed were better educated than their fathers, many of whom were civil servants themselves.[48] Nevertheless, they still felt that they were worse off in terms of their employment conditions than the generation that had joined the civil service before them.[49]

Public spending on education in Egypt reflected a similar rising trend in such spending as part of the overall state budget, as the state came under constant pressure to resolve the problem of education. Between 1940/41 and 1951/52 the budget share allocated to the ministry of education increased from 9.7 to 12.1 per cent of the entire state budget. This percentage was significantly higher than the share of other ministries whose task was to provide welfare, such as the ministry of health, and particularly the ministry of social affairs. Yet, according to the discourse in the effendi middle class press, despite its large share of overall state expenses, education remained the main social crisis in Egypt.

The significant increase in student enrolment further represented a partiality in the Egyptian system of education toward higher, as opposed to mass, education. A clear indication of this gap was the level of illiteracy, its eradication having long been considered a central goal. Between 1940 and 1952, illiteracy in Egypt decreased by 11 percent, a much faster rate of decline than had occurred between 1925 and 1940 (4%), when a system of mass elementary education was first put into place to increase education.[50] Still, illiteracy levels remained high. In 1952, 74 per cent of Egyptians were still illiterate. In all levels of education, there was a considerable gap between female and male education. In 1952, almost three decades after the 1923 constitution guaranteed compulsory, free-of-charge education for boys and girls, 61 per cent of males as opposed to 86 per cent of females were illiterate. Moreover, between 1940 and 1952, the percentage of girls in Egyptian institutions of higher education doubled from 4 to 8 percent, but this percentage broadly indicated a huge overall gap between females and males in these institutions.[51] In education, there existed significant quantitative (number of institutions) and qualitative gaps between rural and urban regions, and between small/provincial and large cities, notably Cairo. Urban dwellers were much better positioned to receive good, quality education that granted entry to higher education. The socio-economic position of fathers remained crucial for their children's, mainly their sons', educational achievements.

In 1951, the Law Setting the Wages for Graduates' Diplomas stipulated a fixed initial salary for graduates holding various diplomas, along with a system of periodic incremental raises based on seniority and level of education, regardless of the position occupied in state service.[52] This reform, which was supposed to resolve irregularities in civil service employment, further established a new practice (already existing de facto, though not yet de jure) in the field that assigned non-market value to education-based, state positions as a fixed principle in public employment. Importantly, this law preceded by about a decade a similar socialist law under Nasser.

Large-scale state employment put significant pressure on state budgets. In 1937–8, following the Anglo-Egyptian agreement that broadened Egypt's independence, expenditures on state employment amounted to 36 per cent of the government's total expenditures (41%, including officials' pensions and bonuses).[53] Charles Issawi, who examined the state budget for the years just before World War II, concluded that this bias in state expenditures barely contributed to increased equity in Egyptian society.[54] Expenditures on effendi employment with the state did not translate to more and better state services for the whole of society. Regardless of a growing call for social justice, this huge budgetary commitment remained high and constant. In 1950, state expenditure on employment constituted 35 per cent of the state budget. The state's bias toward its own employees was very conspicuous, considering their relatively low proportion of the Egyptian population. In 1950, this share was estimated at 2.2 per cent of the Egyptian population.[55] For the year 1951–2, this figure represented an estimated 350,000 Egyptians.[56] Even before the rapid expansion of the civil service, and the establishment of the public sector under Nasser, state employment – while providing public services – had become a state service in itself. Indeed, higher education leading to state employment gradually became part of the state's moral economy, one that was central to the making and socio-economic reproduction of the effendi middle class.

While state employees as a whole benefited from state economic protection, state employment was far from egalitarian. Rather, state employment was hierarchical, centralised, and prone to social and political nepotism. Furthermore, there existed large gaps in pay scale among state employees. Many coveted state employment but resented such employment-based hardships and unfair treatment by superiors, resulting in both a large public outcry in the press against mismanagement in state employment, and attempts to organise state employees. It was this squeeze on white-collar labour that contributed to the contemporary call for social justice among this still-privileged group of state employees.

The state commitment to help its own, and public pressure on the state to go through with this commitment, was especially conspicuous in comparison to the small steps that the state took to bring social justice to the vast majority of Egyptians. A significant case in point is the workings of the ministry of social affairs. As suggested in an earlier discussion, MOSA took charge of two goals. The first was to compete with private charitable associations, but increasingly to coordinate with and co-opt them to the state, in tandem with the dual call for state involvement in society and the economy, including the Egyptianisation of associations. During the early 1950s, MOSA's responsibilities included, according to an official account, the following: legislation concerning labour; cooperative societies; social centres for rural welfare; official charity organisations (waqfs); private charity organisations' remodelling and modernising of villages; reorganising dwellings, estates and farms (*ezbeh*s); an increase in small holdings, the purchase of land from private owners; transfer from congested lands; the Five-Acre Scheme; district experiments (*markaz*) affecting 300,000 people; water supply to Fayoum and elsewhere; housing accommodations for workers at Embabeh; living quarters provided by private manufacturing companies in el-Mahalla el-Kobra, Kafr el-Dawar, and el-Baida; and education – free meals, technical training and so on.[57] Thus, by the early 1950s, MOSA had clearly turned into a regulatory state body supervising a large variety of projects delivering welfare to Egyptians.

MOSA's second goal, based on a rising call for social justice, was to deliver such justice top-down through state redistribution, a goal it achieved much less successfully. In the examples discussed below – the establishment of the Rural Social Centers (RSCs) and an aborted attempt at a comprehensive social insurance scheme – MOSA consolidated and institutionalised various existing ideas of liberal social reform, or productivist welfare. This productivist welfare continued to promote the notion of education, including vocational training, as a panacea for all social and economic ills. Furthermore, while impressive, the scope and scale of the RSCs and the failure to deliver the social insurance scheme exemplified the limits of state readiness to resolve hardship among peasants and workers.

Between 1941 and 1950, the number of RSCs skyrocketed from 5 to 126, while the number of peasants enjoying its services rose thirtyfold, from 50,000 to 1,500,000.[58] Despite this sharp increase – mostly after 1946 – such centres still served only about 10 per cent of Egypt's rural population.[59] Moreover, regardless of an ambitious programme to expand the RSCs, and a significant demand for such centres among peasants, actual financial resources invested in this programme were meagre. Within MOSA, the Department of the Fellah was to 'alleviate poverty, illiteracy and disease' in the rural regions, no doubt a daunting task considering the challenges ahead.[60] For the fiscal year 1950–1, the budget for this department constituted less than 25 per cent of the entire budget allocation to MOSA. The budget of MOSA itself was but a fraction of the entire state budget, averaging around 1.5 per cent of the total, and was a good way off from the massive investment required to bring about such massive change.[61] Even Amy Johnson's favourable evaluation of the RSCs still suggests that this project was limited in scope and slowly implemented.[62] Others saw it in even harsher terms, as an attempt to placate public opinion.[63]

MOSA's failure to implement a scheme of redistributive social insurance further suggests a gap between the outcry in public opinion and the actual implementation of a social policy in response.[64] Before World War II, an employment-based insurance scheme narrowly covered a minority class of urban-based industrial workers, and it was for work-related injuries only. After the war, and turning into a central source of political protest, there was a growing demand for the enactment of non-contribution-based forms of social insurance. In 1950, MOSA suggested a comprehensive social insurance scheme. Promoted by Ahmed Hussein, who headed MOSA, this social security scheme was quite radical in that it included rural workers as well as urban workers in commerce and industry. Moreover, it was to be financed exclusively through government funds.[65] Charles Issawi estimates that this scheme, if implemented, would have benefited half a million people with about a million dependents, and would have cost less than 0.5 per cent of the national income.[66] Indeed, Hussein saw this programme as a centrepiece of his ministry, and a programme over which he resigned because of the Wafd's political inability to make it happen.[67] Noted in Hussein's social security plan, as in the RSCs, was the notion of self-help. In Hussein's own analysis of the programme, 'the objective of the law was not to simply distribute benefits and relief. More constructive measures were envisaged, as for instance, rehabilitation of the disabled and education for the orphaned, with a view to making them self-sufficient and useful citizens'.[68] Neither the RSCs' operations nor even the social insurance scheme actually engaged in a significant redistribution of economic resources throughout society or economic management/regulation that would support social equity. In both instances they were about state measures that would allow those most in need among the lower class to help themselves.

While public health was politicised and became a central topic in Egyptian public discourse during and after World War II, state expenditures on health as part of the national budget continued to trail those of education, particularly as the wartime health crisis seemed to have waned. In 1949, the 5.5 per cent of the national budget spent on health was smaller than the 8.3 per cent spent in 1938.[69] Like other services, health provision continued to be mostly located in urban as opposed to rural areas, thus further tilting social justice in favour of cities. To the extent that the state did get involved with direct help for the poor, this was in the form of flagship projects such as MOSA's RSCs.

Before and especially after World War II, public housing seemed a central means for alleviating poverty, ignorance and disease, as well as for creating a new Egyptian more disposed toward middle class values, or, at least, a citizen the state would not consider a 'threat'. Mirrit Butrus-Ghali suggested this regarding housing reform: 'If a house is cherished by a person and is the object of his care and pride, this person will thereby come to recognize the social order and to respect the rights of his brethren and compatriots'.[70] This line of argumentation was by no means new. As Timothy Mitchel has suggested, experimenting with the making of proper modernity through model villages in Egypt dates back to the mid-nineteenth century.[71] Embedded in the quotation was the (middle class) assumption that property ownership would bring respectability to the conduct of unruly social groups. Social commentators, planners and state officials clearly saw the provision of model housing as an opportunity for social engineering in creating new, modern communities through planned villages and workers' dwellings in cities. Such housing projects were designed to discipline lower classes into a modern way of life.[72] Here too, the purpose of housing provision was as much about enhancing social stability as it was about improving the conditions of the lower classes. During this period, Egypt indeed conducted several flagship experiments involving model villages and public housing for workers. However, no such experiments eventually translated into large-scale housing projects significant enough to transform the living conditions of peasants and workers.

The limited state expenditures on public housing, indeed on all the items of welfare discussed above, were the result of limits on state expenditures as part of the national economy. In the years preceding World War II, the national budget was about 18 per cent of the national income.[73] Though it decreased during World War II, by 1950 the national budget had returned to its pre-war level. According to Issawi, from a comparative perspective this was a large percentage in relation to the size of the country's population. The problem was that this budget contributed little to actually relieving income and wealth inequality.[74] The analysis above indeed shows a bias toward education and state employment and against welfare, vindicating Issawi's claim. Importantly, despite a growing call for state action, Egypt's policy on expenditures remained cautious. Between 1939 and 1952, public debt decreased from an estimated 47 per cent of the GNP in 1939 to 16 per cent in 1952.[75] The state still kept a liberal-economic tradition of budget austerity, a caution soon to be ignored by the new revolutionary regime.

In the period under discussion, Egyptian politicians largely refrained from changing taxation, which could have increased equity through redistribution. Before 1930, Egypt was bound by a series of international agreements that would not allow it to raise taxes, which were then mostly in the form of general customs and certain excise duties, both indirect taxes.[76] In 1930, Egypt gained tariff autonomy, allowing it to raise duties on imported goods. These taxes enlarged state revenues but notably also allowed agricultural and industrial protectionist policies. In 1937 the formal ending of the capitulation system ushered in more changes to the taxation system. In 1939 the land tax was adjusted, but it did not bring a significant change to the overall amount of tax collected, a testimony to the landed elite's grip on politics. A new tax on income was set at 7 per cent, and the same rate was set for industrial, commercial and financial profits and dividends. Taxation on profits and dividends was later raised to 12 per cent.[77] In 1941 a temporary excess profits tax was introduced, followed by an inheritance tax in 1945. It was only in 1947/48 that a more progressive, general, personal income tax was introduced to replace an earlier surtax.[78] Even then, revenues were limited by massive tax evasion. Despite agreement over the need for state command of the economy and society to allow equity, taxation was minimal and often regressive (indirect). Crucially, such taxation could hardly be considered redistributive. In short, a rising demand for social justice in Egypt did not translate into actual readiness among upper- and middle-class Egyptians to financially contribute more, and in a more egalitarian fashion, to closing socio-economic gaps.

The most significant act of redistribution in a largely agricultural economy such as Egypt's would have been land reform. Still, while land reform gradually entered public discussion, it contradicted the interests of the landed elite – as well as those of the effendis, who dominated the public discourse and political activism – and it was mostly rejected in the period under discussion. Such an effendi position, regardless of a constant effendi call for social reform, was well illustrated in the Muslim Brotherhood's approach to this issue. In tandem with other political groups and parties across the political spectrum, land reform was not raised by the Muslim Brotherhood until the late 1940s.[79] In 1939, Mirrit Butrus-Ghali suggested land reform as a voluntary act of landlords, and as a pre-emptive, evolutionary step to alleviate poverty and amend peasant life in Egypt.[80] During World War II, the duress of peasants and fears of social unrest and rural-to-urban migration augmented public discussion about the need for land reform.[81] Nevertheless, even socialist economists Rashid al-Barrawi and Hamzah 'Ulaysh did not see conditions as being ready for the nationalisation of lands, as they stated was the case in Russia (sic) and as was suggested for Britain by the Labour Party.[82] During and after the war, a suggestion to legislate land reform – at the centre of which was a restriction on large landownership – was raised, but it was rejected in the Egyptian parliament in 1947.[83] In 1946, the Wafd introduced a proposal for land reform in a large economic conference in Cairo. By the late 1940s, there was a growing consensus in Egypt over the necessity for land reform, but little actual progress. This consensus was, significantly, the outcome of escalating social unrest that included, in 1951, organised protest in rural regions. In response, MOSA began distributing publicly reclaimed lands. In September 1952, the Wafd included land reform in its platform. Yet comprehensive land reform had to await the Free Officers. Even under their rule, however, this reform was more of a political action against a landowning elite than it was a concerted effort to rapidly bring equity to rural regions.

As Gabriel Baer suggests, land reform was slow to arrive because it was met with broad opposition, and not simply from among the landed elite, or 'feudal class', as it was later dubbed by Nasser's regime.[84] Represented in all political parties, landowners of middle-sized plots and large landowners had significant political clout. Furthermore, landownership was not limited to a landlord elite. The Egyptian and non-Egyptian upper-class bourgeoisie had acquired an interest in land, as did members of the effendi middle class. So, despite much discussion over the need to alleviate poverty in rural Egypt, and a gradual shift in the political discourse toward land reform, this reform was slow to arrive because of the vested interests of the most influential segments of Egyptian society. Some argued that personal and social transformation in rural regions were preconditions for successful land redistribution, without which it was more likely to bring social unrest than to succeed in facilitating poverty alleviation. The thinking was that the irrational, backward peasant first had to be disciplined, educated, and socially uplifted.[85] With regard to the question of land reform, as earlier with the MOSA's RSCs, the peasant lower class required an external agency – effendi middle class action and moral guidance – in order for their poverty to be alleviated.

In Najwa Khalil's analysis, in the aftermath of World War II, the plight of the labourers received more attention than that of the peasants in the political discourse, as well as in the well-publicised political action from within and without the parliamentary system. In addition to contributing to the middle and upper classes' concerns over an onslaught on the cities and resolving urban social malaise and crime, poverty dashed hopes of developing local industry through an import substitute industrialisation model (ISI) based on local purchasing power. It was further harmful to middle-class professionals because poor Egyptians could not retain the health, legal and other professional services the former offered. Equity was therefore an economic precondition for both economic and social development. Still, such arguments had to be balanced against more immediate considerations: cheap labour was a precondition for industrialisation and profiting from industry. Despite the public outcry, there was relatively little improvement in working conditions, wages or welfare for the majority of workers in Egypt. The workers who benefited most from state intervention were often employed in large enterprises and/or enterprises that were under foreign management or ownership.

In comparison to the failed attempt to legislate land reform, the 1947 joint-stock Company Law passed in the Egyptian parliament with relatively little objection.[86] This comparison is significant because under the guise of Egyptianising the economy this law was really about redistributing wealth. Unlike the land reform, this transfer was from non-Egyptians to Egyptians and, importantly, a transfer that if fully implemented would benefit the Egyptian upper and middle classes as opposed to the Egyptian working class. The Company Law required that at least 40 per cent of the board of directors of every Egyptian joint-stock company be Egyptian. It also stipulated that at least 75 per cent of a company's employees be Egyptian. The law defined an employee as a person who performs administrative or specialised tasks or supervises others' work (i.e., white collar workers). Companies were to pay at least 65 per cent of the total salaries paid to workers in this category. At least 90 per cent of a company's workers had to be Egyptians, to whom companies should pay at least 80 per cent of the total salaries paid to workers. The legal definition of workers was not provided in the law; perhaps it was assumed that those who were not employees were workers, but this testifies once again to the marginalisation of workers as opposed to middle-class employees.

While the joint-stock Company Law was seemingly to benefit all Egyptians, a closer look at its implementation presents a clear class bias. Since most workers in these companies were already Egyptians, Egyptianisation mostly pertained to directors and employees. While Egyptianisation was different from the soon-to-arrive nationalisation of foreign enterprises, it clearly set the path to greater state involvement in the economy, and to the benefit of the middle and upper classes.

From the second half of the 1930s, and enhanced during and after World War II and until 1952, both the growing demand for social justice and the emergence of a moral economy based on this social justice were, significantly, about the expectation of more opportunity for socio-economic mobility for the expanding effendi middle class, supposedly without forsaking the social reform of lower-class Egyptians – peasants and especially workers. Socially, as a horizontal agreement among citizens, the social contract moved toward a rising demand for the redistribution of wealth. In practice, the effendi public discourse still focused on effendi-related crises, and state expenditures on social affairs remained heavily tilted toward resolving such crises. Politically, as a vertical agreement between citizens and the state, effendi citizens demanded state action in putting social justice to work through more legislation and regulation. Moreover, though they expected the state to spend more on social services, which effendis provided and from which effendis, more than other social groups, benefited, they refused progressive taxation. For its part, the state was only too happy to cater to a growing effendi demand for social justice as long as it could flex its muscles in the process, and politicians did the same to increase their political clout. As Roel Meijer argues: 'Social justice, the central theme of the 1940s, was to legitimize an increasing interventionist state that would implement reforms to decrease the glaring differences in wealth and opportunities for self-development'.[87]

In 1950, the return of the Wafd Party to power further enhanced public expectations for social justice. Prime Minister al-Nahhas promised a sea change, which, despite notable implementation, turned out to be a far cry from both what was promised and what the government would or could deliver.[88]

By 1952, broad support for statism in Egypt was coupled with a sense of disappointment and alienation from what many began to see as a failed political system that did not make proper use of state resources, notably so in the face of escalating socio-economic unrest. The last Wafd government was swept aside by the 1952 revolution, not because it failed to implement social justice but because it did not implement it fast and far enough. The 1952 revolution was foremost an attempt to change the pace of implementing an existing effendi social contract, not rewrite it. The Free Officers' and Nasser's later emphasis on past negligence and failures of the pre-revolutionary regime as the reason for the military takeover hardly accounted for such a state of affairs.

Notes

1. Linda T. Darling, *A History of Social Justice and Political Power in the Middle East: The Circle of Justice from Mesopotamia to Globalization* (New York: Routledge, 2013).
2. Ibid., 183.
3. Thompson, *Justice Interrupted*, 11–88.
4. Ibid., 61.
5. Ibid., 76.
6. Muhammad Fahmi Lahita, *Ta'rikh Fu'ad al-Awwal al-Iqtisadi: Misr fi Tariq al-Tawjih al-Kamil*, vol. 3, *al-'Adala al-Ijtima'iyya: Misr wa-Mustawa Ma'ishat al-Misriyyin* (Cairo: Maktabat al-Nahda al-Misriyya, 1946).
7. Robert Tignor, 'Equity in Egypt's Recent Past: 1945–1952', in *The Political Economy of Income Distribution in Egypt*, ed. Gouda Abdel-Khalek and Robert Tignor (New York: Holmes and Meier, 1982), 27–32; and Misako Ikeda, *Sociopolitical Debates in Late Parliamentary Egypt, 1944–1952* (PhD diss., Harvard University, 1998), 5. For Abd al-Mughni Sa'id's integration of socialism in Islamism, see Roel Meijer, *The Quest for Modernity: Secular Liberal and Left-Wing Thought in Egypt, 1945–1958* (New York: Routledge Curzon, 2002), 126, 152. Socialism was by no means a newly introduced concept in Egypt. See Mourad Magdi Wahba, 'The Meaning of Ishtirakiyah: Arab Perceptions of Socialism in the Nineteenth Century', *Alif: Journal of Comparative Poetics*, no. 10 (1990), https://doi.org/10.2307/521716; Kamel S. Abu Jaber, 'Salamah Musa: Precursor of Arab Socialism', *Middle East Journal* 20, no. 2 (1966), accessed 26 October 2020, https://www.jstor.org/stable/4323988; and Rami Ginat, 'Early Socialist Thought in Egypt', in *A History of Egyptian Communism:*

Jews and Their Compatriots in Quest of Revolution (Boulder, CO: Lynne Rienner Publishers, 2011).

8. For communist influence on social justice, including later on the Free Officers, see Ginat, 'Revolutionary Ideas and Their Impact', in *A History of Egyptian Communism*; and Selma Botman, 'The Liberal Age, 1923–1952', in *The Cambridge History of Egypt*, vol. 2, *Modern Egypt, from 1517 to the End of the Twentieth Century*, ed. M.W. Daly (Cambridge: Cambridge University Press, 1998), 302.
9. El Shakry, *Great Social Laboratory*.
10. Ilya Harik, *Economic Policy Reform in Egypt* (Gainesville: University Press of Florida, 1997), 9–11.
11. Deeb, *Party Politics in Egypt*, 272–5.
12. Amy J. Johnson, *Reconstructing Rural Egypt: Ahmed Hussein and the History of Egyptian Development* (Syracuse, NY: Syracuse University Press, 2004), 51.
13. Meijer, *Quest for Modernity*, 51–9.
14. Nazih N. M. Ayubi, *Bureaucracy and Politics in Contemporary Egypt* (London: Ithaca Press, 1980), 157–8; and Berger, *Bureaucracy and Society*, 33–4.
15. For associational life and state reaction to it during the pre-revolutionary era, see Morroe Berger, *Islam in Egypt Today: Social and Political Aspects of Popular Religion* (Cambridge: University Press, 1970), 90–126; Robert Bianchi, *Unruly Corporatism: Associational Life in Twentieth-Century Egypt* (New York: Oxford University Press, 1989), 56–81; Ener, *Managing Egypt's Poor*, 99–133; and Pollard, *Nurturing the Nation*. According to Bianchi (*Unruly Corporatism*, 72–81), this associational life was transformed from pluralist to corporatist over time. However, see the analysis of the National Congress of Popular Forces in the current chapter, which exposes class agency in Egyptian corporatism.
16. Muhammad Muhammad Jawwadi, *al-Bunyan al-Wizari fi Misr: Faharis Ta'rikhiyya wa-Kammiyya wa-Tafsiliyya li-Insha' wa-Ilgha' wa-Idmaj al-Wizarat wa-l-Qita'at al-Wizariyya, mundhu 1878 wa-Dirasa li-Tawzi' al-Mas'uliyat al-Wizariyya wa-l-Wuzara' alladhina Ta'aqabu 'ala kul Wizara, 1952–1996* (Cairo: Dar al-Shuruq, 1996), 17.
17. Ibid., 18.
18. The analysis here is based on Floresca Karanasou, *Egyptianisation: The 1947 Company Law and the Foreign Communities in Egypt* (PhD diss., Oxford University, 1993), 19–76; and Deeb, *Party Politics in Egypt*, 321–2; and Ikeda, 'Sociopolitical Debates', 284–99.
19. Ikeda, 'Sociopolitical Debates', 285n71.
20. Deeb, *Party Politics in Egypt*, 321–2.

21. Ikeda, 'Sociopolitical Debates', 284.
22. Najwa Husayn Khalil, *al-Mujtama' al-Misri qabla al-Thawra fi al-Sihafa al-Misriyya, 1945–1952* (Cairo: Al-Hay'a al-Misriyya al-'Amma li-l-Kitab, 1995), 31.
23. Khalil, *al-Mujtama'*. Khalil's analysis covers the period from the end of World War II (May 1945) up to the Free Officers' coup (July 1952). It includes 416 articles and opinion columns in the following publications, which Khalil further divided based on their affiliation/non-affiliation with political parties and organisations: *al-Ahram* (daily, non-affiliated), *Akhbar al-Yawm* (weekly, non-affiliated), *Ruz al-Yusuf* (weekly, non-affiliated), *Bint al-Nil* (monthly, women's magazine, non-affiliated), *Misr al-Fata* (weekly, socialist), *al-Liwa' al-Jadid* (weekly, later bi-monthly and monthly, non-affiliated), *al-Asas* (daily, non-affiliated), *al-Wafd al-Misri* (daily, Wafd), *Sawt al-Umma* (daily, non-affiliated), *al-Ba'th* (monthly), *al-Ikhwan al-Muslimin* (daily, Muslim Brotherhood), *al-Da'wa* (weekly, Muslim Brotherhood), *al-Fajr al-Jadid* (weekly, later bi-monthly, socialist), *al-Malayyin* (weekly, socialist). See Khalil, *al-Mujtama'*, 15–16, for the exact dates and frequency of the publications studied. Khalil was later appointed minister of social affairs and insurance. Unless otherwise mentioned, all translations are my own.
24. Tignor, 'Equity in Egypt's Recent Past'; Ikeda, 'Sociopolitical Debates'; Meijer, *Quest for Modernity*; and El Shakry, *Great Social Laboratory*. Thompson, 'Hasan al-Banna of Egypt: The Muslim Brotherhood Pursuit of Islamic Justice', in *Justice Interrupted*. Published in 1949, Sayyid Qutb's *Social Justice in Islam* further reflected contemporary concerns over social justice in Egypt. See analysis of the book and its translation in William E. Shepard, *Sayyid Qutb and Islamic Activism: A Translation and Critical Analysis of Social Justice in Islam* (Leiden: Brill, 1996), xvi.
25. Khalil, *al-Mujtama'*, 17.
26. El Shakry, *Great Social Laboratory*, 143–94.
27. Khalil, *al-Mujtama'*, 30.
28. I thank Ben Zarhi for helping me in formulating this point.
29. Brynjar Lia, *The Society of the Muslim Brothers in Egypt: The Rise of an Islamic Mass Movement, 1928–1942* (Reading: Ithaca Press, 1998), 209.
30. Richard P. Mitchell, *The Society of the Muslim Brothers* (New York: Oxford University Press, 1993), 291.
31. Joseph, 'Kin Contract'.
32. See Khalil, *al-Mujtama'*, 21–4, for analysis of changing restrictions on freedom of the press between 1945 and 1952.
33. Ikeda, 'Sociopolitical Debates', 182.
34. Ibid., 201.

35. Ibid., 170.
36. Beth Baron, *The Orphan Scandal: Christian Missionaries and the Rise of the Muslim Brotherhood* (Palo Alto, CA: Stanford University Press, 2014).
37. On the establishment of the Ministry of Supply, see Jawwadi, *al-Bunyan al-Wizari*, 64–5. For the impact of WWII on shaping Egypt's food policy, see Eric Schewe, 'How War Shaped Egypt's National Bread Loaf', *Comparative Studies of South Asia, Africa and the Middle East* 37, no. 1 (2017).
38. Sonia M. Ali and Richard H. Adams Jr, 'The Egyptian Food Subsidy System: Operation and Effects on Income Distribution', *World Development* 24, no. 11 (1996): 1778; and Ahmad al-Safati, 'Hisad al-Sinin wa-l-Nahj al-Tanmawi al-Jadid', *Misr al-Mu'asira* 77, no. 404 (April 1986): 5–22.
39. Milad Hanna, *Uridu Maskinan: Mushkila la-ha Hall* (Cairo: Ruz a-Yusuf, 1978), 29.
40. Nancy E. Gallagher, *Egypt's Other Wars: Epidemics and the Politics of Public Health* (Syracuse, NY: Syracuse University Press, 1990), 56–76.
41. Ibid., 3.
42. A notable example of the above was 'Abd al-Wahid al-Wakil, a relative of Mustafa al-Nahhas, who had become minister of health. Ibid., 15.
43. Joel Beinin and Zachary Lockman, *Workers on the Nile: Nationalism, Communism, Islam, and the Egyptian Working Class, 1882–1954* (Princeton, NJ: Princeton University Press, 1987), 257–417.
44. Deeb, 'Labour and Politics'.
45. Calculated from Reid, *Cairo University*, 112, table 11. I use growth per thousand to reflect real growth of student population over demographic increase.
46. Ibid., 112, table 10.
47. Berger, *Bureaucracy and Society*, 43, table 5.
48. Ibid., 43–7.
49. See ibid., 94–108, for different explanations interviewees gave for a sense of decline in status and prestige.
50. Calculated based on Reid, *Cairo University*, 113, table 13.
51. Ahmed Abdalla, *The Student Movement and National Politics in Egypt, 1923–1973* (Cairo: AUC Press, 2008), 26, table 2.3.
52. Ragui Assaad, 'The Effects of Public Sector Hiring and Compensation Policies on the Egyptian Labor Market', *World Bank Economic Review* 11, no. 1 (1997): 91, accessed 17 May 2020, http://www.jstor.org/stable/3990220.
53. Deeb, *Party Politics in Egypt*, 317.
54. Issawi, *Egypt: An Economic and Social Analysis*, 143.

55. Ayubi, *Bureaucracy and Politics*, 240, citing A. P. Sinker, *Report on the Personal Questions of the Egyptian Civil Service* (Cairo: Government Press, 1951), 21.
56. Ayubi, *Bureaucracy and Politics*, 243, table 4.
57. René Francis, *Social Welfare in Egypt* (Cairo: Impr. Misr, 1950), 24.
58. M. Fouad el Bidewy, *The Development of Social Security in Egypt* (Cairo: Ministry of Social Affairs, 1953), 89, diagram 2.
59. Ibid., 87, based on the fiscal budget of MOSA for that year.
60. Johnson, *Reconstructing Rural Egypt*, 71, citing an official report by this ministry.
61. El Bidewy, *The Development of Social Security*, 143, table 9.
62. Johnson, *Reconstructing Rural Egypt*, 68–118.
63. See such a critique in ibid., 249n56.
64. For analysis of early social security schemes in Egypt, see el Bidewy, *The Development of Social Security*, 33–5; and Asya El-Meehy, *Rewriting the Social Contract: The Social Fund and Egypt's Politics of Retrenchment* (PhD diss., University of Toronto, 2009), 76–84.
65. Johnson, *Reconstructing Rural Egypt*, 142.
66. Charles Philip Issawi, *Egypt at Mid-Century: An Economic Survey* (London: Oxford University Press, 1954), 75–6.
67. Johnson, *Reconstructing Rural Egypt*, 140–7.
68. Quoted in ibid., 133.
69. El Bidewy, *The Development of Social Security*, 143, table 9.
70. Quoted in Meijer, *Quest for Modernity*, 53–4. Ghali was a prominent member of the liberal Society of National Renaissance.
71. Timothy Mitchell, *Colonising Egypt* (Berkeley: University of California Press, 1991), 50–4; and Mercedes Volait, 'Réforme sociale et habitat populaire: acteurs et formes (1848–1964)', in Roussillon, *Entre reforme sociale*, 309–11.
72. On the housing project, see Omnia El Shakry, 'Cairo as Capital of Socialist Revolution?', in *Cairo Cosmopolitan: Politics, Culture, and Urban Space in the New Globalized Middle East*, ed. Diane Singerman and Paul Amar (Cairo: AUC Press, 2006); Johnson, *Reconstructing Rural Egypt*, 128–31; Volait, 'Réforme sociale et habitat populaire', 322–8; and Volait, 'Town Planning Schemes for Cairo', 44–71.
73. Issawi, *Egypt: An Economic and Social Analysis*, 141.
74. Ibid., 143.
75. Hansen and Marzouk, *Development and Economic Policy*, 270.
76. Ibid., 246–7.
77. Issawi, *Egypt: An Economic and Social Analysis*, 140.

78. Hansen, *Egypt and Turkey*, 94.
79. Lia, *The Society of the Muslim Brothers in Egypt*, 211.
80. Meijer, *Quest for Modernity*, 57–9.
81. Gabriel Baer, 'Egyptian Attitudes towards Land Reform, 1922–1955', in *The Middle East in Transition: Studies in Contemporary History*, ed. Walter Z. Laqueur (London: Routledge Library Editions, 2017), 80–99.
82. Rashid al-Barrawi and Muhammad Hamza 'Ulaysh, *al-Tatawwur al-Iqtisadi fi Misr fi al-'Asr al-Hadith*, 2nd ed. (Cairo: Maktabat al-Nahda al-Misriyya, 1945), 289–96. Al-Barrawi's agrarian reform would later have many similarities to Mirrit Butrus-Ghali's. Compare al-Barrawi's suggested reform, discussed in Meijer, *Quest for Modernity*, 82–5, with Ghali's, suggested above.
83. See Ikeda, 'Sociopolitical Debates', 67–78, for analysis of the political debate over land reform.
84. Baer, 'Egyptian Attitudes'.
85. Recall the discussion on productivist welfare in Chapter One.
86. Ikeda, 'Sociopolitical Debates', 284–99; and Karanasou, 'Egyptianisation', 77–95.
87. See Roel Meijer, 'Liberal Reform: The Case of the Society of the National Renaissance', in Roussillon, *Entre reforme sociale*, 101.
88. Joel Gordon, 'The False Hopes of 1950: The Wafd's Last Hurrah and the Demise of Egypt's Old Order', *International Journal of Middle East Studies* 21, no. 2 (1989).

PART TWO

THE SOCIAL CONTRACT IN NASSER'S EFFENDI STATE, 1952–70

From early on, and as already noticeable in Nasser's *Philosophy of the Revolution* (written during the second half of 1953 and first published in 1954), the revolutionaries consciously attempted to explain the 1952 revolution against the background of what they depicted as the failures of the Egyptian liberal monarchy. Past hardships were amplified, together with the ineptitude of Egypt's political leadership – particularly the king and the Wafd Party – in resolving them. This ineptitude of the 'old regime' explains why the army came out of the barracks to interfere in politics. Moreover, it illuminates why the initial military coup turned into a full-fledged revolution, and the Free Officers – now led by Nasser – were in place and ready to transform into the new regime.[1] Soon enough, the same arguments would be used to wrench power from former sympathisers, notably the Muslim Brotherhood and the Egyptian left.[2] The revolutionary narrative carried a sense of a 'zero hour' – a new beginning and a seemingly decisive new scheme for bringing change to the pre-revolutionary past.

International analysis of the revolution often echoed this interpretation of the new political beginning and the making of an Egyptian social contract under Nasser. Scholars rightly discussed the political machinations that would eventually allow Nasser to establish his power. However, this did not mean, as is often suggested in such literature, that the Free Officers came into power with little realisation of what they were trying to achieve, often referred to in the historiography as the lack of a coherent ideology.³ Indeed, in such analyses there were often gaps between tracing Nasser and his generation's origins to the effendi middle class and tracing that generation's political formulation to the liberal monarchy, while suggesting that there was such ideological innocence. Since the late 1930s, and more plainly so in the aftermath of World War II, there had been a consensus in Egypt – which the Free Officers shared – regarding what was to be done: deliver social justice under an independent economy and state. Moreover, there was broad agreement as to how socio-economic development should be effected, and therefore, as to the need for a greater state role in the process, an involvement increasingly associated with 'socialism'. Both the ideology and the solutions associated with the zero hour of Nasser's regime had deeper roots than much of the existing literature has assumed. Indeed, it was exactly for this reason that the new regime became increasingly impatient with the implementation of such solutions; the regime's entire raison d'être was that it would be able to achieve what politicians of older generations had not. The Free Officers' propaganda might not have had the precise terminology to convey the revolutionary regime's course of action, but Egypt's new rulers clearly reacted to long-term needs by promoting long-term solutions for them.

After the new regime's assumption of power, historical contingency and changing global best practices further shaped its state-led development policy, which was to implement the social contract. In 1956, the nationalisation of the Suez Canal Company, the sequestration and later nationalisation of British, French and Jewish enterprises, and the increasing institutional state capacity to manage them, surely paved the way for the expansion of direct state management of large enterprises. Cold War politics, and the rise of third worldism, in which Nasser took a central role, no doubt enhanced Arab socialism, as did regional rivalries over leadership of the Arab world.⁴ Nevertheless, the analysis below emphasises the centrality of local over regional and global politics: the search for external economic resources to finance the social contract had become a priority in Egyptian regional and international politics.

The next two chapters argue that there was a great deal of continuity under what I – to emphasise the class origins of state policy and the social dynamics that unfolded after the revolution – term 'the effendi state'. This part of the book joins a widening body of revisionist historiography that bridges Egypt's pre- and post-revolutionary pasts through offering a class perspective on persistence and change between the two periods, and that perspective's implications for the Nasserist/effendi social contract.[5] Chapter Three narrates policy trajectories between the old and new regimes, and Chapter Four focuses on social continuity between the liberal monarchy and revolutionary Egypt.

Both chapters emphasise the continuity of the effendi social contract – from the old to the new regime, and the old to the new society – though not solely for reasons of historical accuracy. They demonstrate historical tracking of the long-term making of the social contract, which would later be hard to unbundle. Put simply, in Egyptian eyes the social contract and its ensuing moral economy would become much more than an authoritarian political bargain. They carried a deeper economic, social and cultural channelling than was implied in such a bargain, one that could not be easily changed through the establishment of a new political coalition. This becomes clear through the analysis of the continuity in the social contract under Nasser, Sadat and Mubarak, despite the changing historical contexts over time.

Notes

1. Hazem Kandil, 'Militarism and its Discontents: March 1954', in *The Power Triangle: Military, Security, and Politics in Regime Change* (New York: Oxford University Press, 2016), https://doi.org/10.1093/acprof:oso/9780190239206.003.0013.
2. Yoram Meital, *Revolutionary Justice: Special Courts and the Formation of Republican Egypt* (New York: Oxford University Press, 2017).
3. P. J. Vatikiotis, *The Egyptian Army in Politics: Pattern for New Nations?* (Bloomington: Indiana University Press, 1961), 67–8, was central to this analysis. See similar references to the lack of coherent ideology in Malcolm H. Kerr, 'The Emergence of a Socialist Ideology in Egypt', *Middle East Journal* 16, no. 2 (1962): 127–44, 127, accessed 24 April 2020, www.jstor.org/stable/4323467; Raymond William Baker, *Egypt's Uncertain Revolution under Nasser and Sadat* (Cambridge, MA: Harvard University Press, 1978), 43; Raymond A. Hinnebusch, *Egyptian Politics under Sadat: The Post-Populist Development of an Authoritarian-Modernizing State* (Cambridge: Cambridge University Press, 1985), 14; John Waterbury, *The Egypt of Nasser and Sadat: The Political Economy of Two Regimes* (Princeton, NJ: Princeton University Press, 1983), 9; and Joel

Gordon, *Nasser's Blessed Movement: Egypt's Free Officers and the July Revolution* (New York: Oxford University Press, 1992), 12. However, see Mourad Wahba, *The Role of the State in the Egyptian Economy: 1945–1981* (London: Ithaca Press, 1994), 24–69, for an alternative narrative that inspired this part of this book.

4. Malcolm H. Kerr, *The Arab Cold War 1958–1967: A Study of Ideology in Politics*, 2nd ed. (London: Oxford University Press, 1967); Nathan J. Citino, *Envisioning the Arab Future: Modernization in US-Arab Relations, 1945–1967* (Cambridge: Cambridge University Press, 2017); Reem Abou-El-Fadl, *Foreign Policy as Nation Making: Turkey and Egypt in the Cold War* (Cambridge: Cambridge University Press, 2018).

5. Shimon Shamir, ed., *Egypt from Monarchy to Republic: A Reassessment of Revolution and Change* (Boulder, CO: Westview Press, 1995); Elie Podeh and Onn Winckler, ed., *Rethinking Nasserism: Revolution and Historical Memory in Modern Egypt* (Gainesville: University Press of Florida, 2004); El Shakry, 'The Revolutionary Moment', part 4 of *The Great Social Laboratory*, 195–222; and Mériam N. Belli, *An Incurable Past: Nasser's Egypt Then and Now* (Gainesville: University Press of Florida, 2013).

3

OLD REGIME, NEW REGIME

Chapter Three contrasts with two previous assertions about the Egyptian social contract: first, that it was established under Nasser, and second, that this social contract was largely the result of a new authoritarian bargain in which the state would boost allocations to citizens in return for political quiescence.[1] Regarding the first assertion, the effendi social contract, at the centre of which was a rising demand for social justice – an increase in equality, opportunity and equity – was by then well established. Indeed, the main reason for the 1952 revolution was the broad consensus that there was a gap between this social contract and the political ability (or willingness) to follow through with it. From this perspective, I concur with Sara Salem's analysis that 'Nasserism, formed in the early 1950s, was an instance of hegemony rather than domination' and initially, at least, was more about consent than coercion because it would be based on a broad agreement regarding the required changes.[2] As I discuss in this chapter and the next, the 1952 revolution did away with the old regime because that regime was accused of sluggishness in making the social contract happen, rather than because of a desire to replace the social contract. Regarding the second assertion, that the social contract was a top-down political dictate, or authoritarian bargain, I argue that this assertion is the result of reading history backward in time, as opposed to events unfolding from past to present. Nasser's regime did turn out to be authoritarian, but by then there was broad popular – read effendi middle class – support for state command of social affairs and economic development. Top-down and middle-up backing for the dominant state closely interacted.

Chapter Three outlines the continuity in Egypt's official, vertical social contract – as found in the state's constitution, as elaborated in the First Five Year Development Plan, and as culminated in the National Charter. As this chapter aims to establish, the Free Officers came to power on a wave of unprecedented effendi middle class expectation of social justice, regardless of the growing use of 'the people' or 'the masses' in official discourse. Despite the seeming lack of a clear ideology, both a greater state role in socio-economic development and the particular development policies that the Free Officers adopted suggest a considerable continuity between the old and new regimes. Egypt's radicalisation was not so much about changing goals as it was about achieving them faster.

The pashas' constitution

In the early 2000s, Salah 'Isa published the by-then forgotten draft of an intended new constitution of 1954.[3] His aim was clearly to contribute to a broadening discussion on the need for democratisation and constitutional reform in Egypt. Despite the abrupt end of the liberal monarchy, the centrality of constitutionalism had not been forsaken. In 1952, when the Free Officers came to power, they suspended the 1923 constitution, which was implicated in the failures of the recently ousted political system. However, they did not abolish constitutionalism as a formal, guiding principle of governance that outlined the interconnected legal rights and duties of both citizens and the state. Rather, the Free Officers set out to write a new constitution that would better reflect the passage of time and the public-political discourse on what this constitution should include in the post-revolutionary age.

The drafting of a new constitution demonstrated an interim stage between the old and new political regimes, with members of the constitutional committee still coming from the old guard of the legal and political elite. This draft constitution – later known as 'the pashas' constitution' – would, in 'Isa's figurative description, find its place in the garbage bin.[4] It ended up in this symbolic garbage bin of history in the aftermath of the 1954 crisis, as Nasser bolstered his position in power, when it had become clear that the democratic governance of the past would not return.[5] Nevertheless, despite this political change, a comparison between the 1954 constitutional draft and the 1956 socialist constitution suggests a great deal of continuity between the two in terms of a vision of socio-economic development. Resemblances between these two documents are especially telling of the ways in which the contractual, mutual obligations of state and citizens continued from the old to the new regime.

In what follows, this chapter compares articles in the 1954 draft with those in the 1956 constitution that refer to two interrelated topics: state management of the economy and the implementation of social justice.[6] The latter notion refers to the economic rights of citizens as suggested by the 1954 draft and the 1956 constitution in articles referring to education, employment, social security/welfare, standards of living, property rights, and planning and taxation. In addition, this chapter makes an occasional reference to the 1923 constitution, notably regarding education, to demonstrate the changes introduced by the pashas' draft that would later be adopted in the 1956 constitution. Such a comparison aims to demonstrate the great similarity between the two documents, and therefore also the continuity in social-economic policy between the old and new regimes.

In the 1954 draft constitution (article 28, under the second part of the proposed constitution, 'General Rights and Duties'), education is the right of all Egyptians, which the state would guarantee. As argued in earlier chapters, the right to education was central to the national struggle under the monarchy, and equality of opportunity through free-of-charge education was a central aspect of the demand for social justice. Article 28 mostly reiterates already existing legislation that followed from the centrality of education in effendi public discourse. Thus, education was compulsory in its elementary stage, as was already determined by the 1923 constitution, and free in state schools, as already determined by previous 1951 legislation. The 1956 constitution (articles 48, 49, 50, 51, under the third part of the constitution, but under the same title, 'General Rights and Duties') similarly emphasises citizens' right to government-sponsored education, and free public education was guaranteed. Additionally, the 1956 constitution mandates that the state take a more active role in educating citizens through the establishment of schools and cultural and educational institutions, and see to their gradual expansion. Under the 1956 constitution, the state was to take more decisive steps in promoting education in Egypt, including through its nationalisation.

Article 38 of the 1954 draft of the constitution reads:

> The state will work to facilitate appropriate standards of living to all citizens, based on adjustments in food and dwelling, and health, culture, and social services, as it will facilitate similar [services] for unemployment, sickness, disability, and old age. It will also ensure these same standards to victims of war and those of other calamities and their families.

Article 17 of the 1956 constitution, under 'The Basic Fundamentals of Egyptian Society,' similarly to article 38 of the 1954 draft, suggests that 'the government will work to facilitate appropriate standards of living to all citizens, based on adjustments in food and dwelling, and health, culture, and social services'. Article 21 of the 1956 constitution ensures the right of citizens to pensions in cases of old age, sickness, or loss of employment. Both the 1954 draft and the 1956 constitution elucidated the state's moral economy, establishing the precepts of a welfare state in Egypt and spelling out the steps that would guide the state on how to fulfil them.

The 1954 draft and the 1956 constitution guarantee the right of citizens to work (articles 40 and 41, and 52 and 53, respectively, and both under 'General Rights and Duties'). Similarly, both texts guarantee work benefits, including vacations and minimum wages for employees. The guarantee of such working conditions was based not only on economic reasoning (presumably based on the law of supply and demand) but also on the contemporary prevalent interpretation of social justice that was to rectify pre-revolutionary structural problems within the Egyptian labour market.

Article 43 of the 1954 draft guarantees state supervision of women's and youth's employment, the establishment of state institutions that would enable women to manage their double role as workers and chief homemakers, and the protection of youth from abuse and exploitation. In the 1956 constitution, articles 19 and 20 make the same state commitments to women and youth (respectively), but now under section two of the constitution, which defines 'The Basic Principles of Egyptian Society'. In both the 1954 draft and the 1956 constitution, intense public discussion over labour conditions and women and youth materialised into a guaranteed, extended state action to resolve such matters. In both cases the state patriarchy guaranteed such rights.

The 1954 draft secured basic tenets of liberal economic initiative such as property rights. However, it did so under specific, restrictive national and social qualifications. Article 32 of the 1954 draft states that foreigners are not allowed to own land in Egypt, unless in cases specified by law. Article 35 allows private economic initiative, unless it is socially harmful or infringes upon the security, liberty, or honour of others. In both cases economic initiative was bounded by (or embedded in) the social rights of citizens, which the state was to uphold. Article 12 of the 1956 constitution, similarly to article

32 of the 1954 draft, prohibits foreigners from owning land in Egypt. In both cases, this was in clear reference to the past dominance of foreigners in investment and ownership in this field, but with little concern regarding a contemporary change in which many of the foreign and Egyptianised communities in Egypt were actually leaving the country. This article further limits overall landownership in Egypt, alongside ongoing land reform, based on the law that would prohibit feudalism (*iqta'*). Article 13 of the 1956 constitution further stipulates state protection of small landownership, and article 8, like article 35 of the 1954 draft, guarantees private economic initiative under similar social and cultural restrictions.

In the 1954 draft, article 36 mandates that the national economy should be based on planning programs that were themselves to be based on the principle of social justice and whose aim would be the development of production and raising the standard of living. According to article 37, the law guarantees coordination between public and private economic initiatives that were based on social causes and had the aim of bringing prosperity to the people. In the 1956 constitution, article 7 is congruous with article 36 of the 1954 draft, and article 10 with article 37. Importantly, neither national planning nor cooperation between public and private initiatives was new. As will be discussed below, Egypt had already had its first economic plan in 1947. As demonstrated in earlier chapters, here as before, the draft reiterated and codified de facto state practice.

The 1954 draft saw a significant change in relation to taxation, in comparison with the 1923 constitution. The latter mandates equity in taxation (taxation without discrimination), while article 46 of the 1954 draft stipulates that 'social justice is the basis for taxation and other financial charges'. This article was adopted in the 1956 constitution (article 22). These articles clearly opened the door for a progressive as opposed to a universal system of taxation. Here again, Egypt's system of taxation had seen the formal introduction of progressive taxation even before the revolution.

The above comparison between the 1954 draft and the 1956 constitution suggests a great similarity in the socio-economic vision that guided the authors of both documents. Both promised state initiative in developing social welfare institutions based on the principle of social justice, and state participation in economic development through planning and direct state initiative. In both texts, public and private economic initiatives were to be coordinated. Private initiative was to remain free – although not allowed to infringe on unspecified social and cultural rights. Notable in the 1956 constitution were references to recent land reform and a limitation on landownership, as well as the protection of small landlords. The state took an active role in regulating labour relations between employers and employees, as well as labour rights, including those of women. From the comparison between the two documents, and with the 1956 constitution being closely based on the 1954 draft, it is clear that the pashas' draft constitution and Nasser's regime had a rather similar vision. Moreover, both re-established the constitution as a vertical social contract in Egypt and were to take over the role of the 1923 constitution as such.

The socio-economic vision of the 1954 draft and the 1956 constitution was commensurate with a public – read expanding effendi middle class – demand for a greater state role in the development of the economy and the implementation of social justice in Egypt that had been around since the mid-1930s, especially during and after World War II. Moreover, this vision and its implementation as contractual justice in Egyptian law was carried from the pre-revolutionary to the post-revolutionary regime through people like 'Abd al-Razzaq al-Sanhuri, who chaired the 1954 constitutional committee.[7] In 1945, al-Sanhuri – then minister of education – had already promoted the expansion of the primary system of education, and the improvement of the elementary system. In 1949 he wrote the New Civil Code for Egypt, in which individual justice would be upheld only if it did not create a social injustice. After the revolution, al-Sanhuri, now, president of the Supreme Court, and Suleiman Hafiz, his deputy, were highly instrumental in bolstering the new regime.

The 1954 constitution ended up in the garbage bin of history because of politics, not because of policies. In 1954, a clash over the return to democratic life in Egypt (the March crisis) – to a large degree a clash within the revolutionary regime – severed the ties between Nasser and his acolytes, on the one hand, and Major General Muhammad Naguib, who had officially led the revolution until then, and his followers, on the other. The 1954 draft was then scrapped when Nasser rose to official power, and he struggled to bolster his regime, including through political show trials in which al-Sanhuri was one of the defendants. Still, this political struggle over power should not disguise the apparent continuity in socio-economic policy, or the broad social agreement on what was to be done, between the pre- and the post-revolutionary regimes, as demonstrated by the many similarities between the 1954 draft and the 1956 constitution.

Unsurprisingly, these similarities were hardly acknowledged in the official rhetoric, such as in Nasser's speech commemorating the new, 1956 constitution.[8] This constitution was supposed to legitimate his regime while delegitimising the former regime from which he actually borrowed more than he cared to admit. Nasser emphasised the people of Egypt's long-term struggle to achieve social justice and national liberation, and he claimed that the 1956 constitution was the successful conclusion of this struggle. The international scholarship that commented on the 1956 constitution mostly adopted the Nasserite narrative and assigned the constitution to Egypt's gradual transition to socialism, with little reference to the intricate ways in which the new constitution corresponded with socio-economic policy and the 1954 draft.[9] The 1956 constitution was itself short-lived. In 1958, the Egyptian–Syrian union, the UAR (United Arab Republic), brought a new, interim constitution that, crucially, closely resembled the 1956 constitution. In 1961, the abrogation of the short-lived UAR created a constitutional gap, soon to be filled by the National Charter and the 1964 constitution.

The birth of Arab socialism?

The July 1961 laws and the National Charter that followed and ideologically justified them are often considered to have launched a new social contract in Egypt, with the latter having constituted the foundational ideological declaration of Nasser's Arab Socialist regime. The 1961 laws nationalised large Egyptian enterprises and initiated a second phase of land reform by further limiting the size of landownership.[10] They also put a cap on ownership of stocks and, through taxation, on earnings. Workers were represented on boards of directors, and a quarter of an enterprise's annual net profits was allotted to workers' welfare. Employment was made more egalitarian by limiting the number of positions one could hold (one person, one job) and limiting working hours. The charter positioned the new legislation on a broader canvas, established through six national goals of the Nasserite regime:

(1) the destruction of imperialism, (2) ending feudalism, (3) ending monopolies and the domination of capital over the government, (4) the establishment of social justice, (5) building a powerful national army and (6) the establishment of a sound democratic system. Less noted but nonetheless significant was the nationalisation of the press that had taken place somewhat earlier. If the charter was to establish broad national agreement and a sound democratic system, this agenda could not to be achieved through liberal democratic principles of governance, of which a free press is central, but rather through authoritarian implementation of the people's will.

The then changing regional and global contexts seem to support the argument for a new start. Regionally, the turn to Arab socialism came in the aftermath of the failed UAR experiment, and Arab socialism was set in the context of an enhanced struggle over regional dominance. Internationally, Arab socialism was part of the new global best practices associated with the development of the Non-Aligned Movement, in which Nasser took a central role. Rami Ginat has emphasised the Yugoslav influence on the July 1961 laws.[11] The turn to Arab socialism could also be set in this context as a new opportunity to acquire political rent associated with the Cold War. Despite the above, I argue that Arab socialism was securely embedded in an evolving social contract – the origins of which lay in pre-revolutionary Egypt and the search for a local socialism – as opposed to its having been launched as a new pact between state and society. Indeed, it constituted a renewed attempt to sustain this contract, although now through more radical steps.

Announced in the aftermath of the breakdown of the short-lived UAR, and part of a larger attempt to unite Egyptians through a one-party system, the July 1961 laws were supposed to invigorate the revolution politically – to give it a new impetus. However, these laws carried much of the socio-economic message and practice of the past. The goals put forward in the charter had already appeared in the preamble to the 1956 constitution and had circulated in Nasser's speeches even prior to that.[12] After 1952, the Free Officers confiscated royal family properties, as well as lands from the landed elite. After 1956, the state first sequestrated and later nationalised British, French and Jewish properties, and in 1961, Belgian property.

The new wave of nationalisations of Egyptian-owned enterprises that followed the July 1961 laws went in tandem with the earlier state experience of transferring capital from private hands to the state. This resulted in a growing state institutional capacity to manage the economy, as well as state motivation to do so. Less noticed but still significant during this period, the state likewise nationalised leading NGOs and closely regulated the rest. This trend also had its origins in the aftermath of World War II. To the extent that the turn to Arab socialism was revolutionary, it was based on the same impatience to bring about social justice, economic development and national liberation that initially drove the Free Officers into action. Indeed, the regime's radicalisation of the early 1960s was based in part on well-established, pre-revolutionary ideological principles and state practices. More simply, the emergence and adaptation of socialism in Egypt was a process that had started at least as early as World War II.

Chapter 6 of the charter, titled 'On the Inevitability of the Socialist Solution' explains the road ahead, which was based on the continuity of content and change in (global) fashion:

> Socialism is the way for social freedom. Social freedom cannot be realised except through equal opportunity for every citizen to obtain a fair share of the national wealth.
>
> This is not confined to the mere re-distribution of the national wealth among the citizens but foremost and above all it requires expanding the base of this national wealth, so as to accede to the lawful rights of the working masses. *This means that socialism, with its two supports, sufficiency and justice, is the way to social freedom.*
>
> [. . .] The socialist solution was a historical inevitability imposed by reality, the broad aspirations of the masses and the changing nature of the world in the second part of the twentieth century.[13]

The quotation above plainly exposes the continuity between the past and present agendas of the Free Officers in fulfilling their interpretation of an effendi social contract. Social freedom was closely associated with social justice. Economic growth ('expanding the base of this national wealth') through self-sufficiency was to further allow this form of social justice. According to this, the basic reasoning beyond greater state involvement with the economy and society did not change. Indeed, the self-narrative of the socialist solution emphasised a changing reality; its inevitability was the result of a popular aspiration and recent changes in international settings. Commenting on the charter, economist and long-time participant in Egypt's efforts toward economic development Bent Hansen observes that 'the charter mainly post-rationalized and codified reform and institutional change actually undertaken since 1952'.[14] As suggested throughout this chapter, both this reform and institutional change had their roots not only in but also before the revolution.

The National Charter became the formative document of Arab socialism. Nevertheless, at this time the charter was announced as an interim means: it explained recent events but also opened the door for popular participation in shaping the socialist road through the public ratification of a new constitution. The charter reaffirmed national constitutional rights, thereby also once more acknowledging the centrality of constitutionalism in Egyptian governance. The July 1961 laws were special measures; the 1964 constitution was supposed to make Arab socialism permanent. Moreover, it turned Nasser's political manifesto (the charter) into a shared agreement between state and citizens, one that the public was actively enlisted to support.[15] Concurrently, however, the 1964 constitution legitimised many of the principles established in the earlier charter.

Clearly emanating from the charter, the first article of the 1964 interim constitution reads: 'The United Arab Republic is a democratic, socialist State based on the alliance of the working powers of the people'.[16] Importantly, despite the seeming centrality of popularisation under Arab socialism and in the form of greater participation from 'peasants and workers', article 3, reads:

> National unity, formed by the alliance of the people's powers, representing the working people, being the farmers, workers, soldiers, intellectuals and national capital, make up the Arab Socialist Union, as the power representative of the people, driver of the Revolution's potentialities, and protector of sound democratic values.[17]

Farmers and workers are noticeably present in article 3. However, so are 'intellectuals', a term that should be broadly read as educated effendis (not simply a limited upper-class intelligentsia), 'national capital' (who were of middle-class origin, as large enterprises were already under direct state control), and soldiers. The people's power in this article stands for broad social solidarity – a horizontal social contract, not an attempt to change the social structure from the bottom up.

Regarding 'soldiers', article 23 of the constitution states: 'The Armed Forces of the United Arab Republic belong to the people and their function is the protection of the socialist gains of the popular struggle, the safeguarding of the country and the security and integrity of its territory'.[18] In this context, 'soldiers' were not merely a category but a manifestation of the people's force. Accordingly, their first duty, perhaps not surprising considering the revolutionary nature of the regime, was safeguarding and promoting the socio-economic achievements of the revolution; their second duty was the more usual provision of national security. In the quotations above, the 'working powers of the people' should not be confused with the conventional socialist 'working class'. In the 1964 interim constitution there was an attempt to integrate the productive social groups of the nation for the sake of progress, rather than securing overall social change through the rise to power of the working class.

The charter and the 1964 constitution were often about rights, including ownership rights. Despite the transition to Arab socialism, the sanctity of private property did not disappear. In the charter, the nationalisation of large Egyptian enterprises, which was an infringement on property rights, is presented as having been made on efficiency grounds and the precedence of social over individual rights. The 1964 constitution (article 13, section C) acknowledges private property, which would share in development as part of a broader, planned effort at development without exploitation. Article 8 of the 1964 constitution states, 'The State guarantees equality of opportunity to all Egyptians'. In article 9, the 1964 constitution guarantees that the transition to socialism will not bring about a squeeze on human labour: 'The economic foundation of the State is the socialist system which prohibits any form of exploitation in a way which ensures the building of the socialist society with its twin foundations: sufficiency and justice'. Although article 21 suggests that 'work in the United Arab Republic is a right, a duty and an honour for every able citizen', the transition to socialism was not supposed to reduce the eligibility of Egyptians to enjoy the fruits of the revolution for the sake of faster industrialisation, or to reduce the intergenerational accumulation of capital required for this structural change.

Citizens' socio-economic rights had a clear presence in the 1964 constitution. Article 20 guarantees social insurance services, old-age assistance, sickness benefits and unemployment compensation. Article 38 further states that education is the right of all Egyptians and that the state will support that right through the establishment of schools, universities and cultural and educational institutions, as well as their expansion. Article 39 states that all state education will be free, including universities. Article 40 guarantees state support of fair employment compensation and working conditions, social insurance, health insurance, unemployment insurance and the right to rest and vacation. Article 42 states that health care is the right of all Egyptians. The state would guarantee such services by establishing and developing hospitals and health institutions. Much like past constitutions, the 1964 constitution formalised existing state policies and regulations, as opposed to determining new guidelines for state conduct in promoting citizens' rights. This constitution reiterated the existing state duties and moral economy; some of these duties, as exemplified in Egypt's newly announced educational policy, dated to the pre-revolutionary era.

Mandated in the 1954 constitutional draft and in the 1956 constitution, Egypt's First Five-Year Development Plan (1960–5) was not really its first.[19] State planning started in the interwar era, with a developing belief in the role, indeed duty, of the state to bring socio-economic development to Egypt. State planning gained momentum through wartime management of the economy.[20] In 1946, further influenced by international enthusiasm over the power of planning,[21] the Egyptian state had announced a Five-Year Plan. As invariably happened in the aftermath of the revolution, and in response to the partial failure of an earlier development plan, the state announced the establishment of the Permanent Council for National Production, presided over by the prime minister. Even before the First Five-Year Plan, this council had begun allocating state funds for economic development.

Like the 1956 constitution, the plan embraced two long-established principles in Egypt, economic self-sufficiency and social justice. The plan required a comprehensive mode of socio-economic development that would serve to balance between these goals. Within this integrated model of development, there remained a strong liberal economic element, as opposed to a socialist agenda. Thus, the government took an increasing role in development through investment in economic initiatives, as well as active participation in and regulation of them. However, it retained 'equality of opportunity' in two central venues of development: education and economic entrepreneurship. The plan brought together current conventional wisdom on how such principles were to be achieved – rational planning, state-involvement with the economy and a strong belief in science and technology. In all this it was the climax of past, including pre-revolutionary, efforts at development, though the plan also constituted an attempt to break away from the past by leapfrogging into a better future.

In preparation for the plan, Egypt significantly overhauled information gathering, notably of statistical information, and planning capacity – both local and international. Despite growing calls for more scientific research, planning, and the building up of state institutional capacity for both during the interwar era and in the aftermath of World War II, it was the concentrated effort leading to the making of the plan that significantly reformulated the state's ability to measure and evaluate the local economy. Moreover, the plan further intensified existing remedies for contemporary ills. It proposed significant investment in education, especially in higher education and research, the modernisation of agriculture and state-led import substitution industrialisation. According to the plan's comprehensive vision, education would facilitate the making of the state cadres required for state engagement with society (welfare) and the economy (planning and management), while simultaneously ensuring equality of opportunity for the many. Agricultural reform would secure better efficiency of production while bettering peasants' standards of living. Import substitution industrialisation carried the promise of rapid industrialisation that would further increase local consumption. In all this, the state would take greater charge of the economy and society.

In setting the scale and scope of the plan, there was a clear gap between planners and politicians. The economists who worked on the plan, ambitious as they were, remained gradualists. Politicians – and Nasser was foremost among them – singled out making a historical breakthrough as crucial to the political credit of the regime. Central to the plan (and the disappointment ahead) was the politically established goal of doubling the national income over a period of ten years, 40 per cent of which was to be achieved during the first five years after the announcement of the plan. As Patrick O'Brien explains, such an objective was the result of a presidential decision to aim for a higher growth rate than had been earlier envisioned by planners. The ministry of information suggested that 'economists have estimated a period of 20 years for the execution of the plan. It has been decided to amend the plan so as to ensure the execution of the programme on a revolutionary basis in a period of 10 years'.[22] Such a high pace of economic growth soon proved unrealistic, not least because the means for achieving it were evolutionist in nature: investment in the economy was balanced against investment in social development, and all social classes were to benefit from the plan. Worthy as these causes might have been, they were to a large extent mutually exclusive.

On 4 July 1960, Vice President A. Boghdady presented the plan to the General Congress of the National Union in a speech titled 'The Plan between the Government and the People'. Boghdady defines the plan as follows:

> The overall national Plan which I present to you in this conference is an expression of the measures taken by the government to realise economic progress and social evolution within the frame-work of a national philosophy. It is an endeavour to maintain the democratic socialist cooperative society we are striving to achieve.[23]

According to Boghdady, the fundamentals of Arab socialism were readily manifested in the plan. He adds:

> The Plan gives a picture of the future we aim at. It does not portray it in words, but in actual projects, figures and objectives. Each one of us will thus know his position in the gigantic framework, and will demand more than just resonant speeches, ringing enthusiasm and hollow words reminiscent of the old speeches from the throne, so full of the promises of partisan politicians of the past regimes.[24]

This quotation, symptomatic of the gigantic effort to establish a zero hour in Egypt, would also ring hollow shortly thereafter, as the plan achieved considerably less than intended.

In discussing the 'inevitability of the socialist solution', the 1962 National Charter stated that 'efficient socialist planning is the sole method which guarantees the use of all national resources, be they material, natural or human, in a practical, scientific and humane way aimed at realising the common good of the masses, and ensuring a life of prosperity for them'.[25] Similarly, article 10 of the 1964 interim constitution suggests that 'the entire national economy is directed in accordance with the development plan laid down by the state'. Here too there would be an ongoing discrepancy between stated goals and reality. During the 1960s, despite the centrality of Arab socialism, much debate over 'scientific socialism', and the increasing role of technocrats in the bureaucracy and public sector, Egypt did not undergo a second development plan. Indeed, there was a broadening gap between official ends and actual means in the execution of Arab socialism.

To the extent that the plan offered a broader scale and scope through an ambitious objective, it was further ready to commit state resources to its implementation. Arguably, the main difference between the pre- and post-revolutionary regimes was the readiness of the latter to commit Egypt to public debt to finance a scheme that involved a concurrent overhaul of public investment and public consumption, where the old regime's more conservative budgets avoided such debt.[26] Moreover, political impatience with the means set for economic transformation was rising. As suggested above, by July 1961, not long after the introduction of the plan, the state had announced a new set of economic decrees associated with socialist radicalisation. Robert Mabro uses strong words: 'With the First Five-Year Plan comprehensive planning died in Egypt'.[27] Despite the plan's achievements, it was to be the first and last such plan under Nasser, not least because a second comprehensive development plan would have exposed the partial failure of the first.

Statism: bureaucratisation and regulation

This section documents two interrelated processes in Egypt: the rapid increase in state ministries that provided the fruits of the revolution to citizens, and their takeover of regulation and management of civil society/NGOs. Analysis of these processes emphasises the continuity with the past, both in the making of this bureaucratic capacity and in state allocation of resources. The section follows institutional histories of five governmental ministries – education, health, social affairs (comprised of social solidarity and religious services), trade and supply, and housing.[28] it explores the context in which they first emerged, and how they developed and changed over time. A study of state allocation through the lens of these ministries suggests the familiar social biases despite the turn to Arab socialism. It later examines a process of centralisation in which the state took over central civil society organisations, including religious organisations, and regulated the rest. No less significant than the creation of new services, the making of state welfare services, much like the creation of a public sector responsible for the economy, was about the nationalisation of private welfare providers.

Increase in the number of ministries and growth in the state bureaucracy were already significant in the period from the mid-1930s until the 1952 revolution. Despite the criticism of growing state expenditures and inefficiency prior to that, and though the Free Officers briefly attempted, as had previous governments, to reform the state bureaucracy, no such reform occurred. Under the revolutionary regime the number of ministries expanded, with twelve new ministries being formed, coming close to doubling the total number of ministries that had existed during the last days of the liberal monarchy. This growth saw further expression in the number of ministers, including deputy ministers and deputy prime ministers. Between 1954 and 1956, Nasser's various governments included about twenty ministers, expanding from eleven ministers under the government of Ali Mahir, who led the first government formed after the revolution.

In August 1961 the state added six new ministries in the aftermath of the socialist laws. After 1961 the number of ministers increased by yet another third or more.[29] Some of the new ministries, such as those of land reform, al-Azhar Affairs, agricultural reform and high dam were task oriented, serving ad hoc purposes. These new ministries were not novel creations, but were new in the sense that they were often at least partly combinations of already existing administrative units in other ministries. Nevertheless, the overall quantitative growth in the number of ministries and ministers over time indicated a rising state role in managing the economy and society. Significant, congruent growth in state employment also took place.

Education was and remained a central effendi demand and state concern.[30] After the revolution, the state significantly increased overall expenses on education as part of the GNP, and this percentage rose between 1952/53 and 1962/63 by 150 per cent.[31] Education still held the familiar pre-revolutionary biases in relation to mass elementary education, and there was a significant gap between quantity and quality. Chapter Four will show how education continued to straddle being a tool for social reform (alleviating ignorance) for the lower class and being a vehicle of social justice (raising equality of opportunity) for the effendi middle class.[32] The study of higher, university education in the current chapter demonstrates a continuing, implicit but effective, effendi agency in determining state policy on education during the early 1960s, even after Egypt's turn to Arab socialism, and the official emphasis on the peasants' and workers' participation in national life.[33] Put simply, in Nasser's effendi state higher education was too consensual in public discourse to be changed.

During this period Nasser invariably pronounced a commitment to education in his speeches. Yet critics, such as Louis Awad in his *University and the New Society*, demanded that the government indeed meet its commitment to enlarge enrolment and develop institutions of higher education. He did so by exposing a gap between such promises and what the state actually delivered. Despite the clear continuity between the old and new regimes with regard to the emphasis on education, the new regime did much to belittle this continuity between pre- and post-revolutionary Egypt. A notable example occurred in 1962 when, on the occasion of the tenth anniversary of King Farouk's abdication, Nasser declared that university tuition would be free from then on.[34]

The rapid expansion of higher education was a particularly glowing achievement in comparison with other areas of social development. Here too, there would be a dual trend of increase in overall expenditures and continuity from pre- to post-revolutionary bias in spending and quality of services. Between 1952/53 and 1969/70, public expenditures on education and health increased at the same rate, by almost 11 per cent on average.[35] However, the significant gap between health and education, in terms of overall state allocations, remained constant. Rural health care, a long-term concern in Egypt, had improved over time. Yet there were two prominent discrepancies concerning the provision of health services. One was between what the Nasserite state promised and what it could deliver. With all the improvements made in the provision of state health services, the promise, for example, in the National Charter for 'comfort and service' in receiving such a service was barely met, owing to budgetary constraints, demographic expansion and the sheer gap between what the state promised and what it could, in reality, provide. The other was the obvious inequality between state provision of health services in cities versus rural regions. This was the result of clear differences in physical infrastructure, but it was also the outcome of reluctance among state-employed, middle-class health providers (therefore, in practice, the state itself) to work in rural regions, both before and after the revolution. Such long-existing hardship persisted despite the already existing, pre-revolutionary compulsory recruitment of doctors and other health professionals to serve in the countryside.[36]

Of the state ministries, the ministry of social affairs (MOSA) was the most closely involved in state provision of services to lower-class Egyptians, therefore ensuring a social revolution from below.[37] Evaluation of MOSA's activities well presents the disparity between an official state commitment to equity and the de facto steps taken by the state to deliver that equity. In October 1953 the government created the Permanent Council for Public Welfare Services (PCPWS), leading to a reorganisation that took place under the leadership of the ministry of social affairs.[38] The ambitious PCPWS's attempt to expand and improve state services encountered myriad administrative difficulties, including that workers, not unlike education and health providers, were reluctant to live in remote rural areas (while villages close to cities were better served). Also similar to the provision of other services, the central impediment here was that while the state allocated significant funds to social welfare services, a large portion of these funds was used to finance wages, the high cost-of-living bonuses and state employees' pensions. From 1960, if not earlier, funding for the project gradually dried up.[39] In January 1967 the PCPWS was officially dissolved.

Significantly, MOSA's main success was in reigning in and dominating associational life in Egypt, a process that had started earlier but that gained pace under the revolution. By the early 1950s, Egypt had a long tradition of private benevolent societies, especially in education and health, coupled with an increasing state tendency to regulate their activities. Since 1945, a series of laws had regulated associational life under the supervision of MOSA. Notably, law 49 of 1945 (further amended in 1952) required the registration of all associations and made MOSA an overseer of their financial and organisational affairs, thus facilitating their control by the state. In 1956, and along the same lines, legislation further consolidated and intensified state control of associational life, and law number 32 of 1964 later enhanced this control over associations, their members and their activities. In addition, the state took over (incorporated) the better-financed and better-organised associations among them.[40] The state also redesignated government workers' unions as social clubs, the result of 1956 legislation (law number 384).[41] All such state actions indicated continuous state interference with civil-society organisations, though not simply growing state authoritarianism. Through the regulation of such organisations the state surely asserted itself in society, but this trend also demonstrated an interconnectedness between state bureaucracy and associational life. Indeed, the two were closely intertwined through their reorganisation along corporatist lines; state-led corporatism became an invisible hand of the government in fulfilling articles of the vertical social contract.[42] Where the state could not afford to officially deliver services, it would let associations handle the providing.

Associational life in Egypt was mostly an urban affair, as is clearly suggested in a 1960 survey conducted by MOSA. In this survey, associations were often located in the larger cities, with about a third of all associations, 50 per cent of all members, and 46 per cent of all associations' incomes located in Cairo.[43] Cairo-based associations likewise received about half of all state subsidies for associations.[44] The centrality of cities was noted in associational membership and service provision, with rural environs served less well. Judging by expenditures, about a third of the associations' budgets went to medical and health services.[45] Recall that this was in a period of free (or almost free) state health services, thus the high rate of expenditures implied a state deficiency in the direct provision of healthcare. In addition, these services were more available to the urban middle class, which had better access to service providers. In comparison, cash assistance constituted about a fifth of these expenditures, while cultural and educational activities took up just below that amount. Judging from information regarding the expenses of associations, they served as a source of middle-class employment no less than of service provision, much like state employment did. According the 1960 survey, over two-fifths of associations' expenses went toward administration, with a similar amount going to actual services.[46] Thus, associational life showed a second, if implicit, tier of bias toward urban, often middle-class, consumers: the associations' activities increased the gaps in provision to the benefit of these consumers and provided them with new opportunities for employment.

The state's incorporation of religious service provision meant that these services eventually became part of the social contract. This was not a new trend. In 1942, for example, a newly appointed sanitation committee for mosques examined this public utility, calling for increased state contribution to its provision, as opposed to mosque management under private charity. This committee further suggested that the ministry of Awqaf could, in turn, abolish private mosques.[47] Since 1953, and becoming a law (157) in 1960, the ministry of Awqaf's annexation policy of turning private mosques into public mosques had been selective. It was also quite similar to the dynamics of state-private associations discussed above, starting with mosques in the best physical and financial condition as opposed to those most in need of improvement.[48] By 1962, 44 per cent of state mosques had been taken over from private management. Also familiar was the higher concentration of state mosques in urban as opposed to rural environments, indicating better state provision of religious services to city dwellers,[49] as well as further state political control over such institutions. In 1964, a ministry of Awqaf report on the ministry's achievements in the twelve years since the revolution testified to religious services turning into a service like any other. In this, state provision of religious services defused their religiosity (making them more mundane). However, it also amplified the religious standing of the state as the provider of these services. Similarly, like any other ministry, the quantitative emphasis of the ministry's achievements before and after the revolution was designed to glorify the revolution's successes and, through this, to further legitimise the regime, in both its own eyes and the public's mind.

Under the revolution, the ministry of awqaf was directly and indirectly stripped of some responsibilities. An example of this is law 247 of 1953, which abolished private waqfs, and therefore the ministry's earlier responsibility for their regulation. In addition, various responsibilities related to education and justice were transferred from the ministry of awqaf to other ministries, notably to the education and justice ministries. The ministry of awqaf remained responsible for charity and the investment of its own funds, and it gained more control over waqf properties.[50] Similarly, the state regulated religious education, notably in al-Azhar University. In reforming al-Azhar, the state allowed it to grow, but it consequently became more reliant on monies received from the state, and the state dictated appointments to the institution.[51] All such steps were a far cry from 'secularisation', in the sense of marginalising religion in the public sphere.[52] Rather, they should be understood as a long-term effendi call for state involvement in modernising religion, or making it into an effendi Islam – reforming religion through the application of rationalism and scientific inquiry.[53] Through this process, the state asserted greater control over religious institutions in return for an implicit commitment to providing them with financial and administrative support.

Food subsidies proved another sphere where the revolutionary regime aimed to strengthen its hold over Egyptian society. As previously mentioned, in June 1940 the ministry of supply was established to secure adequate provision of food to citizens under wartime conditions. After World War II, the state established subsidies for basic foodstuffs, no doubt under the impact of wartime regulation, but also as a result of mounting demand to take active steps to raise local standards of living.[54] In March 1946, the ministry of supply was abolished, and the state transferred its responsibilities to the ministry of commerce and industry. War-led state participation in provisioning was partly waning as wartime pressure on the supply of basic commodities decreased. The ministry of supply regained its independence soon after the revolution, albeit under a joint ministry with the ministry of commerce and industry. By the second half of the 1950s, the ministry of supply was once again independent. In March 1964, the ministry of supply and the ministry of internal commerce had been rejoined to facilitate price regulation of basic commodities and subsidies. Importantly, state regulation and the subsidy of basic commodities remained universal – excluding only various categories of the very rich – as opposed to progressive in supplying those most in need among the lower class. Despite being a hallmark of the Egyptian welfare state during the 1950s and 1960s, subsidies for food and basic commodities were low and included only a few items. For example, in 1970/71, Egyptian food subsidies constituted a mere 0.2 per cent of total government expenditures.[55] Contrary to common belief across the public/political spectrum in Egypt, it was mostly under Sadat's seemingly liberalising economic policy that subsidies significantly increased.

During World War II, the state decreed a rent freeze in urban areas to counter wartime inflation and secure basic standards of living. In 1947, the pre-revolutionary state further legislated a rent freeze based on rent indices dating from April 1941, which prevented owners from evicting their tenants.

This legislation was an attempt to prevent owners from taking advantage of the inflation in housing costs by subletting at higher prices.[56]

In 1952, the newly established Free Officers' regime initiated a series of reductions in urban rents. The state would later (1962) set rents based on a percentage of land and construction costs. Together with rent control, the state legislated tenant protection, which included restrictions on eviction, the right to bring an official complaint regarding the quality of maintenance, the right to inherent, the right to sublet and a prohibition on informal/illegal payment when obtaining the lease. (The latter prohibition related to a common practice of demanding 'key money', or informal payment beyond the official price). Such state regulation of real estate markets meant that other than direct sale of the property, renters de facto obtained property rights. It did not distinguish between different types of rented properties, thereby benefiting renters of more expensive assets and, indirectly, middle- and upper-class renters.

Following the revolution, the public construction of low- and to a smaller extent middle-cost housing was high on the regime's agenda. As with rent control, public construction was not invented by the Free Officers; the last pre-revolutionary Wafd government had already initiated public housing for the working class in Helwan and Imbaba (near Cairo). This Wafd government had also encouraged cooperative housing ventures through subsidies and land grants. Furthermore, the sheer size of the existing and rising demand for housing meant that the state could not really respond to such a demand on its own. Rapid demographic growth and rural-to-urban migration accounted for an ever-growing urban demand for housing. This was particularly so as the state took upon itself ever-expanding financial commitments in its attempt to encourage socio-economic development. A notable example was the construction of the High Dam during the 1960s, which took precedence over the construction of private dwellings in state allocation of building materials. Thus, state constructed and subsidised housing did not exceed 5 per cent of all housing units built during the Nasserite period.[57]

The extensive gap between state commitment and the state's ability to finance housing projects brought about a dual development. The liberal monarchy having provided a precedent, the Nasserite state engaged in flagship-projects such as the construction of workers' dwellings and the renovation of run-down city neighbourhoods such as Bulaq. Concurrently, the period saw a strong outburst of informal construction, which was not documented in official statistics. Such informality was at least partly the inverse result of deepening state regulation. For example, informal housing included circumventing shortages in building materials through substandard construction. While low-cost housing for the lower class was a much-trumpeted state policy, middle-class groups within the military, the police and professional groups such as engineers and journalists formed government-supported housing cooperatives and built using private constructors. A notable site for such construction was the Muhandisin (Engineers) neighbourhood.

The discussion so far has mostly examined direct state provision of services to citizens. No less important for our analysis – and again, dated to pre-revolutionary Egypt, especially since the 1930s – was a growing state commitment to raising local standards of living, primarily middle-class standards of living, through an enhanced policy of import substitute industrialisation (ISI).[58] Under this policy, Egyptian industrialisation was to benefit from local demand, which was predicated on expanding a mostly urban consumption, and to be safeguarded against imports by regulation and tax barriers. In this manner, ISI was supposed to achieve social equity through better citizen access to state-produced commodities, and in the least painful way – with minimal austerity and little curtailing of choice. In return, Egypt was also to achieve what the Free Officers had so sought after and promised: economic self-sufficiency, which in itself was a precondition for national independence.

Since the last days of the liberal monarchy, and despite a shift toward taxation based on personal income and corporate profits, taxation had remained for the most part based on universal, indirect taxation, as opposed to progressive, direct taxation. Moreover, three-quarters of the total state revenue from taxation was derived from the former, and only one-quarter from the latter.[59] As with the state's service provision and industrialisation policy, this system of taxation benefited middle- and upper-class citizens over the rest of society. From the fiscal year 1953/54, Egypt's efforts at socio-economic development were covered to varying degrees by borrowing, as opposed to taxation.[60] When after the mid-1960s, and particularly in the aftermath of the 1967 Middle East War, budgetary constraints lay heavily on Egypt, state development bias toward the middle class became even more pronounced. Moreover, an increase in state expenditures as part of national income meant that there were fewer market-based alternatives for socio-economic mobility, and hence such mobility was increasingly confined to effendi middle class state employment.

If ever there was any proof that Nasser's regime felt obliged to fulfil the social contract, it was the spiralling debt that the Egyptian state encountered as a result of that commitment, coupled with a striving for economic development that was to be brought about with few consequences to citizens. Egypt's growing search for economic rent, indeed much of its regional and international politics, can be explained by the Nasserite regime's need to secure more financing, which stood in a rather sharp contrast to its concurrent call for self-sufficiency. John Waterbury's succinct analysis of this process is quite telling:

> Egypt's costly social welfare programs, overstaffed bureaucracy, and inefficient state enterprises would be paid for by deficit financing and external assistance. There was no call to sacrifice for future generations, no austerity measures other than those dictated by military defeat. Egyptians were promised the fruits of the revolution (*makasib al-thawra*) in their time.[61]

What was less clear in Waterbury's and other's analyses was that the reason for the revolution's dedication to an integrated, and less painful model of social and economic development was that it had promised this moral economy from day one, in tandem with its condemnation of the liberal monarchy's failure to provide the same. In a somewhat paradoxical fashion, the revolution preserved some of the pre-revolutionary social hierarchies it was ostensibly meant to overthrow. Furthermore, it was foremost a promise to an expanding effendi middle class, rather than to all Egyptians, that the authoritarian Nasserite state attempted to uphold.

Notes

1. I have discussed the term 'authoritarian pact' or 'bargain' in the Introduction. See a brief yet effective dispute of this argument in Nathan J. Brown, 'Nasser's Legal Legacy: Accessibility, Accountability, and Authoritarianism', in Podeh and Winckler, *Rethinking Nasserism*, 129–31.
2. Salem, *Anticolonial Afterlives*, 19.
3. Salah 'Isa, *Dustur fi Sunduq al-Qumama: Qissat Mashru' Dustur 1954: Dirasa wa-Wathiqa* (Cairo: Markaz al-Qahira li-Dirasat Huquq al-Insan, 2001). On

this book, including an interview with its author, see Andrew Hammond, 'Cairo Communique: Egypt's Deep-Sixed 1954 Constitution a Reminder of What Might Have Been', *Washington Report on Middle East Affairs* 21, no. 7 (2002): 55, accessed 9 September 2020, https://www.wrmea.org/002-september-october/egypt-s-deep-sixed-1954-constitution-a-reminder-of-what-might-have-been.html.

4. A copy of this draft was deposited at the library of the Institute of Arab Research and Studies in Cairo. 'Isa, *Dustur*, 245.
5. Kandil, 'Militarism and Its Discontents'.
6. See the 1954 draft constitution in 'Isa, *Dustur*, 245–303, and the 1956 constitution in Yusuf Q. Khuri, *al-Dasatir fi al-'Alam al-'Arabi: Nusus wa-Ta'dilat: 1839–1987* (Beirut: Dar al-Hamra', 1989), 559–67.
7. Guy Bechor, 'To Hold the Hand of the Weak: The Emergence of Contractual Justice in Egyptian Civil Law', *Islamic Law and Society* 8, no. 2 (2001): 179–200.
8. Nasser's speech, from 16 January 1956, introduced the new 1956 constitution before a large audience in the Republic Square (*Maydan al-Jumhuriyya*) in Cairo. See this speech in Jamal 'Abd al-Nasir, *al-Majmu' al-Kamila*, 496–511, ALMANHAL, accessed 27 April 2020, https://platform.almanhal.com/Reader/Book/2818.
9. See, for example, 'The New Egyptian Constitution', *Middle East Journal* 10, no. 3 (1956): 304–6.
10. See the laws, including references from relevant ministers and clarifications in the United Arab Republic, Lajnat Kutub Siyasiyya, *al-Thawra al-Ijtima'iyya: Qawanin Yulya al-Majida* (Cairo: Lajnat Kutub Siyasiyya, 1961), 59–128.
11. Rami Ginat, *Egypt's Incomplete Revolution* (London: Routledge, 1997), 16.
12. Baha Abu-Laban, 'The National Character in the Egyptian Revolution', *Journal of Developing Areas* 1, no. 2 (1967): 183n17.
13. See Nissim Rejwan, *Nasserist Ideology: Its Exponents and Critics* (New York: Wiley, 1974), 227, for the translation of the above quotation. Italics mine.
14. Hansen, *Egypt and Turkey*, 115.
15. See the emphasis on popular participation in drafting and legitimising the 1964 constitution in its Preamble: Sami A. Hanna and George H. Gardner, *Arab Socialism: A Documentary Survey* (Leiden: Brill, 1969), 386–7. In quoting from the 1964 constitution, I have used the official English version presented in ibid., 386–408. Egypt retained the name United Arab Republic even after the dissolution of the partnership with Syria in 1961.
16. Ibid., 387.

17. Ibid., 387–8.
18. Ibid., 390.
19. Robert L. Tignor, 'Nationalism, Economic Planning, and Development Projects in Interwar Egypt', *International Journal of African Historical Studies* 10, no. 2 (1977): 185–208; and Wahba, *The Role of the State*, 43–7. For analysis of the plan, see Hansen and Marzouk, *Development and Economic Policy*, 295–316; Charles Philip Issawi, *Egypt in Revolution: An Economic Analysis* (London: Oxford University Press, 1963), 66–75; Robert Mabro, *The Egyptian Economy, 1952–1972* (Oxford: Clarendon Press, 1974), 115–24; and Patrick O'Brien, *The Revolution in Egypt's Economic System: From Private Enterprise to Socialism, 1952–1965* (London: Oxford University Press, 1966), 104–23.
20. Robert Vitalis and Steven Heydemann, 'War, Keynesianism and Colonialism: Explaining State-Market Relations in the Postwar Middle East', in *War, Institutions and Social Change in the Middle East*, ed. Steven Heydemann (Berkeley: University of California Press, 2000), 100–45.
21. Valeska Huber, 'Introduction: Global Histories of Social Planning', *Journal of Contemporary History* 52, no. 1 (2017): 3–15.
22. O'Brien, *The Revolution in Egypt's Economic System*, 105–6. See Kerr, 'The Emergence of a Socialist Ideology', 135, for a rather prophetic analysis of the impossible outcomes of promises made regarding such economic growth.
23. *The Comprehensive Five-year Plan for the Economic and Social Development of the UAR, 1960–1965* (Middle East Publications: The National Publications House Press, 1960), 5. The name spelled 'Boghdady' in this source is commonly transliterated as 'Baghdadi'.
24. Ibid., 6.
25. Rejwan, *Nasserist Ideology*, 229.
26. Hansen, *Egypt and Turkey*, 59.
27. Mabro, *The Egyptian Economy*, 123.
28. See Ayubi, *Bureaucracy and Politics*, 187–93, for analysis of the structural changes in the state bureaucracy since the 1952 revolution.
29. Jawwadi, *al-Bunyan al-Wizari*, 15, table 1.
30. See Belli, *An Incurable Past*, 15–76, for continuity in educational policy between the pre- and post-revolutionary regimes.
31. Calculated from Hansen and Marzouk, *Development and Economic Policy*, 250, table 9.2.
32. On higher education catering to the middle class, see Abdalla, *Student Movement*, 109–10. Mu'min Kamal Shafi'i, *al-Dawla wa-l-Tabaqa al-Wusta fi Misr: Tahlil Susyuluji li-Dawr al-Dawla fi Idarat al-Sira' al-Ijtima'i* (Cairo: Dar

Qaba' li-l-Tiba'a wa-l-Nashr wa-l-Tawzi', 2001), 306–9, discusses Nasserite educational policies as bolstering the middle class.

33. For analysis of higher education under Nasser, including its critics, see Abdalla, *Student Movement*, 101–37; Erlich, *Students and University*, 171–98; and Reid, *Cairo University*, 174–83.
34. Reid, *Cairo University*, 174.
35. Mabro, *The Egyptian Economy*, 159.
36. See Issawi, *Egypt in Revolution*, 103–4, for compulsory service and shortages of health workers in the rural regions; Ayubi, *Bureaucracy and Politics*, 247, for the 1960s preference for employment in Cairo, Giza or Alexandria; and Baker, *Egypt's Uncertain Revolution*, 218–34, for an evaluation of rural health services under the revolution.
37. See Muhammad Muhammad Tawfiq 'Abd al-Fatah, introduction to *al-Dustur al-Ijtima'i li-l-Jumhuriyya al-'Arabiyya al-Muttahida, ka-ma Wada'ahu al-Ra'is Jamal 'Abd al-Nasir*, by Wizarat al-Shu'un al-Ijtima'iyya wa-l-'Amal (Cairo: Wizarat al-Shu'un al-Ijtima'iyya wa-l-'Amal, 1961).
38. James L. Iwan, 'From Social Welfare to Local Government: The United Arab Republic (Egypt)', *Middle East Journal* 22, no. 3 (1968): 272.
39. Ibid., 272–3.
40. Berger, *Islam in Egypt Today*, 117–18.
41. Ibid., 93–6.
42. Bianchi, *Unruly Corporatism*, 72–81.
43. Berger, *Islam in Egypt Today*, 92, table 3.
44. Ibid., 103, table 27.
45. Ibid., 110, table 34.
46. Ibid., 106, table 30.
47. Ibid., 54.
48. Ibid., 56.
49. Ibid., 20.
50. Ibid., 44–6.
51. Malika Zeghal, 'Religion and Politics in Egypt: The Ulema of al-Azhar, Radical Islam, and the State (1952–94)', *International Journal of Middle East Studies* 31, no. 3 (1999): 371–99.
52. Hussein Ali Agrama, *Questioning Secularism: Islam, Sovereignty, and the Rule of Law in Modern Egypt* (Chicago: University of Chicago Press, 2012).
53. On effendi Islam, see Ryzova, *Age of the Efendiyya*, 77–8.
54. Ali and Adams, 'The Egyptian Food Subsidy System', 1778. Interestingly, Ahmad al-Safati argues that a system of subsidies and wage adjustments in

return for political quiet was a system started by the British during World War II to ensure tacit support for the allied war effort. See al-Safati, 'Hisad al-Sinin'.
55. Ali and Adams, 'The Egyptian Food Subsidy System', 1779, table 1.
56. For housing legislation since World War II and under the revolution, see Hanna, *Uridu Maskinan*, 28–31. The discussion here and in the following paragraphs is also based on Harik, *Economic Policy Reform in Egypt*, 157–65; Gehan Selim, 'Instituting Order: The Limitations of Nasser's Post-Colonial Planning Visions for Cairo in the Case of the Indigenous Quarter of Bulaq (1952–1970)', *Planning Perspectives* 29, no. 1 (2014): 67–89, https://doi.org/10.1080/02665433.2013.808580; El Shakry, 'Cairo as Capital of Socialist Revolution?'; Volait, 'Réforme sociale et habitat populaire', 322–8; Volait, 'Town Planning Schemes for Cairo'; and John Waterbury, 'Patterns of Urban Growth and Income Distribution in Egypt', in Abdel-Khalek and Tignor, *Political Economy of Income Distribution*, 339–41.
57. Harik, *Economic Policy Reform in Egypt*, 158, citing Milad Hanna, *al-Iskan wa-l-Misyada: al-Mushkila wa-l-Hall* (Cairo: Dar al-Mustaqbal al-'Arabi, 1988).
58. Ayubi, *Bureaucracy and Politics*, 406–8; and Mona Abaza, *Changing Consumer Cultures of Modern Egypt: Cairo's Urban Reshaping* (Leiden: Brill, 2006), 89–96.
59. Ibid., 256; and Mahmoud Abdel-Fadil, *The Political Economy of Nasserism: A Study in Employment and Income Distribution Policies in Urban Egypt, 1952–72* (Cambridge: Cambridge University Press, 1980), 71–3.
60. Hansen and Marzouk, *Development and Economic Policy*, 253–4.
61. John Waterbury, 'The "Soft State" and the "Open Door": Egypt's Experience with Economic Liberalization, 1974–1984', *Comparative Politics* 18, no. 1 (1985): 69.

4

OLD SOCIETY, NEW SOCIETY

From early on, the Free Officers emphasised that the revolution was a social as well as an economic and political revolution that aimed to create a 'new society'. According to this narrative, the 1952 revolution was a social revolution in the sense that it would bring social justice – equity and equality of opportunity for all Egyptians. Following the formal transition to socialism during the early 1960s, this revolution was also supposed to change the structural base of society by creating a classless society. In such a utopian society, social solidarity would allow social cooperation that would mend previous social problems. This chapter asks the following questions: To what extent did social engineering – the state role in socio-economic development through the formal expansion of the social contract – bring social change to Egypt, and what kind of change? Put differently, what transitions did the promised 'fruits of the revolution' bring to Egyptian society, and to which classes within society? And how did the new society differ from the old?

To respond to these questions, this chapter evaluates social change along three class lines: peasants and workers, or lower-class Egyptians; the middle class; and upper-class Egyptians. It investigates pre- and post-revolutionary transitions among these social classes, throughout the period 1952–70. The chapter first evaluates the notion of a new Nasserite elite and argues that this new elite embraced much of the earlier effendi vision of good government and governance. It then investigates how hierarchies of state redistribution schemes – the state's universal as opposed to progressive social policies and economic development schemes – benefited each social group. Central to the analysis here is an examination of the development of 'middle society' following the revolution. This middle society included the lower and middle echelons of urban, educated and often state-employed Egyptians. It also included organised labour, now incorporated into the newly emerging public sector, and middle-size landowners/peasants. The chapter discusses how, rather than helping the peasants and workers most in need, or creating a classless society, the effendi social contract mostly benefited middle society. Egypt's new society under the revolution indeed reflected an attempt to mend public grievances over the social injustices of the past, but with the same blind spots that such an effendi call entailed.

The new effendis

There is an ongoing puzzle in Egyptian historiography. Historians of the period before the revolution have placed great emphasis on the centrality of the *effendiyya* in promoting socio-economic change through active participation in public discourse and politics. However, this *effendiyya* seemed to have disappeared from the unfolding events that followed the revolution. In 1963, sociologist Manfred Halpern discussed the rise of a new middle class that he regarded as the creation of the new regimes in Egypt, elsewhere in the region and in the postcolonial world.[1] Similarly, when Egyptian historical and sociological analysis from the early 1990s onward returned to studying the middle class, scholars argued that under the revolution, Egypt's middle class grew fast and reached its heyday. As we shall see, this literature reiterated the role of the Nasserite state in facilitating both the social mobility into the middle class and the socio-economic reproduction of this social group. In this analysis too, there is a gap produced by studying the new middle class of the 1950s and particularly the 1960s while ignoring its pre-revolutionary predecessor – the *effendiyya*.

The disappearance of the effendi middle class may be partly explained by the rhetoric of the new regime, whose political zero hour was clearly also going to be a social zero hour. Thus, the Free Officers' regime famously forbade all honorific titles by law. The sartorial diacritics of the effendi middle class – the European-style suit and the tarbush – were also gradually replaced by the popular revolutionary suit. Nevertheless, I argue that the disappearance of the *effendiyya* (both the term and the class) was related to the self-image of the effendi middle class itself, or what Lucie Ryzova terms 'returns'.[2] After the late nineteenth century, new generations of effendis invariably felt alienated from their biological and, more so, 'social' fathers (the generation that preceded them) and sought new ways to reform their society and themselves. The new effendis – Nasser and his generation – rebelled in a familiar effendi fashion and with the same passion for the transformation of Egypt.

During the 1940s and leading up to the revolution, there was a voice in Egyptian public discourse – essentially an effendi middle class discourse – lamenting the contemporary crises of Egyptian society as a whole, but in practice focusing on the hardships of the middle class. Put simply, another reason for the disappearance of the term *effendiyya* in public and political discourse was that from early on the vision of the socio-economic development of Egypt and the interests of this social group became intertwined when the group's members came to dominate the state.

This section explores the large effendi presence in state politics and policy. First, it discusses how existing visions of effendi state leadership and state management informed the new Nasserist elite, the 'new effendis'. This analysis of the making of the new effendi elite complements the argument made in Chapter Three, which demonstrates that the conventional wisdom regarding the Free Officers' lack of a coherent ideology upon coming into power was partially misleading. Second, and also related to the discussion in Chapter Three, it explores the continuity in policymaking between the old and new regimes, under Egypt's growing statism, in support of Egypt's effendi middle class, particularly the educational policy that supported higher education and led to state employment. This policy became central to the expansion of the lower and middle effendi middle class, now frequently referred to by the Nasserite regime as 'the people' or 'the masses'.

In 1948, Rashid al-Barrawi, a socialist who exerted a lot of influence on the Free Officers and on the public image of the revolution itself, directly called for new middle-class action in the face of contemporary hardships. Al-Barrawi was not alone in making this call. As Najwa Khalil suggests in her analysis of the contemporary Egyptian press, there was a rising call for forces outside the political system to take charge, and to take more radical steps in resolving hardships, where an existing political system had failed.[3] In his book *Five-Year Plans*, al-Barrawi suggests that if the ruling class had failed to achieve its economic mission, that is, to supplant a backward system with a more advanced one, another such class was bound to rise and 'carry the bright torch of progress'.[4] In 1952, al-Barrawi's book *The Military*

Coup in Egypt inspired future social analysis of Nasser's regime.[5] In this book, the new middle class's manifest destiny was linked to the Free Officers, albeit with a socialist bent. In al-Barrawi's account, the Egyptian bourgeoisie (i.e., upper-middle class) who led the 1919 Revolution had betrayed its, and therefore Egypt's, goals. These leaders failed to bring national liberation and a stable political system that would check the authority of the palace and the influence of the landed elite. Moreover, this class was now in charge of big monopolist capitalism, which was to the disadvantage of Egypt's socio-economic development. Such failures opened the way for a new generation of effendis (my term) who would lead Egypt to a new beginning. Importantly, according to al-Barrawi, this new middle class would inherit the leadership of the nationalist movement from the bourgeoisie because it would enlist support from the working class and the sympathy of the rural population, a point with which I critically engage later.

The Free Officers plainly fit this bill. A study of the socio-economic background of the Free Officers places them well within the socially mobile lower and middle ranks of the effendi middle class.[6] Al-Barrawi's analysis goes well with Lucie Ryzova's study of the effendi mission. Indeed, the revolution clearly expressed, among younger generations of effendis, a recurring sentiment of alienation from their elders. Moreover, their sense of urgency no doubt came against the background of a seeming failure, in the post–World War II era, to bring social justice and full independence to Egypt. This urgency was enhanced by the outcomes of the 1948 War with Israel.

The revolution indeed gradually swept aside parts of Egypt's old elite: the king and the royal family, the landed elite, and later, after the early 1960s, the large Egyptian bourgeoisie. Another instrumental development in the wake of the 1952 revolution was the mass and, at times forced, exodus of foreign and Egyptianised communities from Egypt, many of whom belonged to the cosmopolitan middle and upper classes of pre-revolutionary Egyptian society. They held senior positions in the Egyptian economy and had a great deal of capital. Their departure opened new employment opportunities with the state and in the private sector, and there was a significant transfer of capital to Egyptian hands and to the state. Hence, the most significant social change under Nasser occurred in the upper echelons of society. Those among Egypt's upper class who kept their economic and social positions re-reintegrated into the new ruling elite through effendication – acquiring merit-based posts in the state bureaucracy and the public sector.

How to interpret the making of Egypt's new elite under Nasser – and therefore its influence on the rest of society – turned out to be a much harder question than accounting for its members. At the core of Halpern's analysis of a 'new middle class' is an attempt to explain the role of the army in Egypt and elsewhere in the Middle East. The army was a regional agent of change because it was often the first sector to modernise. Military coups would, thereafter, turn into socio-economic revolutions because the soldiers who now headed the newly established nation-states would similarly modernise their countries. According to Halpern a new middle class was the outcome of such a process. Thus, Nasser's regime brought comprehensive social change and fast economic growth because 'unlike the traditional elite of landowners and trading bourgeoisie or the tradition-bound artisans and peasants, it is thus the first class in the Middle East that is wholly the product of the transition to the modern age'.[7]

Halpern's favourable account of the role of the army here echoed Nasserite ideology regarding why the Egyptian army turned from formulating change through deposing the old regime to implementing change through an ongoing revolution. In his well-known debate with Amos Perlmutter, who argued that the army was there to bolster its own political power, Halpern for the most part missed this aspect.[8] More pertinent to our discussion, firmly based in the modernisation theory of the period, Halpern's analysis of the new middle class and the social and economic change that it would bring to Egypt assumed the familiar development in stages. It did not really account for the specific historical circumstances in which this take-off occurred: (a) that the Free Officers' vision of progress had long been established in pre-revolutionary Egypt, and (b) that this vision had a social, effendi bias that would shape Egypt's modernisation. The chapter returns to these points below, where it discusses the making of the new middle class as a process of effendication.

Another conventional analysis of elite change in revolutionary Egypt was the study of the new elite as a 'state bourgeoisie'.[9] Unlike the landlord class that it immediately replaced, but also unlike the bourgeoisie that dominated large private enterprises and that it would replace over time, this state bourgeoisie controlled but did not *own* economic resources. Its power and prestige came from managerial and technical/scientific skills (similar to those of Halpern's new middle class) as opposed to property ownership. International and local analysis of the state bourgeoisie, and more broadly, the kind of 'state capitalism' that it promoted, became prominent during the 1960s in discussions of Egypt's transformation to socialism. In this state capitalism, the state allowed ample space for a mixed economy – cooperation between state planning and public sector activity and private sector 'national bourgeoisie' initiatives, and private property. The term 'national bourgeoisie' was in itself reminiscent of an earlier economic nationalism. At any rate, beyond the contemporary Marxist terms of discussion, this state bourgeoisie was often chastised by the Egyptian left for diluting the economic socialist reforms and thereby diverting Arab socialism from its course.[10]

As with the discussion of the new middle class, analysis of the state bourgeoisie in Egyptian and international scholarship has significantly downplayed the group's effendi origins. For a long time, and picking up volume during the 1930s, there had been a growing voice in public opinion demanding the professionalisation of state management, including the introduction of new knowledge emanating, for example, from the social sciences, to facilitate the modernisation of Egypt.[11] During and in the aftermath of World War II, this voice expanded, coupled with an intensifying frustration with the existing political system for not introducing efficient government and therefore frustrating popular hopes for economic development and social justice. It was in this very context that the making of the state bourgeoisie took place after the revolution – not simply a novelty, it was an extension and continuation of pre-revolutionary patterns. Arguably, and very much in line with al-Barrawi's vision of a new middle class in power, such effendication was at the core of the Nasserite social change of Egypt's ruling elite.

Anouar Abdel-Malek's analysis of the newly recruited state management under the Free Officers, particularly with the turn to socialism, is quite telling in how the call for professional management of state services and the public sector was bolstered under the revolution.[12] Before, but mostly after Nasser's first cabinet in 1954, appointments to top state and public sector managerial positions showed a clear preference for specific expertise in fields such as economics and engineering, as opposed to the more generalised training of lawyers that had been prevalent in the pre-revolutionary era. Remarkable here is the fact that among the newly appointed, relatively few were military personnel. Over time, more and more young officers sought professional training in both civilian institutions of higher education, and (after 1961) in the newly established Military Technical Faculty. This trend of professionalisation, as discussed below, also had an important influence on higher education, a precondition for such professional training. An important segment of the new, Nasserite managerial elite was trained abroad, in top universities in the UK and US, despite the regime's turn to Arab socialism and third worldism. Those chosen to manage the state and the public sector needed to have the right educational background, as opposed to merely ideological clearance. It was this enhanced professional elite that would head civilian ministries and the Economic Agency – the core of the future public sector. In addition, the state relied on professional expertise from abroad, notably from Western countries, in enhancing its socio-economic development plans.

Effendication in state appointments is important because it explains a lot about the socio-political dynamics of the new regime – how it operated, but also its internal contradictions. Members of Egypt's old socio-economic elite could be rehabilitated through such a process and reintegrated into state service and the public sector, based on their professional skills.[13] Furthermore, even as political repression of the Egyptian left and the Muslim Brotherhood intensified, sympathisers from both groups could still hold senior positions based on their professional qualifications. Conversely, even at the height of Arab socialism, those managing state ministries and the public sector were by no means devoted socialists themselves. Rather, their educational credentials and professionalism were of key importance in gaining them such positions. From the late 1960s and later, under President Sadat, some of the key position holders at the height of Arab socialism were among those seeking ways to opt out of the enhanced Nasserist/effendi social contract. Indeed, much of the public debate over the revolution's achievements and failures was directed at the discrepancy between official state political goals, as presented in Nasser's and other officials' speeches, and their actual execution by state bureaucracy and managers of the public sector, who were seemingly less committed to Arab socialism.

Professional appointments to senior positions in state service and the public sector may also be considered a form of depoliticization, allowing Egypt's new political elite significant leverage over those who managed the state. This would explain, for example, the frequent reshuffling in state ministries as a manifestation of the political will to perform a quick fix of contemporary hardships. Moreover, political considerations overwrote professional recommendations. An important example here is the restated goals of Egypt's First Development Plan under the revolution. Despite the huge bureaucratic, research and analytical effort it entailed, the overall goal of the plan for how to develop the Egyptian economy was the result of a political dictate. Originally, the First Development Plan had offered a gradual plan. The political need to demonstrate revolutionary action led to Nasser's famous interference in Egypt's development goal, which was set to double the size of the economy in ten years. While planning received more public attention in Egypt when introduced in the National Charter and later legislated in the 1964 constitution, comprehensive planning in Egypt in the form of a second development plan never materialised, at least partly because it would have shamed a past, overly ambitious similar effort.

The effendication of Egypt's managerial state elite did not mean that this elite was devoid of internal conflict. Competition for posts and responsibilities remained fierce. Furthermore, the professionalisation of the bureaucracy and the public sector did not end cronyism and corruption in state appointments and service provision. Fiercely criticised under the old regime of the liberal monarchy, internal conflict, cronyism and corruption prevailed under the seemingly new regime and its managerial elite.

From the *effendiyya* to the masses

The effendication of society under the revolution also took place through the further expansion of higher education leading to state employment. An increase in state-funded higher education and state employment gave the sons and, to a much lesser extent, daughters of the past generation of effendis venues for socio-economic reproduction – to become effendis themselves. However, it simultaneously facilitated a rise in the lower echelons of the effendi middle class, and therefore also the socio-economic diversification of this social group over time. Especially after Egypt's turn to Arab socialism, it was this social group that represented the masses – the people, or ordinary Egyptians, and citizens – in public and political discourse. This section discusses the expansion and dilution of the effendi status in Egypt, which was at the core of Egypt's social revolution at this time. The significance of this discussion will be enhanced below, in the analysis of the socio-economic realities of peasants and workers, that is, most contemporary Egyptians.

By the time the Free Officers reached power, educational reform was well underway.[14] For example, in the last years of the liberal monarchy, the dual system of education in Egypt officially disappeared: elementary education that had previously consisted of selective, primary state schooling for the few was united with basic education for most Egyptians, and such schooling became free of charge. The reform and expansion of Egypt's system of education by the post-revolutionary regime continued apace. Between 1952 and 1972, the number of students in secondary education increased by 223 per cent.[15] Higher education in Egypt increased by 325 percent. Still, Louis Awad, who publicly exposed gaps between the regime's vision and reality in his often-cited *University and the New Society*, thought that even this impressive opening up of higher education was not enough.[16] There was still a gap between the official promise to increase university enrolment and the actual enrolment of students. Indeed, according to Awad, citing pre- and post-revolutionary statistics, there was actually a decline in student numbers under the new regime.

Secondary education, and higher education in particular, were skewed in favour of an existing effendi middle class, as opposed to providing equality of opportunity for all. This was especially so because entry to higher education depended on scholarly achievement at an earlier stage. Even at the height of Arab socialism, private schooling at both elementary and secondary levels expanded, creating clear gaps between those who could afford to improve their child's chances of advancement through education and those who could not. Financing university education further exemplified social inequality. Under the revolution, and in addition to free education, university student privileges included free – or nearly free – dorms, subsidised transportation and movie tickets.[17] Nevertheless, living expenses and the procurement of learning aids still fell on students and their families. Since universities were for the most part located in big cities, primarily Cairo and Alexandria, this meant a further bias against students from rural regions and provincial towns. No less important here was the exemption of students from military service, a central discrimination against those who did not – or could not – undertake the course of higher education.

As a result of the above-mentioned gaps, there was a close, direct correlation between parental earnings and the level of their offspring's education. In a series of surveys conducted in the years 1955, 1962, 1966 and 1968, a father's lucrative economic position often correlated with his children's university attendance and entrance to better-paid state employment; the only exception here was the humbler economic background of parents of students at al-Azhar.[18] By the end of the 1960s, only about 10 per cent of university students were the offspring of workers and peasants who, nonetheless, represented over 82 per cent of the country's population.[19] At the same time, over 85 per cent of the students came from within a broadly defined middle class that constituted just over 15 per cent of Egypt's population. From the analysis above, while education at all levels expanded quickly under the revolution, education remained a far cry from the revolution's promise of social justice for all.

Between 1952 and 1972, the number of students attending basic, elementary education increased by 234 per cent.[20] However, school attendance remained low, and dropout rates remained high.[21] Regional disparities were similarly large. Insufficient schools and teaching aids further frustrated the quality of this education. The most explicit indicator of the relative failure of basic education in Egypt was the ongoing high level of illiteracy; expenditures on illiteracy campaigns and adult education significantly declined under the revolution. Despite a much-trumpeted national need – pre- and post-revolutionary alike – to overcome illiteracy, a strong social and political bias toward higher education took precedence over campaigns to improve elementary education, to fight illiteracy or to expand adult education. As a result, between 1947 and 1969, illiteracy declined only slightly, from 77.2 per cent to 65 per cent, with an overall increase in absolute illiteracy as a result of overall population growth.[22] The inferior quality of elementary education and the poor achievements of its graduates further testified to the middle-class bias of Arab socialism and its half-hearted effort to resolve both problems.

An important exception here, and to a degree the main beneficiary of the growth in student numbers, was Egypt's lower-middle class, whose sons, and to a much lesser extent, daughters, enjoyed some new educational opportunities, the result of the expansion of universal, free education.[23] To cater to this group the university system became bifurcated. Since the 1930s, the prestige of law and the humanities had eroded, a process that the Nasserite regime institutionalised.[24] The 'theoretical' faculties (as opposed to 'practical' faculties such as engineering and medicine) increasingly served to facilitate the entry of more students to university. Furthermore, beginning in 1953, attempts to expand higher education brought about the development of external studies, which allowed students to study on their own and be physically present for exams only. By 1962/63, about a quarter of the freshmen admitted to Egyptian universities were external students. Meanwhile, technological and scientific education, notably engineering and medicine, became more exclusive and led to more lucrative state employment.

While higher education was open to the lower echelons of the middle class, the same process brought the graduates diminishing returns. As with education, demand for employment with the state was already rife before the revolution, and the state was hard pressed to employ graduates. Pre-revolutionary governments attempted reform, as did the Free Officers when they came into power, because it was clear that the capacity of the economy and the state to absorb so many graduates was limited. Both soon succumbed to the same public pressure for state jobs. Between 1951/52 and 1969/70, state employment grew by 343 per cent, about the same rate of growth as the number of students in universities.[25] Despite the growing role of the state in socio-economic development, the rise in state employment further enhanced the chronic, already pre-revolutionary problems of a bloated state bureaucracy, hidden unemployment and a constant drain on the state budget. This trend exemplified the effendication of the state-led economy, as well as its becoming quasi-socialist.

Entry into state employment displayed a trend that paralleled that of entry into education, inasmuch as family background was paramount in ensuring placement. This trend was also not new. The socio-economic background of both pre- and post-revolutionary civil servants (studied for the year 1966/67) remained similar.[26] Then and later, the vast majority of civil servants were born and resided in urban regions. Their fathers' occupations were often comparable to their own. Indeed, with a slight decrease over time, about a third of these fathers were themselves state employees. As may be expected, there were fewer children of landlords in state service (a decrease from 24% to 8%). However, the proportion of peasant fathers also significantly decreased

(16% to 10%). Instead, during that period there was a notable increase in fathers who were businessmen and independent professionals (9% to 15% and 6% to 13%, respectively), army officers (4% to 7%), and especially, non-civil servant white-collar workers (3% to 16%). These transitions indicated an uptick in the state's importance as a white-collar/middle-class employer in a period of rising state involvement in socio-economic development.

State employment became divided between those with more rewarding technical/scientific educational credentials and the vast majority of the university educated, or between the state bourgeoisie and those increasingly becoming, according to Nazih Ayubi, the 'white collar proletariat'.[27] This was because the level of education determined waiting periods for state employment, the placement and entry level for such employment, and the pace of promotion in state service. Despite the gap, and owing to few economic alternatives, demand for these lower-paid positions remained strong.

Between 1952 and 1972, and primarily during the 1960s, the state's combined policy of education and employment allowed for the fast expansion of middle-income brackets in urban regions, which led to a reduction in urban poverty.[28] Nasser's renewed social contract brought social justice to this social group in particular. Most employees in the lower echelons of state employment would, however, live too close for comfort to a real or imagined poverty line. Indeed, commenting on the poor civil servants, Ayubi suggests that

> the days are long since gone when the mere fact of belonging to the *effendiyya* group indicated not only social distinction but also a relative degree of financial affluence. The large bulk of bureaucrats today are small civil servants who struggle in conditions of ever-rising prices to sustain their families, which are usually large.[29]

As suggested in this quotation, the fast expansion of state services and employment that was to lead to socio-economic development also enhanced a moral economy according to which the state was responsible for guaranteeing the well-being of employees living close to the poverty line.

The state's widening inclusion of the expanding effendi middle class was also a venue for disciplining this group. Those benefiting from the state through education, employment, and provision of services likewise had much to lose. Both aspects of citizen–state relations were enhanced by the lack of civil society alternatives, as the state incorporated NGOs and curtailed both blue- and white-collar labour unions. The state further co-opted students by supporting higher education while regulating student activism through the universities' unions and popular organisations, which allowed students to be indoctrinated by the state.[30] All such actions had already started to take form under the liberal monarchy, but they intensified under greater state participation in economic and social development. The state's increased role in enlarging and securing middle society meant an increase in state power that was interconnected with a broadening of citizen dependence on the state.

Peasants and workers

From 1952, the revolutionary regime took some well-trumpeted measures to alleviate poverty, especially through land and agricultural reforms, labour laws and social security measures. The state also further expanded social services and subsidies. In undertaking these steps, the revolution demonstrated a continuity with pre-revolutionary attempts to alleviate poverty and to avoid social unrest. Such state action mostly benefited 'middling' peasants and workers – small and, more so, medium landowners, and employees of large, often public sector enterprises, as opposed to those working in the smaller enterprises that dominated the private sector. The outcomes of these state steps were limited socio-economic mobility among peasants and workers, under the intensifying control of an effendi state. During the early 1960s, a much-publicised attempt at popular power sharing – the National Charter, and later, the rewritten constitution – and actual management of public assets, did not bring significant change to the relations between the state and the majority of citizens in Egypt, or to the social bias those relations entailed.

Already discussed and partly originating before the revolution, land reform was a decisive act that the Free Officers took toward alleviating poverty.[31] The land reform allowed the redistribution of land to many peasants, who owned little or no land. But it was no less an immediate political move against the Free Officers' political rivals: the landed elite, who also constituted the backbone of the constitutional monarchy's political elite, including the Wafd and the royal family.

A careful look at the implementation of the reform will further demonstrate its middle-class bias. Land reform in pre-revolutionary Egypt targeted landlords with large, as opposed to medium-sized, landholdings. This pattern remained in force in the post-revolutionary era, until July 1961, when under Arab socialism, the regime introduced new laws regarding land reform and further limited landownership. Moreover, because the land reform mainly targeted landlords with large holdings, it left a vacuum for families with middle-sized holding to flex their economic muscles and political influence in rural regions. A significant, if officially unintended consequence of the Free Officers' land reform was an enhanced rural middle class. This further developed through growing state involvement in agricultural production, and notably, the establishment of agricultural cooperatives that soon followed. At the same time, the expansion of state participation in agricultural production brought urban supervision by bureaucrats and experts to the countryside. Finally, sequestrated land went first to the state, and was later – and only partially – redistributed to peasants. The rest, retained by the state and the army, provided a significant economic boon for those managing it.

Recipients of redistributed lands joined agricultural cooperatives, but they did not face collectivisation. The land reform was essentially part of a long-established liberal economic reform, or productivist welfare, through which the state would resolve the crisis of landless peasants by putting them to work on their own plots of land. The establishment of agricultural cooperatives – to modernise agricultural production but also to better tax it, and to discipline and educate peasants – had an even longer pre-revolutionary history than did land reform.[32]

The state avoided a drastic squeeze on agriculture that would have transferred funds and resources to industry, despite a significant attempt at industrialisation. However, after 1952 the state's increasing ability to supervise the countryside resulted in a flow of resources out of agriculture, including the migration of the most talented to the cities. This migration was further enhanced by state provision of services and subsidies that clearly benefited city over village dwellers. Being mostly universal as opposed to progressive, these state measures disadvantaged Egypt's poor rural population. This was especially true for education – the main venue for mobility in Egypt – and the same bias in state provision could be found in health services and state investment in physical and human infrastructure in rural regions. State employment was also the prerogative of city dwellers.

The social and economic development that took place in rural regions did not result in qualitative structural change.[33] Such development initially brought some improvement in poverty levels, lessened inequality and increased agricultural productivity. However, these changes did not produce significant technological or institutional transitions in rural regions. The result was a rather unimpressive growth in agricultural output and much continuity in social and political relations that further stalled it. Estimates of poverty in rural Egypt initially showed a reduction in poverty during the 1950s and early 1960s as the result of land redistribution. Yet land redistribution was limited to 13 per cent of the total cultivated land and to 9 per cent of the rural population.[34] Furthermore, land redistribution had come to an end by the mid-1960s. This, coupled with a new state policy in the wake of the 1967 War that diverted agricultural products to cities, meant a significant increase in rural poverty between 1967 and 1973. Overall, between 1952 and the mid-1970s, rural inequality showed little or no improvement.[35] After that period, opportunity to work abroad and in the fast-emerging Egyptian informal economy provided unprecedented economic opportunity for peasants, albeit with little state interference.

From the above analysis it is evident that despite land reform and the larger state role in agricultural production, and regardless of the overall expansion of state services, human and physical infrastructure, and subsidies, rural regions did not experience the social revolution promised by the Free Officers' regime. Rather, rural socio-economic development lagged behind urban development, as it had in the past. Also familiar was an exit from village to city. There were continual waves of local peasants migrating to cities in search of economic relief and better employment opportunities. The spread of mostly city-oriented welfare state services enhanced this trend.

Beginning in the late 1930s, and significantly during and in the aftermath of World War II, effendi public opinion, and parliamentary and extra-parliamentary politics, became preoccupied with working conditions and working-class standards of living. In a sense, 'the labourer question' came to replace the past 'peasant question' in an emerging agenda designed to bring social justice to Egyptians. The gradual expansion of local manufacturing, the rising demand for labour in cities during World War II and unemployment in the aftermath of the war were among the main reasons for this political interest. Such matters were of concern to effendi city dwellers and the state because – dating back at least to the nineteenth century, but becoming more acute as Egypt's modernisation and industrialisation intensified – urban poverty was more conspicuous than rural poverty, and it constituted the ever-present danger of social and political unrest. Furthermore, labour was central to the national protest against foreign domination in Egypt. In this regard the struggle to improve working conditions in foreign-dominated enterprises formed part of the national cause. Nonetheless, the demand to improve working conditions stood in contrast to labour relations that experienced friction between labourers and effendi employers.[36]

In 1947, a textile workers' strike at al-Mahalla al-Kubra, 'the largest collective action in the history of Egyptian labour to that date',[37] and a strike at the Misr Spinning and Weaving Company, an enterprise at the centre of the national industrialisation project, set alarm bells ringing throughout Egypt. Organised action of this nature had previously often taken place in foreign- and local minority-owned enterprises, and it was encouraged by the national movement. However, the strike at Misr Spinning and Weaving was publicly condemned by the government and in the press. In August 1952, two months after they seized power, the Free Officers crushed a similar strike at the Fine Spinning and Weaving Mill. In the aftermath of this strike, and 'acting out of the same corporatist and paternalist understanding that had informed the relations between most of the *effendiyya* and workers',[38] the revolutionary regime implemented a reform that contained labour's demands, while obliterating the independent trade unions and collective action. This dual policy continued throughout the Nasserist era, despite changes in economic orientation. In state planning and managerial decision making, industrialisation took precedence over working conditions in state-controlled enterprises. Despite the above, workers in the public sector were still privileged in comparison with those employed in the private sector/informal economy.

After 1956, the rapid expansion of the public sector contributed to a widening structural duality in the Egyptian economy between formal/organised and informal enterprises. In the formal economy, now mostly part of the public sector, medium and, particularly, large enterprises dominated the scene.

In 1964, such enterprises – having 100 or more workers – employed 32.5 per cent of Egypt's workers. At the height of Arab socialism, Egyptian-owned small and medium enterprises still continued operations; the activities of the so-called 'national bourgeoisie' in the free market were exempt from state interference. Small and medium enterprises, which employed up to fourteen persons and mostly belonged to the private sector, employed 51.2 per cent of workers.[39] The state was mostly not involved with such enterprises: it did not systematically regulate working conditions, wages or benefits, nor did it secure access to social security. A structural duality in employment meant that the state implicitly disengaged from a large portion of the working class, who did not receive state protection and provision of services like those labouring in the public sector did. This state of affairs had long-term socio-economic ramifications, as private sector employment was often the least desirable form of occupation because of both the low status of those employed in it and the small remuneration such occupation brought.

In November 1961, President Nasser announced a new initiative that, if implemented, would change Egyptians' political and managerial participation in power through rewriting Egypt's social contract, the National Charter.[40] For this purpose, a National Congress of Popular Forces (NCPF) was convened – to better represent, as suggested by its title, the Egyptian social fabric in more cooperative political and economic decision making. As such, it was to interlink a new vertical (state–society) social contract with a new horizontal social contract between social groups within society. Beforehand, a preparatory committee of 250 members was appointed by presidential decree. It received a draft of the charter and debated it prior to submitting it for ratification by the NCPF. This procedure was intended to broaden social participation in constitutional decision making – the constituency of this preparatory committee was to equally represent the whole of society, as opposed to its socio-economic elite.

Among the committee's 250 appointed members, twenty-four were representatives of peasants, twenty-nine were labourers, thirty-seven were from white-collar professions, twenty-one from business, twenty-three were members of the old Council of the Nation, ten were women, fifty-nine were administration officials and fifty-seven were unclassified members.[41] Just over 20 per cent of the Preparatory Committee members were of peasant and working-class origin – a far cry from their actual number in the population. Hence, despite a declared attempt at drafting the National Charter by the entire nation – to make a fresh national start – this list of participants, in itself, already suggested a rather distorted representation of the so-called Popular Forces, especially of peasants and workers, and a continued bias in favour of the middle class.

As narrated by Abdel-Malek, the main public debate surrounding this initiative, led by Khalid Mohammed Khalid – a well-known author and public intellectual – centred around the call for the return of civil liberties and democracy. This debate reflected criticism of the recent repression of the Muslim Brotherhood and the Egyptian left, and Nasser's response to that criticism. Though the making of a National Charter was supposed to offer a new start, it was clearly bogged down by recent politics.

More pertinent to our discussion, the Preparatory Committee was to establish a formula for social representation for the forthcoming congress that would determine the National Charter. Tellingly, this formula was primarily based on two principles: the size of the membership of various social groups in organisations representing their profession (and social background), and the relative, measured contribution of each such group to the national economy.

Based on these criteria, the total 'social value' of peasants' representation was reduced from 44.3 per cent of the delegates to the congress to 35.4 per cent, and later to 25 per cent. Workers (presumably in the public sector), who constituted 17.9 per cent of the organised labour force but contributed more to the national income, were granted a 20 per cent share of the representatives in the congress. Another group of workers (presumably in the private sector), both non-unionised and those unionised in trade unions, received slightly higher representation (9% as opposed to a demographic size of 7.5%) in the congress. The social category of 'national capitalism' received 10 per cent, representing a parity between membership and economic contribution. Members of the professional (white-collar) associations, comprising 6.6 per cent of organised members, received 15 per cent of representatives to the congress, based on their superior economic contribution. University teaching staffs – 0.4 per cent of organised members, and 1 per cent in terms of economic contribution – received no less than 7 per cent of the seats in the congress. Students, 11.7 per cent of the organised members, who made no economic contribution, similarly received 7 per cent of the seats. Women, only 1 per cent of the organised members and whose contribution to economic activity went unrecorded also received 7 per cent of the congressional seats.

In the list above, the Congress of Popular Forces well reflected existing social biases in which peasants were significantly underrepresented. Labour received a more-or-less equal share of representatives to the congress, as did national capitalism and non-unionised workers and members of trade unions. Members of professional, white-collar associations, and notably, university teaching staff, as well as students, were significantly overrepresented. Women, who were arguably also represented by male representatives according to their professional affiliation, were by far the most marginalised in the congress, which under the corporate model was supposed to include all Egyptians in national decision making.

Overall, this proportional social representation in the congress would no doubt have been further skewed if actual demographic size, as opposed to membership in official professional organisations, had been taken into account. Furthermore, the subcommittee that determined the above ratios removed undesirable social categories – enemies of the people, and those whose interests were in opposition to those of the people. These were rather broad categories that included landlords with large holdings and people who had been subjected to sequestration of property and arrest in the past, as well as anyone seemingly posing a potential economic and political threat in the present. Arguably, most damning to this experiment in national participation in the congress that was to determine the National Charter was the fact that the charter ended up being a largely top-down dictate – read by Nasser in a six-hour speech before the congress – as opposed to a cooperative action. As suggested in Chapter Three, the 1964 constitution that eventually replaced this interim charter was destined to a similar fate. Despite great emphasis on popular participation, peasants and workers continued to be underrepresented in such top-down endeavours, which, under the guise of Arab socialism, still embodied a restrictive regime combined with an effendi social bias.

Nasserism has often been described as a populist regime – a regime benefiting from wide support among the lower echelons of society often portrayed as the 'masses' or 'people'.[42] Under the call to enhance social solidarity, this populist regime was supposed to redirect state redistribution toward bringing social justice, and it was therefore also supposed to rewrite the pre-revolutionary social contract both vertically and horizontally. Yet, as the last two chapters have shown, despite the regime's frequent use of the phrase 'social justice' in public discourse, and of terminology that centred on the people and solidarity, the existing social contract was, at best, only widened rather than changed. The analysis of state policies provided here has shown ample similarities between the old and new regimes; equally, there were similarities between the old and new societies of pre- and post-revolutionary Egypt.

The most notable socio-political changes to take place under the revolution were the displacement of Egypt's royal family, the Egyptian socio-economic and political elites, and large tracts of the non-Muslim upper and middle classes, which Egypt's new effendis came to replace.[43] In tandem, the effendication of middle society through an enhanced system of higher education and state employment continued in earnest. Under Nasser's regime, the terms effendi and *effendiyya* were dropped from public use, having been associated with the pre-revolutionary, monarchical socio-political regime. However, there was nevertheless a great deal of continuity in Egypt's social contract with this social group. Here too, the transformation to socialism, already publicly and politically upheld in the last days of the liberal monarchy, was less about building a classless society than it was about enhancing the effendi middle class. Social solidarity was a conservative effort at avoiding the social tension associated with class struggle, not a basis for a new horizontal social contract.

And yet the Egyptian state did not simply become isolated from society or become a state supported by an authoritarian bargain whereby the state provided services and employment in exchange for political quiescence. Such familiar interpretations of the Egyptian state under Nasser and since fail to capture the nature of the vertical Nasserist/effendi social contract – its contours and the kind of socio-economic channelling it enhanced in Egypt. Under Nasser, Egypt became an effendi state committed to promoting the long-term vision and interests of Egypt's expanding middle class, but with some practical consideration for middling groups among the peasants and workers who the state attempted to co-opt with various degrees of success. Moreover, social justice, by now an explicit part of the social contract, tilted toward equality of opportunity in state employment, as opposed to general societal equity. Social services, the construction of physical and social state infrastructure, and state price regulation and subsidies further exposed a continuing gap between rural and urban regions. Growing state involvement with social development was universal as opposed to progressive, and it therefore benefited middle Egyptian society more than other sectors. While repression of the opposition under Nasser was rife, the social contract with the effendi middle class did not produce less support for Nasser's regime, as is amply demonstrated in the kind of middle class, populist support that underwrote this regime's darkest hour in the aftermath of the 1967 War.

By the mid-1960s, and especially in the aftermath of the 1967 defeat, Egypt's integrated socio-economic development project had proved unsustainable. The country's expanded social contract had promised more than it could deliver, which led to increased state debt. Nevertheless, it was maintained because by then it had become a strong moral economy bonding not only citizens to the state but also the state itself to its own earlier commitment. Under Nasser, Egypt sought ways to partially liberalise the economy – to redirect economic responsibility from the state to the market, and to partially unload the burden of state provision, thereby reducing debt. This search brought about a widening rift within Egypt's ruling elite, and later between Nasserites and President Sadat's new regime. Arguably, the most significant change from Nasser to Sadat was the search for a new social contract for Egypt, or so it originally seemed.

Notes

1. Manfred Halpern, *The Politics of Social Change in the Middle East and North Africa* (Princeton, NJ: Princeton University Press, 1963). Halpern's is the most comprehensive analysis of the new middle class but far from the only one. See also Morroe Berger, *The Middle Class in the Arab World*, Princeton University Conference (Series) 9 (Princeton, NJ: Princeton University Conference, 1957). Nathan J. Citino's analysis of historian and Middle East expert Richard Roe Polk's understanding of the 'new men' further combines sociological analysis of this dynamic social group with US–Egyptian Cold War politics of the period. Indeed, Halpern's book was sponsored by and prepared for the Rand Corporation, a think tank with close ties to US foreign relations decision making at that time. Citino, *Envisioning the Arab Future*, 212–50.
2. Ryzova, *Age of the Efendiyya*, 237–58.
3. Khalil, *al-Mujtama'*, 345–61.

4. Analysis of al-Barrawi is based on Meijer, *Quest for Modernity*, 66–95. Find the quotation from al-Barrawi on page 87. This book was published in Arabic: Rashid al-Barrawi, *Mashruʿat al-Sanawat al-Khams min al-Nahiyatan al-Nazariyya wa-l-Tabiqiyya* (Cairo: Maktabat al-Nahda al-Misriyya, 1948).
5. Rashed El-Barawy, *The Military Coup in Egypt: An Analytic Study* (Cairo: Renaissance Bookshop, 1952).
6. Vatikiotis, *Nasser and His Generation*, 23–46.
7. Halpern, *The Politics of Social Change*, 59.
8. See the Halpern–Perlmutter debate in the pages of *Comparative Studies in Society and History* – volumes 10, no. 1; 11, no.1; and 12, no. 1 – between 1967 and 1970.
9. See Waterbury, *Egypt of Nasser and Sadat*, 247–60, for an elaborate discussion of this social group.
10. Mahmoud Hussein, 'The Nasser Regime and State Capitalism', in *Class Conflict in Egypt, 1945–1970* (New York: Monthly Review Press, 1973); and Anouar Abdel-Malek, *Egypt: Military Society: The Army Regime, the Left, and Social Change under Nasser* (New York: Random House, 1968), 363–71.
11. El Shakry, *Great Social Laboratory*.
12. Abdel-Malek, *Egypt: Military Society*, 174–8. My analysis is further based on Zeinab Abul-Magd, 'Socialism without Socialists (1950s–1970s)', in *Militarizing the Nation: The Army, Business, and Revolution in Egypt* (New York: Columbia University Press, 2017); H. A. Akeel and Clement M. Henry, 'The Class Origins of Egyptian Engineer-Technocrats', in *Commoners, Climbers and Notables: A Sampler on Social Ranking in the Middle East*, ed. C. A. O. Van Nieuwenhoijze (Leiden: Brill, 1977), 279–92; Ayubi, *Bureaucracy and Politics*; and Mahmud A. Faksh, 'Education and Elite Recruitment: An Analysis of Egypt's Post-1952 Political Elite', *Comparative Education Review* 20, no. 2 (1976): 140–50, accessed 26 October 2020, www.jstor.org/stable/1187158.
13. See two examples in Robert Springborg, *Family, Power, and Politics in Egypt: Sayed Bey Marei – His Clan, Clients, and Cohorts* (Philadelphia: University of Pennsylvania Press, 1982); and Omar D. Foda, *Egypt's Beer: Stella, Identity, and the Modern State* (Austin: University of Texas Press, 2019).
14. Belli, *An Incurable Past*, 15–76.
15. Mahmoud Abdel-Fadil, 'Educational Expansion and Income Distribution in Egypt, 1952–1977', in Abdel-Khalek and Tignor, *Political Economy of Income Distribution*, 353, table 11.1. The figures in this table were normalised to account for demographic growth through a measurement of rise in student numbers per thousand as opposed to an absolute increase.

16. Reid, *Cairo University*, 177–8.
17. Erlich, *Students and University*, 177.
18. Ayubi, *Bureaucracy and Politics*, 411–17.
19. Ibid., 414.
20. Abdel-Fadil, 'Educational Expansion', 353, table 11.1.
21. Ibid., 354–5.
22. Ayubi, *Bureaucracy and Politics*, 406.
23. Saad Eddin Ibrahim, 'Social Mobility and Income Distribution in Egypt, 1952–1977', in Abdel-Khalek and Tignor, *Political Economy of Income Distribution*, 375–434.
24. See analysis of this process in Abdalla, *Student Movement*, 105–13; Erlich, *Students and University*, 179–81; and Reid, *Cairo University*, 174–83.
25. My calculation is based on Ayubi, *Bureaucracy and Politics*, 243, table 4.
26. Ibid., 360–70.
27. Ibid., 377. For earning gaps in state employment for the year 1967, see ibid., 378, table 24.
28. Ibrahim, 'Social Mobility'.
29. Ayubi, *Bureaucracy and Politics*, 377.
30. Abdalla, *Student Movement*, 105–13; Erlich, *Students and University*, 179–81; and Reid, *Cairo University*, 174–83.
31. Analysis of the land reform is based on Leonard Binder, *In a Moment of Enthusiasm: Political Power and the Second Stratum in Egypt* (Chicago: University of Chicago Press, 1978); Hamied Ansari, *Egypt, the Stalled Society* (Albany: State University of New York Press, 1986), 79–95; and Waterbury, *Egypt of Nasser and Sadat*, 263–304.
32. Johnson, *Reconstructing Rural Egypt*, 23–7.
33. Richard H. Adams Jr, *Development and Social Change in Rural Egypt* (Syracuse, NY: Syracuse University Press, 1986).
34. Ibid., 13, citing Mahmoud Abdel-Fadil, *Development, Income Distribution, and Social Change in Rural Egypt, 1952–1970: A Study in the Political Economy of Agrarian Transition* (Cambridge: Cambridge University Press, 1975), 10.
35. Adams, *Development and Social Change*, 20.
36. Joel Beinin, *Workers and Peasants in the Modern Middle East* (Cambridge: Cambridge University Press, 2001), 99–113; and Hanan Hammad, *Industrial Sexuality: Gender, Urbanization, and Social Transformation in Egypt* (Austin: University of Texas Press, 2016), 27–55.
37. Beinin, *Workers and Peasants*, 110.

38. Ibid.
39. Calculation based on Abdel-Fadil, *The Political Economy of Nasserism*, 91, table 6.3.
40. Analysis based on Abdel-Malek, *Egypt: Military Society*, 180–6.
41. See full list in ibid., 180–1. The numbers do not add up to exactly 250.
42. Elie Podeh and Onn Winckler, 'Nasserism as a Form of Populism', Introduction to *Rethinking Nasserism*. See their detailed analysis of the historiography of this term.
43. How the departure of non-Muslim communities influenced the Egyptian economy (and was influenced by contemporary changes in it) is yet to be fully studied. However, see Najat Abdulhaq, *Jewish and Greek Communities in Egypt: Entrepreneurship and Business Before Nasser* (London: I. B. Tauris, 2016), *ProQuest Ebook Central*, 158–200, for one example of such analysis. I thank Yoram Meital for bringing this source to my attention.

PART THREE

THE TORTUOUS SEARCH FOR A NEW SOCIAL CONTRACT, 1970–2011

Part three of this book explores the long, tortuous and largely unsuccessful attempt to bring about a new social contract in Egypt, through a comparison with how the old, effendi social contract was established. This comparison is based on three questions that drive the discussion in the next three chapters. The first question, which looks into the changes within the effendi middle class that supported the old social contract over time, asks what happened to this group during the oil-boom era of the 1970s and early 1980s (Chapter Five). The second asks why a long-term plan designed to offer a new social contract largely remain just that – a planning initiative with little impact on the actual process of economic reform and structural adjustment in Egypt (Chapter Six). The third question examines why – despite constant public and political outcry over the crises that it entailed – the old social contract was so entrenched and central to the moral economy of the period (Chapter Seven). Overall, Part Three investigates why attempts at socio-economic reform, which were not dissimilar to the past calls for alleviating poverty, ignorance and disease under the liberal monarchy, became an elusive search for a new social contract under Sadat and Mubarak.

The period under discussion saw the return of the Muslim Brotherhood as a dominant social force in politics and in the Egyptian economy, where an Islamic economic sector became more distinct and Islamic service provision took over in places where the state retracted from offering education, health and welfare. Nevertheless, despite giving voice to a growing political opposition, the Muslim Brotherhood – as a broad social umbrella with various, sometimes conflicting, economic interests – did not come up with a clear alternative new social contract either. The Muslim Brotherhood was central to the opposition that would stall state-led socio-economic reform, voicing concern for the struggling effendi middle class and adding an important religious undertone to the moral economy that upheld a growing coalition of discontent against the regime. However, and in a somewhat contradictory fashion, it also promoted the neoliberalisation of Egypt through private economic entrepreneurship and service provisioning.[1] The Muslim Brotherhood was also part of the rising demand for democratisation in Egyptian public discourse. However, the regime's apprehension of their political clout stalled this process.[2]

Notes

1. Hesham Al-Awadi termed such service provision to the middle class an 'Islamic social contract'. However, in his description of this social contract too, service provision by Islamists filled an existing void in state provisioning. As such, it constituted an attempt to gain political support from society, as opposed to being an alternative contract to that of the state. See Al-Awadi's *In Pursuit of Legitimacy: The Muslim Brothers and Mubarak 1981–2000* (London: Tauris Academic Studies, 2004), 89–98.
2. The analysis above is based on: Joya, *The Roots of Revolt*, 139–66; Relli Shechter, *The Rise of the Egyptian Middle Class: Socio-Economic Mobility and Public Discontent from Nasser to Sadat* (Cambridge: Cambridge University Press, 2019), 194–230; Bjorn Olav Utvik, *Islamist Economics in Egypt: The Pious Road to Development* (Boulder, CO: Lynne Rienner, 2006); Carrie Rosefsky Wickham, *Mobilizing Islam: Religion, Activism, and Political Change in Egypt* (New York: Columbia University Press, 2002).

5

THE SOCIAL CONTRACT BROKEN TWICE

During the oil-boom of the 1970s and early 1980s, the effendi social contract broke down in an unlikely period when the Egyptian state had regained resources that would allow it to sponsor this social contract as never before. This chapter, therefore, predates the breakdown of the effendi social contract, which is often associated with post-oil-boom economic retrenchment and the implementation of economic reform and structural adjustment (ERSA) programs in Egypt. At the same time, fast socio-economic mobility – the result of informal liberalisation of the Egyptian economy – saw the creation of a broad middle class or a middle-class society, despite the seeming demise of the effendi middle class in public discourse. In this discourse – in reality a discourse dominated by the upper-middle class – the effendi social contract broke down twice: first, as a vertical political agreement between citizens and the state and its accompanying moral economy, and second, as a horizontal social agreement among members of Egyptian middle-class society.

This chapter begins by exploring Sadat's Corrective Revolution, through an analysis of Egypt's new, 1971 constitution and the 1974 October Working Paper that officially launched the Open Door policy (*infitah*). In a rather paradoxical fashion, the notion of revolution here stood for preserving an existing political economy associated with Nasser and Arab socialism through its partial liberalisation by amendment or correction. The second part of this chapter, 'Oil-Boom Populism', further corroborates this argument by analysing growing state spending on various articles of the effendi social contract. The third part of the chapter shows that the 1977 Food Uprising enhanced the state's commitment to the provisioning of citizens. Finally, 'Socio-economic Mobility and Its Discontents' suggests that the effendi social contract broke down during the oil-boom era not as a result of the demise of the middle class but owing to the rapid expansion of that class – estimated to have constituted some 45 per cent of Egyptians by the mid-1980s – and the social unrest that this caused.[1]

The Corrective Revolution

In the literature on political change in Egypt, Nasser's Arab socialism is often associated with populism, while Sadat's liberal Open Door policy is discussed as post-populist – an era in which the state retrenched employment, services and subsidies to citizens.[2] Nevertheless, Sadat's regime was more populist than Nasser's both in bolstering the effendi social contract and extending state provision down the social ladder. Sadat's Corrective Revolution sought to liberalise the economy in order to support an expanding, if inadequate, welfare state. During his reign the state spent more on various articles of the social contract – notably on subsidies, increasing student enrolment in universities and state employment – while it was simultaneously publicly criticised in the media by spokespersons of the effendi middle class for not doing enough for its citizens.

In 1970 Sadat's main struggle was to strengthen his power, an uneasy feat considering Nasser's enduring political shadow. To do so Sadat engaged in bold, dramatic changes to Egypt's political leadership, or a purge in which he replaced Nasser's loyalists with his own.[3] Alongside and supporting these changes, Sadat launched the 'Corrective Revolution' (*Thawrat al-Tashih*), which was – if indeed it was to be a revolution – to bring a no less swift change to Egyptian governance than the 1952 revolution had. This was not to be the case. The Corrective Revolution and the Open Door policy that soon followed it were evolutionary as opposed to revolutionary in nature. 'Revolution' in Sadat's Corrective Revolution did not mean radical social change in Egypt, but rather securing the president's internal power (within the ruling elite) while keeping and even expanding older, economic state commitments to its citizenry. Put differently, the revolution in the Corrective Revolution aimed to retain the legacy of the Free Officers' revolution, while taking steps toward amending what went wrong with that revolution over time. This often entailed replacing Sadat's detractors (or Nasserists) within the regime with his supporters, as well as the search for a way out of the impasse of economic recession in the aftermath of the 1967 War.

The 1971 constitution well exemplified the above. While it replaced the interim, Nasserite 1964 constitution, the new constitution was a part of a familiar Nasserite trope to accompany the pronounced changes in Sadat's regime with a new constitution that would legalise these changes. Within the context of a political struggle against powerful Nasserite elements entrenched in Egypt's ruling elite, the drafting process that led to the 1971 constitution exposed the 'flaws and excesses of the Nasserite regime',[4] thereby providing justification for Sadat's political purge. Furthermore, as in the past, the constitution presented a new agenda aimed at facing contemporary Egyptian socio-economic challenges, ostensibly without discarding Arab socialism. Finally, it enlisted popular support for such actions through public participation in the drafting process, which, as in the 1964 constitution, gave it a democratic veneer.[5]

In the 1971 constitution, 'social solidarity' – as an ideal for making and maintaining an organic society (promoting organic unity of the nation, rather than a site of political contest) – remained in place.[6] Article 7 of the 1971 constitution, 'social solidarity is the basis of the society', contains the exact same wording as article 4 of the 1956 constitution. Delivering and maintaining social solidarity had been a principle reason for implementing social justice in the past, and it remained so under the 1971 constitution. This social justice – past and present – was about allowing 'equality of opportunities for all citizens' (article 8 in the 1971 constitution), as opposed to creating the means for equality through radical redistributive measures. Similarly, although article 38 mandates taxation based on the principle of social justice, the wording was rather vague and did not articulate a progressive system of taxation that would result in a more egalitarian society. Sadat's 1971 constitution facilitated social justice based on pre-existing social stratifications in the name of social solidarity, as opposed to promoting deeper change in Egypt's layered social order.

Article 12 of the constitution maintains 'socialist conduct' as a principle to which Egyptian society was to adhere. Once more, as was the case during the Nasserite era, what this term meant in Egypt's socio-political reality was not clarified. Arab socialism remained central to the 'foundation of the economy', the section of the constitution relating to economic matters. Thus, in article 33, for example, the state maintains that public ownership of enterprises is a central attribute of Arab socialism. Alongside continuity in public ownership, articles 34, 35 and 36 introduce some novelty by enhancing the sanctity of private property, notably against state encroachment. Past Arab socialism had emphasised public- and private-sector collaboration with elements of the 'national bourgeoisie'. In the 1971 constitution, however, the new emphasis on the sanctity of private property constituted a novel voice from among Egypt's managerial elite to promote private initiative along with public initiative. Put differently, the principle of the sanctity of private property was layered side by side with state commitment to a large public sector.

In article 23 of the constitution, the state remains committed to central planning that would facilitate economic growth. It further commits to securing the citizenry's standard of living, and to fair employment, all of which were – under Egypt's revolutionary discourse – regarded as attributes of Arab socialism. Nevertheless, this article also links wages with productivity, spelling out a future attempt to make state employees more efficient. This attempt to increase efficiency in the workplace would potentially contradict the citizens' right to employment, to which the state remained committed (article 13). If so, workplace efficiency was another example of the layered meaning in the constitution – adding new intent to it without getting rid of the old. In article 15 the state further expands state employment to 'war veterans, those injured in war or because of it, and the wives and children of those killed'. This article expands employment as a welfare measure, in clear contradiction to article 23, which emphasises more connectivity between efficiency and remuneration. Once again, a step toward economic reform was layered side by side with an earlier state commitment to the citizens. In this regard, the 1971 constitution was not simply layered, but layered with contradictions emanating from the complex political situation in which Sadat's regime found itself in its early days – that is to say, the need to publicly uphold the revolutionary concepts and moral economy from which it was gradually distancing itself.

Another example of such layering was the establishment of trade unions and federations (article 56). This step toward workplace democratisation allowed economic actors a greater say in economic conduct – seemingly a relief from the tight, Nasserite corporatist model that had previously demoted organised labour and professional organisations, turning them into social clubs. However, in article 56, these trade unions and federation were supposed to 'bolster the socialist conduct of their members'. Here too, while not specified, 'socialist conduct' no doubt meant maintaining loyalty to the Arab socialist state and its then current leader; therefore, workforce democratisation was conditional upon political loyalty to Sadat's regime. The 1971 constitution was not subservient to a past political economy, but was subversive in manipulating it for the purpose of supporting a new president.

Contrary to the future charges made by mounting local opposition to Sadat, which suggested that the 1971 constitution would decrease state welfare, this constitution was more populist than the previous, Nasserite constitutions in its commitment to the provision of state services to citizens. Indeed, the section of the constitution related to 'social foundations' extends that provision down the social ladder. Article 20 offers to expand education in Egypt by making it compulsory beyond elementary schooling, albeit 'according to the ability' of the state. This article went further than a previous state commitment to free education at all stages, as legislated in the earlier 1964 constitution. Furthermore, article 21 constitutionalises the state's commitment to the eradication of illiteracy. Although an official state commitment to this already existed, it was constitutionalised to amplify that state commitment under Sadat's new regime.

Article 16 guarantees state-sponsored cultural, social and health services to citizens. Article 17 guarantees state-sponsored social, health and work insurance, and pensions. In both cases, as in the renewed state commitment to eradicate illiteracy, the 1971 constitution reaffirms past state duties toward citizens. A novelty in article 16 was the state's commitment to extend these services to the countryside 'in particular' – that is, with more emphasis on the provision of such services further down the social ladder.

The above analysis suggests that the 1971 constitution did not really offer radical change over the past, 1964 constitution,[7] but it did offer a change in Egypt's political economy. The premises of Nasser's effendi social contract remained intact, as various articles of the social contract were retained and even expanded. To the extent that this constitution implied liberal economic reform, that reform was layered side by side with older, Arab socialist principles of socio-economic development. Yet, alongside seeking legitimacy through Nasser's legacy, the constitution also cautiously led the way toward a new economic road.

In the aftermath of the 1973 War, the October Paper that celebrated Egypt's victory also launched the Open Door economic policy. As Mourad Wahba has suggested, the search for such a policy reform had already begun during the late 1960s, and it gradually came into being during the early 1970s.[8] Like the 1971 constitution, the Open Door policy was also about layering new plans for socio-economic development alongside existing, Arab socialist conventions. The Open Door was designed to facilitate economic growth through enhancing the profitability of the public sector, as opposed to a reversal of state–market relations. Moreover, and a central reason behind the introduction of this policy, an increase in the profitability of the public sector would allow the state to meet its financial commitments to its citizens. More accurately, still very much committed to the educated and state-employed middle class, the state initiated an economic reform that would maintain the effendi social contract and its underlying moral economy, rather than break it.

From the perspective of maintaining the social contract, I argue that Sadat's Open Door policy was logically closer to Nasser's 'third worldism' than initially thought. Both Nasser and Sadat operated to maximise political rent based on Egypt's geostrategic position and seniority in the region – increasingly, by attempting to tap regional oil wealth. Internationally, both presidents attempted to raise economic rent, albeit via different partners. Nasser envisioned economic opportunity by means of postcolonial activism and a reliance on the USSR, while Sadat identified such an opportunity with the United States. In both cases, Egypt's regional and international policy was immediately connected to its most central domestic policy of maintaining the social contract with the effendi middle class – the regime's mainstay and, increasingly, a growing opposition.

Not unlike Nasser's National Charter, Sadat's 1974 October Working Paper – the official announcement of the new economic policy – outlined an economic policy already set in motion. Like the charter, it was submitted to an abrupt plebiscite to broaden its social base of support, was canonised as a document of the revolution, and it structured future debates on the Open Door reform.[9] As with the charter, Egypt's history was mobilised and linearly arranged to explain the future change. Furthermore, in the October Paper, the call for a new 'comprehensive civilizational strategy' and its implementation was rather familiar in its attempt to advance simultaneous social and economic development and to enlist a national effort in doing so.[10] As in the past, planning remained central to socio-economic development.[11]

Also familiar was the political impatience to bring fast economic growth and social development.[12] In short, despite the change in Egypt's leadership, Nasser's National Charter and Sadat's October Paper were similar in both form and intent, if not in detail.

The main purpose of the Open Door economic policy as outlined in the October Paper was to enhance industrialisation.[13] By this time the project had been the central goal of Egypt's model for economic development for about four decades, and it changed little despite its limited success. Also similar to past economic development, agricultural development was of secondary importance, and it was mainly used to support industrialisation and to reduce dependence on food imports, as opposed to being an engine of growth of its own accord.

In the October Paper, Sadat outlines past mistakes, especially concerning the public sector. These mistakes provided the rationale for the economic correction under the Open Door policy, as the Corrective Revolution had earlier done to politics. In particular, and along the same lines adopted in the 1971 constitution, it was through reform that the public sector was destined to become more efficient, freed from previous shackles of price caps and the state's commitment to full employment. Here too, and despite past mistakes, Sadat was careful to stress that the Open Door policy would enhance a long-term Egyptian goal of development, one that reached back to the beginning of the 1952 revolution itself.

Sadat emphasised recently introduced economic initiatives, such as the free trade zones, the further development of the energy sector and greater emphasis on tourism. In all such initiatives, and layered alongside the public sector's reinvigorated initiatives, the private sector was allowed more freedom of operation but also had to take larger steps toward the shared cause of economic development. The free trade zones – areas that allowed extraterritorial initiative in commerce, an initiative not bound by existing legislation in matters such as labour or taxation – were a good example of contemporary layering in the economic reform. They seemingly allowed the reintegration of Egypt into the world economy, while still containing that integration so as to protect state-led industry.

Arab and foreign investment were encouraged, with Arab investment taking centre stage. When referring to foreign investment, a highly controversial topic that was closely, and negatively, associated with past imperialism, Sadat quotes the charter itself, later suggesting that 'the Charter has made it clear that we accept unconditional aid and loans, as well as direct investment in such fields of modern development as require world expertise'.[14] Such a direct reference to the charter further indicated that Sadat was well aware of the need to obtain legitimacy for his actions, based on the legacy of the 1952 revolution, regardless of the large changes that the October Paper introduced to the Egyptian economy in encouraging private enterprise and investment.

In the October Paper, social development carried the familiar templates of the effendi social contract. According to the paper, people are Egypt's main economic resource. Sadat suggests that 'the development of manpower means first and foremost increasing its capacity to give and to work by providing food, clothing, health services and housing and improving its human potential through culture, education and training'.[15] Sadat committed the Open Door policy to similar, Nasserite articles of the social contract, and to articles that the 1971 constitution also embraced.

Education, historically the central preoccupation of the social contract, received special attention in Sadat's October Paper. Here too, like the above emphasis on industry as central to economic rejuvenation, education took centre stage in the comprehensive improvement of Egypt. Sadat argues: 'Our country is neither lacking in educated young people nor in technical and administrative expertise. Still, the tasks lying ahead call for more'.[16] In this quotation it is clear that despite the obvious over-supply of educated Egyptians, Egypt needed even more. Moreover, according to Sadat, educational reform would now simultaneously train professionals, bureaucrats and skilled labour, as well as alleviate illiteracy. The latter, was a recent constitutional commitment, if not a policy change over past educational policy. Furthermore, as in the past, the state continued to commit to a dual system of education – both mass education and higher education – both causes that the regime found noble but difficult to simultaneously obtain.

According to the paper, education itself needed to be reformed – to move away from 'rigid study curricula' to become 'organically linked to the action and requirements of society'.[17] Central to Sadat's suggested educational reform was the call to correct an 'overwhelming disease whereby many consider education as the instrument for acquiring a special social privilege, while the principal target for some educated people has become office-jobs irrespective of their value in the movement of society'.[18] Instead of acquiring a special social privilege, education, according to Sadat, was supposed to provide the required economic skills and to teach work discipline. How this would check the desire for office jobs among some of the educated remained unclear. While education required reform, education and academic research were to be further expanded. Under the Open Door policy, education remained the remedy for all ills that it had been in the past.

The state remained committed to social development through 'affording maximum employment opportunities'.[19] In an era of large-scale labour migration, the state also had to organize the conditions of labour abroad in order to uphold 'the dignity of the citizens' and preserve 'the value of their work'. Such formulations were an implicit response to the rising criticism in Egyptian public discourse of labour migration and its negative impact on the economy, as well as on Egyptian migrant labourers and Egyptian society. Labour migration, Sadat emphasised, was only a short-term solution for 'surplus manpower'.[20] Once more, Sadat pre-empted public outcry against a state that was sending its citizens abroad instead of fixing the local economy. Regardless of Sadat's above remarks, the labour migration that took place during this period was hardly treated in a comprehensive way in the October Paper. This cursory treatment was typical of both state action and public attention to labour migration and remittances sent home. The latter brought important economic changes that were hardly discussed and, if so, were often denigrated as interfering with Egyptian economic development.

According to the October Paper, the state had to take steps to allow women to participate in 'our comprehensive strategy for progress'.[21] Hence, the relation between social justice and the place and role of women in society during the Nasserite era was reasserted.[22] Sadat referred to article 9 of the 1971 constitution to reiterate this state commitment to women's participation in the economy and society. As follows from article 9, this participation was conditional upon being compatible with the role of women in the Egyptian family and with religious belief. Alongside equality of opportunity for women in the economy, and similarly to the past, this equality was bound by women's roles as mothers and wives, which the state safeguarded – past and present – through gender-specific labour laws, as well as religious, personal status laws.

Under Sadat, women entered the education system and state employment in growing numbers, but under the familiar, patriarchal double-bind of working outside the home while still maintaining full responsibility for the household and the welfare of spouses and children. State feminism carried a similar logic under Nasser and Sadat. Sadat further reiterated a familiar past trope of centring Egypt's development efforts on youth: the younger generation took a central part in facilitating reform and was to benefit from it accordingly.

The 1974 October Paper, like the 1971 constitution, demonstrated a commitment to the past goals and actions of Arab socialism and its model of socio-economic development. Both officially attempted to correct rather than replace Arab socialism. The Free Officers' revolution was held up as a source of legitimacy for Sadat's regime, together with the social contract that determined state–citizen relations and continued the state's commitment to the moral economy that supported the effendi middle class. Nevertheless, in both there were also various measures of reform that were not compatible with the Arab socialism model of socio-economic development. These measures were layered alongside an existing paradigm and practice. The 1971 constitution and the October Paper together portrayed continuity in Egypt's political economy and legislated and promised much change. This duality, as we shall see in the following chapters, was perhaps politically savvy in the short term, in bolstering Sadat's and later Mubarak's legitimacy. However, such inconclusiveness would further haunt any attempt to successfully introduce a new social contract in the future, despite significant socio-economic and political transitions over time.

Oil-boom populism

Prior to 1973, Egypt was a small oil exporter, however state earnings were augmented by the huge rise in energy prices in the aftermath of the October 1973 War, and especially with the return of the Sinai oil wells to Egypt after 1979.[23] Furthermore, the state benefited from hikes in oil-related earnings, such as from the Suez Canal, state-owned tourism and state-to-state transfers (donations and loans from the Gulf states and international development aid), and remittances. As a result, the state was able to raise its expenditures on social services, employment and subsidies while the oil-boom lasted (1973–83). Throughout this period, the effendi social contract was extended to accommodate population increase and socio-economic mobility into the middle class.

By the end of the oil-boom, Egypt had been transformed into a middle-class society. One illustration of this change is that there were more graduates of institutions of higher education, particularly university graduates, than in the past. The number of white-colour state employees had also swelled. Overall employment saw a rise in services at the expense of agriculture. Material standards of living improved for many under the contemporary housing boom, including the suburbanisation of rural regions, and new consumer items, notably electric household appliances, were introduced to Egyptian homes. The media, including new television sets and VCRs, spread a new middle-class lifestyle and increased consumer expectations. An Islamic consumer culture dovetailed with these changes. Nevertheless, many in Egypt's middle-class society – particularly members of the state-educated and state-employed (effendi) middle class – were struggling, living uncomfortably close to a real or imagined poverty line and fearing that worse would come. The oil-boom created temporary economic opportunities for citizens and the state, but these were not sustainable for long.

The spread of higher education, long the central venue for mobility in Egypt, but also part of the social contract and its ensuing moral economy, provides a first glance at the transformation of Egyptian society during the oil-boom. Analysis of contemporary changes in education reveals a concurrent increase in the number of students and rising public discontent over the deteriorating quality of state education. Despite the expanding enrolment in universities under Nasser, it was under Sadat that this growth turned into a flood. In the early 1970s, Sadat improved the existing regional universities and ordered the opening of new ones, broadening higher education beyond the large cities and into regional hinterlands. Between 1971 and 1985, university enrolment more than tripled, a huge increase even considering population growth and the upsurge in numbers of college-age Egyptians. While women accounted for only about a third of the total student population, their absolute number increased as fast as that of their male peers, faster than it had in the past. Despite the expansion of state resources, per capita state spending on education diminished. Without increased spending to accommodate the expanding enrolment, the ratio of students to various types of university infrastructure such as classrooms and laboratories went up, as did the student-to-faculty ratio.

The quantity versus quality dilemma in Egypt's higher education – reminiscent of a dilemma regarding education since the liberal monarchy – did not fail to register in Egyptian public discourse, which had long been dominated by the upper-middle class. As suggested in Sadat's speech above, the state was also keenly aware of the economic trade-off associated with over-expanding education. However, once the floodgates of student enrolment opened, it was politically impossible to reverse the trend. Free-of-charge education for all was both a pre-revolutionary national call for independence and later part of the Free Officers' legacy, and it had recently been reiterated in the 1971 constitution and the 1974 October Paper. There was broad public consensus in favour of free-of-charge education, and it was an article of the social contract that no politician or government would publicly breach. Popular demand and state commitment had long turned higher education into a goal in and of itself, with some vague hope that economic development would catch up at some point with the growth in student enrolment, a hope that was not met over time.

This decline in the education system, compounded by the limited carrying capacity of the economy, meant that future economic improvement for graduates could not be as guaranteed by higher education as it had in the past. Nevertheless, this process of effendication, or the attempt to gain social mobility through higher education, was still growing strong. Despite diminishing returns, for young Egyptians and their families in rural areas, lower-class urban environments, and provincial towns, the expansion of higher education still facilitated mobility, notably through access to state employment and state benefits provided through the workplace. The propensity of families from these socio-economic backgrounds to enrol and keep their children in school was enhanced when economic conditions in Egypt improved during the 1970s. Families partially dispensed with child labour and managed to finance private classes for them, often a precondition for success in schools. Socioculturally, higher education remained a key factor in the formation of middle-class identity, distinction and respectability. In Egyptian public discourse, the educated were cultured (*muthaqqafin*), as well as professionally trained to occupy more refined (white collar) jobs. Contemporary discourse in the press, films, academic writing and other literature invariably conveyed this impression. Moreover, such discourse established the centrality of higher education in determining the social hierarchy, not least in facilitating class reproduction through marriage.

Despite the official state goal of efficiency in the workplace, Sadat reaffirmed the state's commitment to state employment of graduates, in line yet again with the effendi social contract and its ensuing moral economy. Between 1974 and 1976, the state extended guaranteed employment to former conscripts, as part of demilitarisation in the aftermath of the October War. Under Sadat, between 1971 and 1978 alone, employment in the Egyptian government administration (not including the public authorities and public enterprises, i.e., the public sector and the army) rose fast, amounting to a 73 per cent rise in state employment, while 'formal' employment increased by only 16 per cent.[24] By 1984, state employment in government had reached about one-fifth of all those officially employed in Egypt, and public enterprise employed about one-tenth of the working public. This means that about one-in-three officially employed persons worked for the state. While this phenomenon began under Nasser, such high levels of state employment were unprecedented in Egypt, notably in a period that saw large labour migration and an attempt to enlarge the private sector.

In the decade between 1976 and 1986, state employment of women grew almost four times faster than that of men. Women's share of state employment expanded from 15 to 26 per cent, raising the overall state employment of women by more than half.[25] The state became the dominant employer of middle-class women in the formal economy. This increase was due to the intensification of men's labour migration and the fact that private sector employment in some professions had become more lucrative, luring the men away. Moreover, educated women had fewer employment alternatives in the private sector, and government wages and benefits for women were higher than in the private sector at all levels of education. This gap widened as women became more educated. The more egalitarian state compensation created women's strong preference for state employment, even though they were not equal (owing to gender bias) with regard to seniority and wages.

Like higher education, state employment turned into an implicit form of welfare for the middle class because it clearly and increasingly offered remuneration with little relationship to the economic contribution of these white-collar employees. While the numbers of state employees – both men and women – rose, state wages deteriorated under the oil-related economic conditions, particularly because of inflation. Nevertheless, state employment was far from being an employment of last resort, and it remained coveted by many. To understand such preference in employment, one should consider existing employment alternatives. Positions for graduates were limited in the private sector, and while wages in the private sector were higher, state employment offered benefits, job security and a pension, which the private sector did not. State employment also offered a certain social respectability and the potential for social mobility, regardless of its low economic value. For example, male state employees ranked higher in social hierarchies as suitable marriage candidates. Women's state employment was better tolerated by Egyptian society and, in public opinion, was often the only employment venue deemed proper for educated women. Graduates placed their names on waiting lists for positions having state-sanctioned waiting periods; by 1984, a university graduate could expect to wait three-and-a-half years for a job, while graduates of secondary schools waited four years.[26] This gap between waiting periods for employment further suggests a hierarchy in state welfare for the middle class that was biased toward the more educated.

Both Egyptian public discourse, which was a middle-class discourse, and the state were occupied with the economic hardships of state employees, who had long been associated with the 'average' Egyptian. The state periodically increased their wages – adjusting employee remuneration to contemporary price increases – which caused further inflation. State subsidies of food and basic commodities, while universal, were often associated with indirect support for state employees on meagre wages, at times providing these subsidised commodities directly to these employees through work-based points of sale.

During the 1950s and 1960s, subsidies for food and basic commodities were low and included only a few items. This changed dramatically with the fast rise in basic food prices – the combined result of an oil-related upsurge in prices, changes in agricultural production and the rising demand for new types of food. In 1974, expenditures on subsidies, as part of overall governmental expenditures, reached 16.5 per cent and remained high until the aftermath of the oil-boom.[27] This steep incline in state expenditures was even more striking because Egypt was enjoying the windfall of oil-related earnings that increased its GDP.

Most economists agreed that, in monetary terms, overall food consumption (both quantity and quality) in Egypt improved during this period, reducing poverty but also supporting the rise of the middle class. Although Egyptians continued to spend a large percentage of their household budgets on food (about 50% and 60% in urban and rural regions, respectively) in order to live near the subsistence level, according to standardised statistical definitions of poverty, the diets of many improved.[28] Oddly, this meant that Egyptians experienced an ongoing food crisis – hikes in food prices combined with temporary shortages in state-regulated commodities – alongside an overall improvement in their food consumption. Furthermore, subsidies contributed to poverty alleviation, but as they were universal (provided to all as opposed to targeting those most in need) and with better allocation of subsidies in urban regions, they substantially benefited the middle class. This was even more true of the indirect state subsidisation of energy prices.[29] In 1979, indirect energy subsidies were estimated to be three times higher than the expenditure on food subsidies.[30] Here too energy subsidies were universal and therefore also disproportionately benefited car owners, those connected to the electrical grid and those who owned electrical appliances – that is, the middle and upper classes. Because of their centrality in the budgets of the majority of households, an abrupt attempt to abolish subsidies would have led to a major clash between citizens and the state – which is what happened in the 1977 Food Uprising.

Since 1947, and with several adjustments over time, urban rent control had been another long-term article of the effendi social contract. Rent control was often criticised for being skewed or regressive in various ways: in depriving middle-class owners of an important source of income, in unjustifiably benefiting older rather than younger generations of urbanites and those who lived in more expensive properties yet paid little rent, and for the general depletion of real estate where owners had little incentive to invest. Since the early 1970s, high inflation that eroded fixed rents had further exposed the inadequacy of rent control. The reformation of state rent control – allowing private owners to demand higher rents – was too politically risky to be considered, because many urbanites depended on cheap rent. Facing a mounting public uproar over the housing crisis, the state, in cooperation with private developers, initiated state-led housing projects. Moreover, the state increasingly let informal construction – in reality, still significantly under state control and patronage – to close the gap between the rising demand for housing and the limited supply.

As the above discussion of state provision during the 1970s and 1980s suggests, the state increased its expenditures on different articles of the effendi social contract, expanding it down the social ladder. Sadat's Corrective Revolution indeed partially delivered what it implicitly promised – to reinvigorate this vertical social contract. Furthermore, under oil-boom conditions, and despite the call for economic liberalisation in the October Paper, Sadat turned out to be more of a populist than Nasser had been under Arab socialism. This, however, barely registered in the contemporary public discourse and academic analysis, according to which Egypt's social contract was eroding, not expanding.[31] This is hardly surprising in a period during which higher education expanded, but deteriorated in quality; state employment also quickly expanded, but its remuneration decreased under steep inflation; the state increased subsidies for basic foods and commodities and their distribution, but food prices remained high; and when the state took steps to relieve the rising pressure on housing, the measures taken did nothing to ease the price hikes of dwellings. In short, Sadat's oil populism was not accorded favourable commentary in Egyptian public opinion. Broad improvement in local standards of living, from calorie intake to the reduction in illiteracy, and the spread of mass consumption scarcely registered in contemporary public discourse. Moreover, under oil-boom conditions the Egyptian middle class expanded while many lamented its demise – a 'struggling middle class' had become a fixture of Egyptian socio-politics.

It was crucial for contemporary living standards and the hopes for socio-economic mobility that the existing articles of the effendi social contract could be elaborated but not restructured. Under these conditions, and with continuous pressure on the state budget, there was a growing official call to put forward a new social contract to overcome this impasse. Nevertheless, the effendi social contract was still going strong in the public's eyes, as the Egyptian state was about to discover during the January 1977 Food Uprising.

The 1977 Food Uprising

In February 1975, Prime Minister Hijazi gave an extended interview to the semi-official daily, *al-Ahram*.[32] Boldly titled 'Prime Minister Discusses Commodity Shortages, Popular Complaints', the journalist Fahmi Huwaydi opened the article by suggesting that Hijazi, since his appointment, had been – rightly or wrongly – on continuous trial by the Egyptian street. Since pharaonic times, Huwaydi explained, whenever the state took charge of the water supply, governments managed Egyptians' needs in return for political power. This social contract (Huwaydi referred here to Montesquieu as the person who had coined the term) had now become a burden for Hijazi's government because of the multiple shortages and economic hardships that Egypt suffered, and for which the government only had partial solutions.

Popular complaints as reflected in *al-Ahram*, as well as in the broadening opposition press – including that of the Muslim Brotherhood, which was a growing mainstay of middle-class opposition to the state – came in a period of relative ease with regard to freedom of speech and an easing of political censorship between 1976 and 1980. The relatively free press allowed many across the political spectrum to assert that the state was not doing enough to support the average Egyptian, or 'the people' – in reality, the lower segment of the middle class – in the face of multiple economic crises. President Sadat's economic policy initially enjoyed the support of the old vanguard of the Muslim Brotherhood. The general mistrust toward the Egyptian state (in which Nasser had persecuted so many people), added to their growing support for state liberalisation in economic and political affairs. Nevertheless, a broad national consensus remained (among religious and secular Egyptians alike) that the state should adhere to the existing articles of welfare in the social contract – its core moral economy – regardless of the economic liberalisation under the Open Door.

Hijazi's appearance in the press was not unique. The prime minister, the minister of supply and various other officials gave frequent interviews to the press in which they also explained the challenges ahead and defended ministerial action. President Sadat appeared in the press in times of crisis, such as when meat prices significantly increased, promising immediate government action – a clear indication of the political importance he attached to such matters. More and more, the state found itself in a bind. Faced with a contemporary public uproar against multiple economic crises, the state promised more resolutions than it could deliver – a broad public consensus on state provisioning left the state with little room to reform or adjust its expenditures to what it could realistically afford. This resulted in chronic, mounting state debt, which Egypt experienced despite a significant rise in state revenues. Bound by the social contract, the state increased its expenditures well beyond its financial means.

In the interview in *al-Ahram*, Hijazi expressed typical official exacerbation over the state's diminishing ability to continue providing for its citizens at the then-current level. The prime minister highlighted the significant state efforts to fix the results of economic hardship, including his own insomnia, which was brought on by constant worry over such affairs. These efforts and Hijazi's own personal concern clearly highlighted the state's commitment to the social contract. Along with this commitment, he reprimanded the citizenry for its irresponsible practices, such as refusing to be more frugal in consumption, for example, by wasting food. Hijazi further complained that Egyptians would not compromise in matters of higher education and state employment – adjusting both to the economic realities of Egypt as he saw them, especially in face of the state's growing inability to cover its expenses, resulting in state debt. The rather reprimanding tone of the interview exposed the familiar paternalistic style of state discourse. It also suggested an official sense of public moral betrayal – Egyptian citizens were breaching their end of the social contract.

Almost two years later, the underlying tension between state and citizenry perspectives on the broken social contract, reflected in Hijazi's interview, came to a boiling point. In January 1977 three days of violence and protest shocked the Egyptian public and the political establishment. The Food Uprising ostensibly took place in reaction to an abrupt government decision to follow the advice of the International Monetary Fund (IMF) and drop the subsidies for basic foods and non-food household items.[33] After a few days, the uprising was ended by a combination of military repression and the government's retraction of its misguided, IMF-inspired plan. However, it would remain a watershed in Egyptian politics thereafter because it reflected broad public agreement that such a breach of the social contract was misguided. This agreement was expressed by the fact that many across the political map, including the Muslim Brotherhood, alluded to their role in the unfolding events.

Egyptian and international commentators attributed the uprising to a political failure, which it was. In a period of relative freedom of expression, Deputy Prime Minister Abdel Aziz Qaisunni, who was in charge of economic affairs, delivered a speech on 17 January before the People's Assembly announcing the subsidy cuts, which quickly disseminated through the press and ignited the protest.[34] Egypt's political leadership did not anticipate such a harsh reaction, and was taken by surprise. The uprising was, in part, a response to Sadat's Open Door policy, which had received much criticism following its announcement. Sadat's own public support, based on the successful 1973 War against Israel, was waning, which further set the stage for the protest. However, this account of the immediate background of the uprising fails to convey the full extent of the public sentiment that brought about the huge public outcry.

Anthropologist Nadia Khouri-Dagher suggests a more nuanced explanation of the Food Uprising along these lines: 'In Egypt, the price of bread plays the role of a gold standard, a kind of monetary unit in the food price scale', while the price of meat represented 'the maximum tolerable price for food items'.[35] The uprising was about holding the government responsible for its own commitment to keep essential food costs low, and therefore, for preserving the existing social contract. The protest against cancelling food subsidies was not simply about hunger. Because food was the largest household expenditure, food prices determined the standard of living for most families – lower and middle class alike. Building on Khouri-Dagher's analysis, the Food Uprising can be understood as a government miscalculation in breaking with an existing if unwritten agreement over the price of food, often referred to in Egypt as 'food security'. Moreover, this breach of the agreement was done under seeming IMF international pressure that threatened national sovereignty, which constituted another breach. Many in Egypt resented this pressure, which they considered unjust (neo-imperial) interference in Egyptian national affairs.

On 5 February 1977, President Sadat made a speech to the nation commenting on recent events.[36] He congratulated the state – both the political leadership and the army and security forces – on the actions taken to restore order. Diverging as he often did from formal Arabic to colloquial Egyptian and informal speech, Sadat later reprimanded the Egyptian left, particularly the communists, whom he blamed for being the main perpetrators behind the destructive events. According to Sadat's narrative, rather than putting forward their grievances through official state institutions, according to the law and in accordance with democratic principles, these alleged perpetrators were to blame for diverging into urban violence and causing disruption in Egypt's main cities. In his speech Sadat flipped the argument above, regarding the breaching of the social contract, on its head. Rather than being a popular protest against the state reneging on its part of the agreement, Sadat lashed out against those engaging in street protests for violating the social contract, claiming that they deserved the state's wrath. Furthermore, in targeting the communists, Sadat refrained from admitting the public's wide-scale participation in and support for the protest, in an attempt to minimise the rupture in state–citizen relations.

In his speech Sadat consistently emphasised that destructive opposition was not an acceptable means for the public expression of dissent, and he returned again and again to the physical damage to public and private property and to the hardships that the unfolding events had caused citizens. Sadat used the religious notion of *fitna* – a rebellion against the just ruler – here, to religiously discredit the uprising and relegate it to an act of unlawful, anti-state violence. Sadat argued that this 'Uprising of Thieves' (*intifada haramiyya*, as he referred to it) was not a legitimate political expression of citizen or national freedom. Rather, Sadat juxtaposed street violence with his own and the state's lawful conduct. Here he cited specific articles of the 1971 constitution that mandated state use of force to put down an uprising when bringing back national unity. Sadat added that whatever the differences in opinion over economic reform (the Open Door policy), such a reform was necessary because Egypt was facing significant budget shortages. In all the above, he clearly attempted to discredit the uprising as an authentic public manifestation of discontent against the state.

Sadat concluded with a formal, presidential decision on how to protect this national unity (and the social contract), in a familiar, paternalistic carrot-and-stick manner. In the aftermath of this huge street protest, this decision included a clause that secured some political participation – the right to establish political parties based on the law – therefore, the right to express political opinion but in accordance with what the regime regarded as an 'orderly fashion'. The government further introduced progressive taxation based on a law (progressive here meant taxation based on relative personal wealth) that would bring equity among Egyptians. Thus, Sadat stipulated a greater political openness that would allow citizens a greater say in politics, while maintaining public safety, together with a new way to ensure a more economically egalitarian society. Alongside the above, he put forward several disciplinary acts in retribution against those who perpetrated violent acts against the state. He emphasised the hard hand of the government – based on the law – including the detention and arrest of those disturbing the public order, and acting against strikes. This was a direct threat that such street protests would not be tolerated and that those involved would be punished. The supposed purpose of such measures was to provide security and to protect public and private property, all under the firm guidance of the state.

Tellingly, the government's retreat from its earlier decision to cut subsidies – the central reason behind the uprising – was not mentioned. Had it been mentioned, it would have revealed the uprising's success in turning around a government decision. In the aftermath of the Food Uprising, various political groups, from the Egyptian left to the Islamists, were happy to claim leadership in the protests – a clear indication that in public opinion the uprising had been a successful political act against the regime. The Food Uprising would remain a vivid memory in Egyptian politics regarding public sensitivity to rolling back state provisioning. Moreover, it fuelled a great deal of awareness of the political repercussions of economic reform from then on, including in future discussions between the government of Egypt and international financial institutions (IFIs).[37]

While, or because, the Food Uprising brought about the reaffirmation of the social contract, it was also the turning point in which a government call for a new social contract first emerged. If the Open Door policy was about maintaining the old social contract, the Food Uprising signalled the failure of that policy, which could not deliver on its promises. A new, paradigm shift was required, as opposed to the Corrective Revolution, of which the Open Door policy was a part.

Socio-economic mobility and its discontents

Under the intertwined influence of the oil-boom and the Open Door policy, many a commentator felt that the effendi social contract had broken down twice. First, as discussed above, this policy abrogated an agreement between the state and society, particularly with the state-employed effendi middle class. Second, and somewhat paradoxically, commentators were alarmed by the rapid expansion of a new middle-class society through labour migration, as well as by the spread of the informal economy (i.e., economic activity not accounted for by official statistics or regulated and taxed by the state). They associated such transitions with various sociocultural ills and the rise of what they considered new, parasitic social groups from below and above the middle class; the commentators also associated these transitions with the rise of this new middle class that ruined the effendi middle class from within. According to many, the period experienced the destruction of the Egyptian person, the Egyptian family, and society at large.[38] Implicit in all such critiques was a public outcry against these social transitions that broke the existing, horizontal social contract between citizens.

During the 1970s and the early 1980s, Egypt indeed experienced quick socio-economic mobility through a significant market turn that was neither planned nor immediately directed by the state.[39] During this period, Egypt went through an 'industrious revolution', as opposed to a much hoped for 'industrial revolution', an argument inspired by economic historian Jan de Vries.[40] Barely recognised in positive terms by public commentators then or later, the industriousness of many in Egypt – from all social groups, including more participation of women in both the formal and the informal economies – produced a significant part of the contemporary economic growth. Egypt's industrious revolution started with mass labour migration to oil-producing states in the Gulf and Libya. During the early 1970s, after a few years of increased labour migration, one estimate put the number of migrant workers at fewer than 300,000. By 1980, however, the estimated number of such migrants had increased by a multiple of five, reaching about 1,600,000. Soon after, during the first years of the Iran–Iraq War, labour migration almost doubled when Egyptian rural workers migrated to Iraq and replaced Iraqi draftees, bringing the total to approximately 2,900,000. Between 1975 and 1982/83, the percentage of migrant workers within the official Egyptian labour force was estimated to have increased more than fourfold, from 5.4 to 23.9 per cent, or nearly one in four.[41]

Labour migration tended to have a transitory and somewhat repetitive nature, suggesting that the actual volume of labour migration was probably even larger than the above estimates indicate. Contrary to contemporary social commentary that associated migration with peasants, unskilled labourers, and lower-class urbanites, it was the Egyptian middle class, including state employees, who first sought work abroad, and in relatively larger numbers than other social groups. By 1976, almost 30,000 Egyptian teachers were working in foreign countries. That same year, a quarter of all the faculty members from Egypt's most esteemed universities held positions abroad. Between 1973 and 1984, the estimated remittances in the Egyptian economy rose approximately threefold. To grasp the magnitude of this new sum, suffice it to say that these remittances went from about 1 per cent of Egypt's GDP to approximately 10 per cent, while Egypt's GDP was already growing quickly.[42]

Migrant workers used a significant portion of their remittance funds for private consumption, to improve their families' standard of living. These remittances also served as an important source for local investment, albeit not in the large-scale, state-owned industry envisioned by both the supporters and the critics of the Open Door policy. Such informal investments were not readily quantifiable. However, collated data from various sources, not least contemporary ethnographies, suggest the magnitude of the transformation that remittances brought to a large socio-economic mobility during this period.

Contemporary public discourse in the press, arts (cinema and literature), and academia in Egypt – all bastions of the upper-middle class – rarely discussed labour migration and remittances in favourable terms. To the extent that labour migration was commented upon – and contemporary public discourse by and large avoided in-depth engagement with this topic – it was mostly through outlining the negative consequences of migration. For many, labour migration was not an acceptable form of socio-economic development for Egyptians or for Egypt, because its immediate benefits derailed the long-term development of both. According to the critics, working abroad actually dulled professional skills. The money earned easily abroad – there was little reference to the hardships these migrants endured – corrupted the work ethics of labour upon their return. The fact that employment abroad eased the pressure on the state to provide employment and services (as would become painfully clear in the mid-1980s, in the wake of the oil-boom) was hardly acknowledged. Moreover, according to the critique, forsaking the country for work abroad implied betraying local patriotism, despite this employment practice becoming normative in Egypt.

Similar to labour migration, remittances – a huge source of earnings for all Egyptians – did not sit well with critics. Labour migration raised the price of blue-collar labour, causing great resentment among middle-class commentators. Furthermore, according to many, remittances in foreign currency contributed to local inflation and to the rising economic gap between the owners of capital and those living on their wages – the latter often being the middle-class state employees now also economically threatened by those previously lower down the social ladder. The fact that they greatly shared in migration was often ignored. This social group was absolved for taking part in migration because it had little alternative in the face of its current economic hardship.

Criticism often ignored the marked improvement in the standards of living among peasants and lower-class urbanites provided by these remittances. The latter further contributed to investment in Egypt's informal economy, which was at the core of the socio-economic mobility of urban and rural lower-class Egyptians to middle-class status. Here, bias toward large-scale industrialisation brought criticism that associated informal small and middle manufacturing, construction, and commerce with harms caused to the 'real' economy that was led by the public sector. Middle-class critics further associated the local production of commodities in the informal economy with low quality and high prices. They complained about the quality and prices of services, for example, in household maintenance. Construction workers were denigrated for the same reasons. Informal commerce was associated with the black market, and again with exorbitant prices and the low quality of commodities sold, mainly foodstuffs. Commentators further contrasted the fortunes of peasants and lower-class urbanites who migrated or worked in the informal economy with those of state officials on fixed wages, ignoring the fact that these officials also labour-migrated in large numbers.

While many complained about cronyism and corruption among public officials, public opinion tended to view such practices among the lower echelon of state bureaucracy as a survival strategy, and therefore as acceptable. Complaints mostly targeted 'fat cats' (*qitat samina*) – a new upper class consisting of pre-revolutionary elites, state officials, politicians (a Nasserist 'state bourgeoisie' gone awry) and parvenu social climbers – as opposed to average state employees. These fat cats were the forerunners of a future generation of crony capitalists who gained ascendency during Mubarak's presidency. Having become socially, economically and politically dominant, they were more visible during the period of new economic opportunities, spreading cronyism between private capital and administrative/political power, and corruption. They, according to this critique, had driven Egypt back to economic dependency on the West, while promoting their own interests by illegal means, to the detriment of the local economy and society. The proximity of the fat cats to state officials and politicians brought many to charge the state itself for all such wrongdoing. Indeed, the public condemnation of these fat cats complemented political protests against the state. According to these critics, state officials and their cronies had forsaken the social contract made with the nation, and sought only their own self-enrichment. Public demonstrations of their wealth enhanced the fat cats' public visibility and marked economic inequality, further stimulating mounting discontent regarding their role in Egyptian society, the economy and the state.

A rural middle class had already developed under Nasser. However, after the 1970s, and especially during the 1980s, it grew rapidly. The long-term trend of rural-to-urban migration in search of better living conditions and employment was reversed. This happened with some state help, through growing investment in infrastructure such as running water, sewage systems and electricity. Rural areas, however, experienced a 'red-brick revolution' – a construction boom – primarily thanks to remittances that raised the quality of those residences, thus slowing the rural-to-urban migration. Changes in rural Egypt, when noted (public commentary in Egypt – past and present – has tended to be city oriented), were associated with the loss of both agricultural production capacity and cultural authenticity, as opposed to the improved standards of rural living. Middle-class commentators complained that the Egyptian village, with its newly built dwellings and commercialised outfits, had become like the city. Commentators overlooked the pattern of many peasants and lower-class urbanites educating their sons and, increasingly, their daughters to join the ranks of the state employees. In short, they resented a seemingly improper process of socio-economic mobility through which rural dwellers attempted to enter the middle class, thereby breaking the earlier 'organic' structure of society and its stratification. These commentators implicitly associated such mobility with the breakdown of a horizontal contract between citizens, according to which each social class had previously kept to its place in the existing social hierarchy.

In the Egyptian public discourse and across the political spectrum and the religious–secular divide, a marriage crisis epitomised all that had gone wrong for the middle class. Under contemporary economic conditions, male youths had to postpone marriage because their earnings did not allow them to start a family. Commentators suggested that this was particularly true under emerging Western-style consumerism, which had raised inauthentic, sometimes secular, social expectations regarding the standards of living among the newly wed. Socio-economic mobility among peasants and lower-class urbanites exacerbated the practice of polygamy. Furthermore, migrants and those operating in the informal economy sometimes married into middle-class families and 'corrupted' this class from within. In existing families, economic hardships and budding consumer expectations strained married life and created cross-generational tensions regarding the spending of family earnings. The combination of growing household needs and demands drove many wives and daughters to work outside the home, which further strained family life.

As a result of the above, many came to feel a sense of growing disappointment with the state for failing to guide (or regulate) this new consumer culture and to protect the middle class. Such guidance previously existed in the social contract through state regulation of the supply side of the economy. Now there was also a call to introduce such regulation of consumer demands because the latter brought growing economic inequality and immorality, and yielded a rise in social tension and anxiety. Spokespersons for the contemporary Islamic resurgence in Egypt were, alongside others, critical of the social and moral havoc that socio-economic transitions brought. This came despite that fact that a new religious consumer culture came into being together with the spread of mass consumption. Moreover, an Islamic economic sector and Islamic NGOs supported the process of economic liberalisation from below, not least through replacing state services with those provided by these organisations themselves.

Escalating social tension is usually associated with an increase in economic scarcity – social divisions come to the forefront in any society under economic duress. The research above suggests a somewhat more nuanced explanation, based on perceptions of relative deprivation in the effendi middle class public discourse. It was during the oil-boom that 'peasants and workers', long placed on a national pedestal but mostly left out of the effendi social contract, had a real chance for a breakthrough, through a combination of a larger share in state provision and oil-boom economic opportunities. New social climbers from rural and urban backgrounds, however, attracted much negative commentary, according to which the respectable middle-class way of life was breached by the expansion of this new middle class. The many condemnations of peasants and lower-class workers suggest that a great deal of social tension was created by contemporary socio-economic mobility, which many critics associated with the breakdown of social solidarity in Egypt. Implied in all such critiques was the accusation that the horizontal social contract was breached from below no less often than by the fat cats from above. Further implied was a moral social breakdown – a combination of inauthenticity and secularisation, both often meaning 'Westernisation' – the result of the creation of a rampant and unregulated consumer society.

Despite these changes, and much lamentation in the public discourse, no new middle class came to replace the old. Under such confusing conditions, the Egyptian social contract expanded down the social ladder as never before, while the Open Door policy was simultaneously criticised for eroding it. The oil-boom- and Open Door-induced socio-economic mobility did not create a new social coalition that openly supported contemporary changes. Under such conditions, this social contract could not be changed – regardless of the broad recognition in the government and in public discourse that it had malfunctioned.

Notes

1. Shafi'i, *al-Dawla wa-l-Tabaqa al-Wusta*, 216.
2. For the use of this term see, for example, Hinnebusch, *Egyptian Politics under Sadat*.
3. On the 'Corrective Revolution', see Waterbury, *Egypt of Nasser and Sadat*, 349–53; Baker, *Egypt's Uncertain Revolution*, 124–6; Hinnebusch, *Egyptian Politics under Sadat*, 40–6; and Robert L. Tignor, *Anwar al-Sadat: Transforming the Middle East* (Oxford: Oxford University Press, 2016), 73–8.
4. Kristen Stilt, 'Constitutions in Authoritarian Regimes: The Egyptian Constitution of 1971', in *Constitutions in Authoritarian Regimes*, ed. Tom Ginsburg and Alberto Simpser (Cambridge: Cambridge University Press, 2014), 120.

5. See the analysis of the constitutional process, ibid, 115–20.
6. See the 1971 constitution in translation: 'Constitution of the Arab Republic of Egypt', *Middle East Journal* 26, no. 1 (1972): 55–68. See the original document in *Bibliotheca Alexandrina*, accessed 28 April 2020, http://modernegypt.bibalex.org/NewDocumentViewer.aspx?DocumentID=DC_38388&keyword (Arabic).
7. Stilt, 'Constitutions in Authoritarian Regimes', 118–19.
8. For analysis of the origins and aims of the Open Door policy, see Wahba, *The Role of the State*, 147–73.
9. Mark N. Cooper, *The Transformation of Egypt* (Baltimore, MD: Johns Hopkins University Press, 1982), 88–90.
10. Anwar El Sadat, 'Tasks of the Stage; or a Comprehensive Civilizational Strategy', in *The October Working Paper* (Cairo: Ministry of Information, State Information Service, 1974), 50–88. See the October Paper at 'Written Works', University of Maryland, Anwar Sadat Chair for Peace and Development, accessed 12 September 2020, https://sadat.umd.edu/resources/written-works.
11. Ibid., 84–8.
12. Ibid., 55–6.
13. Ibid., 64–5.
14. Ibid., 63.
15. Ibid., 67.
16. Ibid., 68.
17. Ibid., 70.
18. Ibid., 71–2.
19. Ibid., 75.
20. Ibid., 76.
21. Ibid.
22. For the state's protective role of women's socio-economic rights under Nasser, which was often termed 'state feminism', see Laura Bier, *Revolutionary Womanhood: Feminisms, Modernity, and the State in Nasser's Egypt* (Stanford, CA: Stanford University Press, 2011); and Mervat F. Hatem, 'Economic and Political Liberation in Egypt and the Demise of State Feminism', *International Journal of Middle East Studies* 24, no. 2 (1992), 231–51. In contrast to Hatem, this chapter argues for much continuity in state feminism under President Sadat.
23. For an elaborate discussion of this topic, see Shechter, *Rise of the Egyptian Middle Class*.

24. Shechter, *Rise of the Egyptian Middle Class*, 59–60. 'Formal' employment stands here for the employment accounted for in official state statistics.
25. Ibid., 62.
26. Ibid., 61–2.
27. Ibid., 87.
28. Ibid., 89.
29. These state energy subsidies were indirect, because they were embedded among the 'opportunity costs' of energy (i.e., the revenue gap between selling local fuels at cheap prices versus higher gains from exports to international markets). By comparison, imported foods required actual withdrawals from the State Treasury and expensive payments in foreign currency.
30. Shechter, *Rise of the Egyptian Middle Class*, 89.
31. Ibid., 82–110.
32. Interview with Prime Minister Dr 'Abd al-'Aziz Hijazi: Fahmi Huwaydi, 'Prime Minister Discusses Commodity Shortages, Popular Complaints', *al-Ahram*, 7 February 1975, 3, 8. Translated in 'Middle East and North Africa: Global Perspectives, 1958–1994', *Readex* (Naples, FL: Readex, 2015), accessed 25 December 2017, https://www.readex.com/content/middle-east-and-north-africa-global-perspectives-1958–1994.
33. For the Food Uprising, see Husayn 'Abd al-Raziq, *Misr fi 18 wa-19 Yanayir: Dirasa Siyasiyya Watha'iqiyya* (Beirut: Dar al-Kalima, 1979); Ansari, *Egypt, the Stalled Society*, 185–93; Cooper, *Transformation of Egypt*, 235–46, 278; Hinnebusch, *Egyptian Politics under Sadat*, 71–2; Tignor, *Anwar al-Sadat*, 140–2; and Waterbury, *Egypt of Nasser and Sadat*, 229–31.
34. Tignor, *Anwar al-Sadat*, 140.
35. Nadia Khouri-Dagher, 'The State, Urban Households, and Management of Daily Life: Food and Social Order in Cairo', in *Development, Change, and Gender in Cairo: A View from the Household*, ed. Diane Singerman and Homa Hoodfar (Bloomington: Indiana University Press, 1996), 124.
36. See this speech: Anwar El Sadat, 'Khitab al-Ra'is Muhammad Anwar al-Sadat ila al-Umma', *Bibliotheca Alexandrina*, accessed 29 April 2020, http://modernegypt.bibalex.org/NewTextViewer.aspx?TextID=SP_568 (Arabic).
37. Khalid Ikram, *The Egyptian Economy, 1952–2000: Performance, Policies, and Issues* (London: Routledge, 2006), 60, 63.
38. For a more detailed discussion, see Shechter, *Rise of the Egyptian Middle Class*, 111–93.

39. I have borrowed the term 'market turn' and its analytical framework from Avner Offer, 'The Market Turn: From Social Democracy to Market Liberalism', *Economic History Review* 70 (2017): 1051–71, https://doi.org/10.1111/ehr.12537.
40. Jan de Vries, 'The Industrial Revolution and the Industrious Revolution', *Journal of Economic History* 54 no. 2 (1994): 249–70.
41. Shechter, *Rise of the Egyptian Middle Class*, 68.
42. Ibid., 69.

6

PLANNING A NEW SOCIAL CONTRACT

This chapter explores the emergence of a 'new social contract' – a planning initiative among Egyptian planners and international developers – and the social reform envisioned in it. The chapter first traces the emergence of the new social contract to planning initiatives conducted during the second part of the 1970s, particularly, to the 1978–82 Development Plan. The chapter later outlines the continuity in planning for socio-economic change in Egypt over time, and the re-emergence of the call for a new social contract in the Egypt Human Development Report project between 1994 and 2010. The second part of this chapter asks why, despite more than three decades of active planning, the new social contract continued to put forth similar policy recommendations when the government clearly did little to follow through with their application. I demonstrate that planning turned into a tool for obtaining economic and political rent that postponed or diluted the introduction of a new social contract in Egypt.

The birth of the new social contract

In 1961, the same year in which Egypt's initiative for the National Charter was introduced, the Egyptian Ministry for Social Affairs and Employment published a book titled *The Social Constitution of the United Arab Republic*.[1] In the 'Introduction', Muhammad Muhammad Tawfiq 'Abd al-Fatah, the responsible minister, explains that the purpose of this book is pedagogical – to enlighten the people, but also educators and decision makers, on the various venues available for achieving the social goals of national development. The social constitution here was a meta-text on how to guide society, as the constitution was the source of all laws. This meta-text constituted a social contract, according to 'Abd al-Fatah, that had been narrated by the leader of the revolution and the president of the state. Arranged in ten thematic chapters, this book includes quotations from President Nasser's various public expressions that reflect different aspects of this social contract regarding social culture, the social revolution, the basic principles of society, social justice, the family, youth, rural areas, work and workers, production, cooperation and Arab nationalism.[2]

Interestingly, the notion of a social contract does not appear directly in any of the quotations in this book or, more broadly, in Nasser's speeches.[3] Nasser made ample references to citizen–state relations and, notably, to citizens' newly acquired rights under national liberation and social justice, though this term is not used. 'Social contract' as a key term used to discuss state–citizen relations in Egypt only emerged during the mid-1970s, particularly in the aftermath of the 1977 Food Uprising. This does not preclude the prior existence of the social contract, as is demonstrated throughout this book. But the fact that 'social contract' emerged during this period and has remained in use since suggests a continuous search for an alternative political economy for Egypt – a combination of economic and political reform.

The term 'social contract' surfaced as a call for broad liberal reform in Egypt (though not yet the full-fledged call for neoliberalisation that would arrive later, during the 1990s) and was closely intertwined with the global use of this term. According to Google Books Ngram Viewer, the 1970s saw a rise in the frequency of the term's appearance in English, indicating a broader, global trend in its employment during a period in which a global change of heart regarding the post–World War II comprehensive welfare state took place.[4] In Egypt and elsewhere, 'social contract' in public discourse became very noticeable when an existing – even if without overt, official state recognition – social contract was challenged. The search for a new social contract meant that the old one had to be spelled out, if only so it could be contested and changed.

The January 1977 Food Uprising was, somewhat paradoxically, a turning point in the formulation of the new social contract. This uprising was both a high point of public resistance to an abrupt change in the old social contract and a starting point in state planning for such change. In August 1977, several months after the uprising, the 1978–82 Egyptian development plan explicitly used the term 'new social contract' to present urgently required transitions in Egyptian socio-economic development in the aftermath of the

Food Uprising.⁵ The official introduction of a planning initiative for a new social contract suggests the Sadat regime's de facto recognition of the past social contract, and hence, a commitment to putting forward a new contract. The introduction of a new ruling party – the National Democratic Party – during the same period suggests an attempt to develop a new, democratised politics alongside the new liberal socio-economic plan.

Khalid Ikram, earlier the World Bank's chief economist in the Middle East (1975–79) and a keen observer of Egypt's political economy since, suggests that Abdel Razzak Abdel Meguid, who would go on to be appointed minister of planning and later deputy prime minister in charge of economic matters, was the principle author of the plan.⁶ This plan partly constituted a political defence of the government economic ministers who took the controversial decision to proceed with the subsidy cuts. However, the plan also detailed a new course of economic action, one that clearly deemed the Corrective Revolution, with the Open Door policy as its centrepiece, to be insufficient to face the challenges ahead. The plan now suggested that what was required was comprehensive transformation. Rather than attempting to stimulate the economy so as to enable Egypt to keep the social contract, as in the past, the plan for liberalisation advocated for changing central elements of this contract.

The 1971 constitution and Sadat's 1974 October Paper layered economic reform side by side with the ostensible continuity of Arab socialism. The Open Door policy was an attempt to make gradual economic and political changes that would continue to emphasise a strong affinity with the Nasserite social contract. The 1978–82 development plan was a potentially radical initiative in that it detailed this social contract for the purpose of offering an alternative, new social contract for Egypt. The 1978 establishment of the National Democratic Party as a new ruling party for Egypt further suggested a large political change (democratisation), as implied in its title.

According to the plan, the old social contract included the following:

1. The government guarantees unconditional employment and earnings to all;
2. It provides social welfare through housing, health, education and other services;
3. It protects the consumer from the increase in the cost of living;

4. It administrates all public utilities and most units of national production;
5. It provides the public with both necessities and luxuries, from bread to motion picture films. These are available at prices much lower than their actual cost to the government.[7]

This succinct description successfully outlined the contours of the existing social contract, if not its actual implementation. Concurrently, it exposed the enormity of the state commitment involved in fulfilling the old social contract, as part of a new attempt in the plan to offer an alternative, smaller-in-scope social contract, one that would be more sustainable in the long run. For this same reason, the plan mostly remained a plan rather than an actual roadmap that would bring significant change.

The 1978–82 development plan was much more in sync with a global transformation in how international (read Western) scholars and planners working for IFIs envisioned socio-economic and political reform than it was with the feasibility of actually implementing such reform under Egypt's prevailing political economy. Indeed, the plan reflected a congruency between global and local expertise and 'glocal' visions of change. Egyptian planners were by and large part of this international group in their training and career trajectories, as well as in their professional worldviews. They all shared similar socio-economic mobility through education, especially through new economic opportunities in a globalising world, and they therefore had similar global upper-middle-class membership and interests. Abdel Meguid, with his Oxford training and several years of successful work at the United Nations Development Programme (UNDP), was no exception.[8] As I outline below, the 1978–82 development plan was the first, but hardly the last, comprehensive initiative to introduce a new glocal social contract to Egypt that would have little success in bringing such a transition about.

By the early 1970s, scholars and planners had become uncomfortable with the earlier model of state-led economic development. Many started to doubt the overwhelming emphasis on economic growth, which had led to rising inequality. As in many other developing nations, even when economic growth took place, it left many behind. An earlier assumption that economic growth would trickle down the societal ladder failed to materialise. Income and wealth inequality often remained high, as did unemployment among the poor. Developers began searching for ways to assist 'those most in need' through better targeting of 'basic needs'.[9] These two terms became central to a new approach called 'basic needs' in developmental studies, and a new international best practice among development institutions, notably the International Labour Organization (ILO). Starting in the early 1970s and throughout that decade, 'basic needs' showed a sharp increase in use, according to Google Books Ngram Viewer, an indication of this prevailing mode of development.[10]

At its core, the basic needs approach suggested and lobbied for two, interrelated processes. First, a focus on poverty alleviation through directing available state resources to those most in need. Second, the development of new tools to assist the poor to help themselves. Implicit in this approach, and enormously controversial as we shall see below, was the redirection of state help to those *most* in need as opposed to members of middle-class society. Put plainly, the basic needs approach favoured alleviating deep poverty over facilitating socio-economic mobility into or the social reproduction of the effendi middle class. The latter was left to fend for itself via more participation in the free-market economy. For the purpose of alleviating deep poverty, the basic needs approach further called for reform within development economics itself, from centring measurements and policy recommendations on aggregate, national economic growth, to collection and analysis of data related to the poor, and the development of new tools to provide their basic needs.

One motivation behind the basic needs approach – a motivation not readily admitted but clear in its implementation – was an intertwined, worldwide crisis of state management of the economy and state provision of social services. This crisis had become severe under the oil shock of the early 1970s and the following world recession, especially in developing nations. State debt – the result of earlier state-led economic development and a growing state financial commitment to finance welfare projects – and contemporary stagflation that halted economic growth while also bringing price inflation, brought many developing nations to an economic standstill. The basic needs approach offered a tacit solution to the state welfare commitment by offering to redirect dwindling resources to those most in need, while putting the poor to work.

The basic needs approach indirectly underwrote a change from state-led economic development to a market-led economic solution to poverty. In this change the state retrenched state employment and state-owned industries. Importantly, basic needs legitimised state disengagement from the earlier model of import substitute industrialisation (ISI), a central justification of which was to provide (middle-class) citizens/consumers with affordable goods. Instead, the state would attempt to enhance informal, often small and medium enterprises operating in the free market. The state would also refocus state expenditures – shifting them from universal to progressive welfare provision for those most in need – yet again, at the expense of middle-class society.

By the mid-1970s, the ILO was the main facilitator of the basic needs approach, as seen notably in a 1976 international conference on employment and a report on this topic from the same year.[11] Egyptian scholars soon picked up on this new trend in development and adapted it to Egypt. In 1978, Samir Radwan, who also worked at the ILO, copublished an article on how to best to adjust a household survey of basic needs.[12] In 1980–1, he was deputy chief of an ILO mission to Egypt. The mission published a report on employment and equity in Egypt that incorporated basic needs into its analysis. In 1980, Youssef Butrus-Ghali – not to be confused with his uncle Butrus Butrus-Ghali, the future the UN secretary-general – co-authored an article on the macroeconomics of basic needs.[13] Significantly, Youssef Butrus-Ghali and his cowriter at MIT, Lance Taylor, used Egypt to explore the efficacy of this approach. Both Samir Radwan and Youssef Butrus-Ghali, the latter after working for a few years at the IMF, took senior economic positions in Egypt, including as ministers of finance.[14]

The basic needs approach and its successor, the human development approach, defied any attempt to differentiate between global and local expertise. Indeed, both approaches hinted at a shared upper-middle class, glocal perspective in setting a development agenda for Egypt. Moreover, this shared perspective and the development paradigm it put forward were often structurally congruent with early twentieth-century effendi prescriptions for social reform.

Egypt's new social contract, as illustrated in the 1978–82 development plan, carried many of the explicit and implicit attributes of the basic needs approach by putting forward a comprehensive vision of socio-economic reform. Astonishingly, because it was presented only a few months after the 1977 Food Uprising, the plan recommended eliminating both the direct subsidies of food and basic commodities and the indirect subsidies (the latter being indirect subsidies to public sector enterprises, which in turn sold consumer goods below market prices). The plan therefore advocated a remedy similar to the one that Egypt, cajoled by the IMF, had attempted to implement a few months earlier. In return for accepting the elimination of universal subsidies, the plan suggested compensating those most in need through the direct transfer of funds in the form of a wage increase. Those most in need, according to this plan, were living on a fixed, limited income that had eroded under mounting inflation. Such compensation, the plan reasoned, would more closely target the poor – those most in need, as outlined in the plan – than the current system of provision, which targeted, the plan claimed, the 'undeserving few'. Another advantage of folding back the subsidy system was that this would allow public sector enterprises to raise prices of consumer goods, hence improving profitability – a central goal of the Open Door policy.

How much real change in the social contract did the above suggestion bring? From the perspective of an existing, effendi social contract – seemingly, not much. The plan defined those most in need as being both state and public sector employees and those employed in agriculture (small landowners and agricultural workers), as well as private sector workers (who subsisted on close to the minimum wage). How, exactly, those not receiving their wages from the state would receive wage increases was not clear; raising the wages of those most in need targeted state employees alone. This, however, was only to be an interim solution for state employees as well, since their numbers – according to other parts of the plan – were soon to be reduced.

No less significant for the social contract, the 1978–82 development plan outlines two other critical areas of reform – employment and education. According to the new principles put forward by the plan, public employment would be placed under continuous evaluation, achievements rewarded and unsatisfactory performance punished, including through firing state employees.[15] Early retirement would be introduced and encouraged for workers deemed less productive, including those in management, and wage structure would be connected to job productivity. Importantly, tying the wage scale to the level of the certificate of education (legislated in the early 1950s) was to be abolished. The government's commitment to employing all graduates would also be reconsidered in light of contemporary changes in the economy. Through such steps, the plan explains, 'We aim for a system of both short- and long-term policies for absorbing excess employment and for providing real work for the labour force, for the correction of the present situation of massive under-employment in many sectors'.[16] This would also include enforcement of state employment policies. As examples of required enforcement, the plan refers to the case of veterans who refuse to go back to agriculture and 'craft professions', and university students who refused employment in rural areas.

In accordance with the above aims, Egypt's system of education would also be reformed. University enrolment would be limited; vocational training would be developed and promoted; and new technical training centres would also be developed and promoted, their purpose being to 'produce exportable employees for African and Arab Countries'.[17] The plan further explains:

> Reevaluation of present educational policy must be based on the actual needs of society. [Notice the use of society here, not the economy.] The government obligation to employ graduates must be geared to providing real productive work for the graduates and seeing that the universities train graduates for specific societal functions, instead of serving the social prestige goals for which so many students now desire university degrees.[18]

In the above quotation, the main articles of the effendi social contract were to be significantly curtailed. Higher education as a central venue for socio-economic mobility into the middle class was to be limited and state employment downsized and 'rationalised' – the latter, in practice, meant a greater squeeze on employees.

The plan does not shy away from making recommendations for a reform of what it terms 'political affairs':

1) The reintroduction of political parties must be followed by the stabilisation of their function, and a clear sense of their respective roles in the working of the government. At present there is a disjuncture, as each group seeks to achieve its own limited ends.
2) Political organisation should not be based on obligations and personal preferment, but on national goals; electoral support should be rallied behind clearly defined objectives.

3) A deeply entrenched characteristic of our political organisations has been the gap between their performance and their slogans. Because of this hypocrisy, the public has had a long-standing distrust of political organisations.
4) Our parties need to articulate their ideological stands clearly. We can learn from previous experience the consequences of not doing so.[19]

Despite the rather convoluted language used, the overall message here is quite clear. The plan suggested partial democratisation in exchange for curtailing central economic articles of the existing social contract. Such an exchange was not to be abused: the opposition was to be loyal, support national goals and work with the government to achieve them. It also meant that the opposition should enhance the existing political system, as opposed to fomenting distrust in the system. Greater political say would come with the responsibility to avoid rocking the political boat. In short, political participation was to underwrite the economic reform twice: first, as a form of currency – less state provision in exchange for more political say – and second, through assigning political agency (responsibility) for the success or failure of the reform to citizens and their responsible conduct.

The plan recommends that the new social contract be published and negotiated publicly – to avoid being perceived as a top-down dictate, as had happened a few months earlier during the Food Uprising. The new economic social contract was further to be openly debated in the People's Assembly.[20] Nevertheless, and as suggested in the quotations regarding political reform above, this public negotiation and debate was to take place in a rather confined manner in which actual public participation would be severely restricted. The introduction of the new social contract – seemingly an agreement between citizens, and between citizens and the state – was still very much by government dictate.

The 1978–82 development plan outlines the main features of a new social contract that scholars and planners would reiterate for years to come. At the core of the new social contract was a dual effort. First, it was an attempt to move away from the past social contract with the educated and state-employed middle class – historically, the effendi middle class, and now often the much larger and nearing poverty lower-middle class. Second, it indicated a return to a past mode of productivist welfare in which the state supports those most in need during a period of structural change, particularly through vocational training or retraining. Social justice, as defined by the earlier, effendi social contract, was to be significantly retracted because past socio-economic mobility into the middle class and its reproduction through higher education and state employment would now be conditioned upon productivity. If anything, 'real productive work for graduates', as recommended by the plan, no doubt meant their proletarianisation, either through migration of graduates to labour in the private sector or a greater squeeze on their labour in state employment. This attempt to restrict state-sponsored mobility into the effendi middle class was, therefore, to reverse the past trend of channelling into this stratum based on the old social contract. What was left of the latter now became a state obligation toward a moral economy, supporting those who failed to achieve socio-economic mobility, especially through productivist welfare for those most in need. In short, with little real participation in decision making, the new social contract meant that large tracts of society were to give up on the still extant, if eroded, state provision of socio-economic benefits in return for promised (but yet to be delivered) better jobs and a rosier economic future for Egypt.

In September 1981, Khalid Ikram published an article on the 1978–82 development plan in the joint IMF-World Bank organ, *Finance and Development*, titled 'Meeting the Social Contract in Egypt'.[21] The abstract of this article states:

> Egypt has combined a strategy to stimulate the private sector to spearhead growth and a determination to direct resources to meet the needs of the most deprived. This dual approach, balancing private enterprise and public involvement, may have implications for many mixed economies.

As suggested in this abstract, Egypt was at the forefront of a global shift in development with this combination of economic liberalisation and redirection of available state resources to the poor. As outlined below, the plan was more of an intellectual exercise involving putting forth new ideas. It would never be fully executed and indeed was soon replaced by an extended, new development plan for the years 1980–4. Nevertheless, abolishing the subsidy system and reforming education and state employment became a long-term prescribed planning strategy in an attempt to cut down state expenditures, along with liberalising the economy by shifting the balance in economic growth from the public to the private sector.

In July 1979, the director general of the ILO visited Egypt. Invited by Egypt's prime minister and supported by President Sadat, the ILO sent a mission to Egypt the following year to produce a report on the future of employment in the country.[22] As was frequently the case, this report, part of the global ILO agenda, was the eighth in a series of such ILO reports, with Egypt standing at the vanguard of innovation in the field of economic development.[23] In 1980–1, economists Bent Hansen and Samir Radwan, the ILO's chief and deputy chief respectively, headed a mission to Egypt that produced a report titled *Employment Opportunities and Equity in a Changing Economy: Egypt in the 1980s*.[24] Hansen and Radwan were anything but strangers to Egypt. Hansen was the most senior international economist working on Egypt and was married to an Egyptian, while Radwan was a foreign-educated Egyptian economist.[25] The mission's work relied heavily on preparatory work undertaken in various Egyptian ministries, and was based on background papers by Egyptian economists employed by the state.[26] Among these economists, Osman Mohamed Osman and Heba Handoussa are names worth noting for their role in a future ILO report (Handoussa) and, more so, in the UNDP's Egypt Human Development Report (EHDR) project. The ILO's initiative of sending missions to study employment conditions in developing economies was, in itself, the result of cooperation between the UNDP and the ILO.

Like the national 1978–82 development plan, the official aim of the *Employment Opportunities* report was to facilitate a planning process in Egypt that would allow it to better develop its labour market. While the report offered a labour market approach to macroeconomic reform in Egypt, the welfare aspect of the reform was redirected toward those most in need, as in the plan.[27] The authors of the mission's report pointed out many of the employment imbalances in the labour market – from overstaffing in state employment to the scarcity of well-trained, blue-collar workers in the economy, to underemployment in agriculture, to the potential hardships associated with the large-scale return of labour migrants from oil producing states. All these areas needed reform and overhauling to increase efficiency and generate more income for employees. Nevertheless, the authors also invariably emphasised that the main concern of their recommendations was to improve income redistribution and the satisfaction of basic needs for those most in need. This no-doubt worthy cause meant, significantly, a less-acknowledged redirection of Egypt's employment policy, from one centring on the increasingly struggling, state-employed middle class to one centring on the poor, again in line with the plan.

According to the *Employment Opportunities* report, the payment scale for state employment should be more closely tailored to productivity. A hiring freeze was recommended for lower-level state employees. 'Natural attrition would then slowly reduce the overstaffing without creating insurmountable social problems' – a clear sign that the authors of the report were aware of the political risk that such a recommendation would entail.[28] After 1978, the public sector was placed outside the guaranteed employment scheme. Alongside the trimming of state employment, private sector initiatives were to be encouraged, ostensibly to absorb such employees into this sector. In urban regions, a reformed taxation system would combat tax evasion, and the system was to be more redistributive, or progressive, as were state provision of services and subsidies.[29] Both steps would redirect resources to the poor, who often worked in the informal economy.

Because of the close connection between education and employment opportunities, the mission investigated and made specific recommendations regarding the future development of Egypt's system of education. The mission kept these recommendations in line with the above shift from the state-employed middle class to the poor employed in the informal economy. It strongly recommended that vocational training and education should be dedicated to preparing the latter for more productive employment in agriculture and export-led manufacturing. Notably, the mission supported an overhauling of Egypt's basic education system, aimed at all children aged six to fifteen.[30] The university system that channelled middle-class students to state employment, 'should not be expanded further in quantitative terms'.[31] To conclude, the ILO mission reiterated the main recommendations of the development plan.

In 1988, barely seven years after the ILO mission published its report, the Egyptian government invited another, rather similar ILO intervention in the form of a conference in Cairo titled 'Employment Strategy:

Egypt in the 1990s'. The outcome of this conference was later published in an American University in Cairo (AUC) edited volume: *Employment and Structural Adjustment: Egypt in the 1990s*.[32] While the ILO's earlier report attempted to gauge the employment challenges ahead, this conference outlined transitions that were urgently required in the job market to allow for broader economic reform and structural adjustment in the aftermath of the oil-boom. However, the volume's recommendations were rather similar to those of the earlier mission and the development plan.

In the introduction to the AUC volume, the editor, Heba Handoussa, who had earlier also contributed to the mission's report, suggested that if the employment programme were to succeed, it would require boosting the employment productivity of those employed with the state and the public sector.[33] Here too, productivity spelled a squeeze on public sector employment that would no doubt limit future participation in the public sector and push labour to search for private employment. White-collar state employees faced an even grimmer future of being proletarianised, because the programme for employment reform made no real alternative provisions for these employees. The suggestion that white-collar state employees should shift to blue-collar labour was not explicitly expressed in Handoussa's introduction, but it was amply made in the text. To the extent that Handoussa represented a class perspective on structural adjustment in employment, this perspective was an upper-middle-class call to downsize the state-employed middle class, and an attempt to bring it to its past, seemingly more manageable, proportion.

In the introduction Handoussa (rightly) argues that contemporary state employment 'can best be characterized as an extension of its [the government's] subsidy system'.[34] Indeed, by then, state employment was fully part of the state's moral economy, which the old social contract underwrote. Overall employment reform would, in the long run, improve compensation for state employees, the low rate of which was a long-standing complaint in Egyptian public discourse. However, this change would significantly reduce employment with the state. The reduction would be achieved through attrition, early retirement and retraining, as well as by creating new jobs in the private formal and informal economies. Neither the type of retraining nor the kind of employment opportunities awaiting state employees in the private sector were specified.

Also mentioned in the introduction, and similar to the recommendations of the ILO mission's report and the development plan, was that for the employment reform to succeed it was necessary to shift away from secondary school and university education, 'in order to reduce the problem of open and disguised unemployment among holders of diplomas and university degrees, and to help the government to phase out its guaranteed employment scheme with the minimum of social instability'.[35] Instead, the state should promote technical education and training.

Although seemingly outside the jurisdiction of an economist, Handoussa made a remarkable observation regarding the successful implementation of the revolutionary change embedded in employment scheme above:

> There is an important role to be played by the mass media and the educational system towards the changing of attitudes and aspirations. The value attached to private initiative and self-employment must be enhanced, and a national consensus reached on the need to bear collectively the burden of transition to an economy where productivity with equity is the basis for growth and welfare.
>
> The concept of equity itself must be reformulated to mean explicit transfers by the government to the most vulnerable groups in society, rather than the indiscriminate distribution of subsidies which characterises the system today. The government's role as paternalistic provider must also, of necessity, change to become that of a regulator and an arbitrator in the shared task of national reform and regeneration.[36]

In the quotation above, Handoussa summarises all the basic tenets of the new social contract for Egypt, which she, as the coordinator of the Egypt Human Development Report project during the 2000s, would later help to formalise.

In 1991, the same year in which *Employment and Structural Adjustment* was published, the World Bank published a report titled *Egypt: Alleviating Poverty during Structural Adjustment*.[37] This report was a part of a broader World Development Report that focused on poverty that year,[38] and it was a lively testimony to the diffusion of fashions in economic development across international institutions. Importantly, the report was published during the year in which Egypt signed a new economic reform and structural adjustment (ERSA) programme with IFIs. While written by World Bank staff, this report was heavily based on data provided by Egyptian ministries and the Central Agency for Public Mobilization and Statistics (CAPMAS). With the exception of the fourth, practical recommendation, the report's principle recommendations for 'a comprehensive Alleviation Strategy' were by now quite familiar:

- structural measures to increase income-earning opportunities for the poor through improved access to productive employment and assets;
- structural measures to improve the equity and cost-effectiveness of public expenditures in health and education to increase opportunities for human capital formation for the poor;
- structural measures to achieve a more equitable and efficient targeting of all secondary income transfers, including consumer subsidies, producer subsidies and direct welfare transfers; and
- an Emergency Social Fund to protect the low-income population groups directly affected during implementation of macroeconomic reforms.[39]

The first three recommendations testify to important required policy changes: The state should focus more closely on facilitating income-earning opportunities for the poor (first recommendation), which corresponded closely with the change in the state's focus on employment in small and medium enterprises and in construction suggested by Handoussa above. Accordingly, the state should promote opportunities for self-help among the poor (second recommendation). State provision of social services should strive to do more with existing (or reduced) public expenditures; to improve equity in the provision of these services would therefore mean that a larger share of funds for health and education should be diverted to the poor, rather than to the middle class. Complementing the second recommendation, state direct and indirect transfers should refocus on the poor (third recommendation). Here and elsewhere in the discussion on alleviating poverty in Egypt, who the poor or those most in need actually were was never clearly defined, and whether they were the absolute poor or lower-middle state employees remained ambiguous. This ambiguity enabled the state to direct welfare resources more toward the latter than the former. Of the recommendations above, only the fourth recommendation was immediately directed at alleviating the poverty that was to increase during the structural adjustment, as opposed to being part of the structural adjustment itself. The Social Fund was to cushion the poor during this period of change. Unsurprisingly, it was this recommendation that was the first priority of the Egyptian government.

In the World Bank report, financial unsustainability and the persistence of poverty required the government to move toward selective targeting of state provision, instead of having general equal opportunity policies for all Egyptians.[40] This, in turn, meant significant cuts in universal subsidies, in free access to health and education and in the guarantee of government employment and an egalitarian (as opposed to differential) salary scale. While the four recommendations above promised more to the poor, the resources required for better social services and larger transfers to that group would have to be acquired by diverting state resources from the middle class to the poor – the latter to be joined by the lower echelons of the former – in a period of intensifying constraints on state resources.

Between 1994 and 2010, the EHDR – a project led by Egyptian experts and financed by an international development institution – set an agenda for socio-economic development under financial constraints, with an eye toward the new opportunities that would emanate from economic reform and structural adjustment. The EHDR, part of a wider UNDP Human Development Project, became the flagship of planning in Egypt.[41] Cooperating with this project, Egypt's Institute of National Planning (INP) supervised the research, analysis and writing of the reports, which were conducted by top-ranking Egyptian scholars working under the auspices of the INP. This made it a close collaboration between the Egyptian state and Egypt's academic elite, in that the demarcation line between the two (state officials and independent academics) was not always clear. Thus, Osman Mohamed Osman, who was involved with the EHDR from its inception – first as project coordinator, and later as the head of the project – would later be appointed minister for economic development and the INP's chairman of the board. (One can observe here a similar career track to that of Abdel Razzak Abdel Meguid, who was originally the driving force behind the 1978–82 development plan and was appointed to the position of minister of planning. This path from working in development to a government position was a common feature in Egyptian politics.) EHDR researchers further enlisted the help of state ministries in the collection of data and evidence, and consulted state officials on how to implement the report's recommendations.

Starting in 1990, the UNDP began publishing annual reports on how to measure, evaluate and improve human development.[42] Inspired by a new voice in economic analysis, the purpose of the Human Development Report (HDR) was 'expanding the richness of human life, rather than simply the richness of the economy in which human beings live. It is an approach that is focused on people and their opportunities and choices'.[43] This approach, most closely associated with Nobel laureate Amartya Sen's work, was further developed and institutionalised through the work of UNDP economist Mahbub ul Haq.[44] It was operationalised into a series of world and country-specific reports on human needs such as food, shelter and health. Reports also focused on gender, education, employment and environmental issues. They emphasised voting and participation in communal, economic and political life as social and political enablers – all allowing people to improve their socio-economic capabilities.

The *EHDR 1994*, one of the first national reports (only four other countries published such national reports during that year), adapted the HDR to Egyptian contexts. The abstract of the 1994 report states: 'The report focused on introducing the concept and measurements [of the HDR] in addition to an assessment of the status of human development in Egypt'. Moreover, 'it gave some guidelines on how the concept of HD [human development] can be operationalised in Egypt'. In line with the HDR, 'the Report linked the human development approach to other development strategies. It noted that the concept advocates a new way of thinking, with a development strategy that is more comprehensive and more humanitarian than ever before'.[45] This new way of thinking was not that far from the old.

Since their initiation, the EHDRs have closely echoed the HDR project – from an attempt to develop new measurement tools associated with the HDRs' Human Development Index (HDI), to thematically following the UN's agendas of development. Yet, an examination of the EHDRs in terms of their institutional context and their content reveals much continuity with earlier planning initiatives, including the re-emergence of the new social contract as the focal point of Egypt's planning for socio-economic development. Hailed as the new development panacea, the EHDR in fact included many of the earlier existing glocal calls for socio-economic reform. As in the past, the new social contract that the EHDR came to advocate was the result of a planning dictate, as opposed to a negotiated agreement between citizens or between citizens and the state. This happened despite the report's frequent preaching in favour of freedom and citizen participation. It was also a project guided by an upper-middle-class intellectual elite that joined the state in search of remedies for the unsustainable growth of middle-class society, in an attempt to contain it.

As suggested by the earlier analysis of planning initiatives before the EHDR, the institutional setting of the EHDR was not entirely new. However, previous institutional collaborations were often in the form of ad hoc missions and reports. Despite the self-congratulations of the HDR officials and the Egyptian scholars in charge of the EHDR regarding the report's novelty (and that of the HDR project as a whole), it did not simply constitute an entirely new introduction of the human development approach to Egypt.[46] The following analysis also suggests a great deal of continuity between the EHDR and past planning of broad socio-economic and political transformations, including a central thrust to partly dissolve Egypt's bloated effendi middle class.

While the EHDRs emphasised putting a human face on economic development, economic development through economic neoliberalisation was central to the reports, as was the case with earlier development schemes. In the words of the *EHDR 1995*, a main thrust of the EHDR was 'adjusting adjustment programs', or in other words integrating human development more closely with economic reform.[47] Significantly, the measures put forward in the EHDRs, while often trumpeting the cause of human development, saw economic growth as central to the endeavour. As the *EHDR 1996* suggests, 'economic growth would enlarge the opportunities for the poor to enjoy the benefits of increases in output. Hence, the report concludes, poverty reduction requires enhanced growth'. Put simply, despite an attempt to soften the ERSA programme, the report argues that Egypt could not do without economic reform and structural adjustment. Economic choice and participation of the poor were closely tied to tenets of neoliberal economic change, which anticipated the trickling down of wealth in a process of macroeconomic growth.

In the EHDRs, as with earlier planning schemes, alleviating poverty took centre stage and was to take place mostly by raising the 'capability' of the poor to engage in self-help. 'Capability' was the contemporary buzzword then used to describe multiple improvements in education and vocational training (human capital), in access to markets through loans to SMEs and reduction of state red tape (facilitating private sector initiatives), and through state decentralisation of service provision and focus on the poor and deprived regions of Egypt. These measures, taken to increase the capability of the poor to help themselves, were often associated in the EHDR with 'participatory development', particularly after the *EHDR 2003*.[48]

The *EHDR 1997* suggests increasing efficiency in state mechanisms for helping the poor, but also better targeting of public spending toward poverty alleviation. The call for emphasis on self-help carried the underlying assumption that through such measures the state would be able to reduce the scope of services – from assisting all of society to helping only the poor. As in the past, measures to increase capability among the poor implicitly and, more rarely, explicitly, involved dedicating a larger share of state expenditures to those most in need. Moreover, helping the poor to help themselves through market initiatives, as opposed to via direct state support, allowed state financial retrenchment to take place. State efficiency meant smaller government, and hence a reduction in state employment. Overall, the focus on poverty alleviation was tantamount to a significant change in state redistribution and an at least partial state retreat from its earlier, comprehensive commitment to all its citizens, particularly to the effendi middle class.

The *EHDR 1998/99* cautiously discusses educational reform in Egypt. The report suggests the important role of education in both developing human capital and redistributing wealth through facilitating socio-economic mobility. In doing so, it treads between the economic benefits of higher education for the middle class and the broad Egyptian consensus over it, and a human development logic of poverty alleviation for the lower class through expanding elementary and vocational education. The report therefore refined but did not retract earlier suggestions to reform Egypt's system of education through a shift in the balance between the two.

While 'participation' as a theme in the EHDR had been present since the early reports, it came to the forefront of the EHDR project after the

2003 report. Heba Handoussa, who headed the EHDR team, writes in the 'Preamble' of the *EHDR 2003*:

> The previous six Egyptian (NHDR's) tackled the basic human development approach, concepts, and strategies, in addition to thematic issues like poverty, social spending, and education. The present report focuses on participation. It pays great attention to the relationship between participation and human development with special emphasis on grassroots participation and its role in local development.[49]

From the perspective of the analysis here, the call for participation singled out the return of the new social contract to centre stage. In the *EHDR 2005*, titled *Choosing Our Future: Towards a New Social Contract*, this notion fully re-emerged.

In the EHDRs and, more broadly, the HDR project, what connected capability (alleviating poverty) and political participation was the neoliberal notion of 'choice'. In this context choice was constructed from above: the citizenry is allowed to choose between options allotted by the EHDR and sanctioned by the regime. Furthermore, this choice was to quickly become the duty of citizens, under a national effort at socio-economic reform. For alleviating poverty, choice meant that the poor could better help themselves, but only if allowed to do so by an increase in state options for self-improvement through education and other state redistributive means. In economic terms choice was synonymous with free-market initiatives, which would facilitate socio-economic mobility among those most in need, as well as in the rest of society. Choice in politics was to be the result of citizens' participation through a more transparent system of governance in Egypt, and citizens having a larger say in the daily management of state affairs, or decentralisation. In both instances, choice emphasised Egyptians' rights in the economy and, more implicitly, in politics (in choosing between various policy options). Nevertheless, such rights could be easily turned on their heads to become citizens' duties, as would be in the *EHDR 2005*.

The *EHDR 2005* was the culmination of previous reports in its attempt to synthesise past research and policy recommendations into a broad scheme. In the words of the report, 'What is proposed is a complete departure from a "business as usual scenario" to embark on a comprehensive assault on each and every problem facing Egyptian society'.[50] In line with past reports, the new social contract in the *EHDR 2005* focused on the poor. However, it offered other social groups venues for participation:

> The EHDR 2005 defines the social contract as an integrated rights-based program of action that is tailored and targeted to the poor but which provides choices and alternatives for other citizens so as to enable all Egyptians to raise their capabilities to realize the ambitions that they value.[51]

The emphasis on 'all Egyptians' here clearly shows an emerging awareness by the EHDR of the need to draw in support for human and economic reform from a larger constituency of middle-class Egyptians. In putting forward a call for a new social contract, as opposed to an improved plan for socio-economic development, the *EHDR 2005* also had to account for the politics of its implementation. As the following quotation taken from the report's 'A Vision for Egypt' suggests, 'What is projected is to reinvigorate the legitimacy of the political regime by reforming the principles of entry and participation in national life'.[52]

Crucially, in the report political rights are mostly discussed as economic rights under the neoliberal assumption that economic participation would 'reinvigorate the legitimacy of the political regime', which was anything but democratic. In such a state of affairs, as in past planning, it was for the government to implement the new social contract from the top downward, including through bestowing economic, if not political (democratic), participation on its citizens. Embedded here is the assumption that a fundamental of democratic choice — the possibility of change in government — would, as a result, be excluded from the future realm of possibility.

Despite a growing call for democratisation in the EHDRs, this new social contract promised economic neoliberalisation partly detached from political freedom. While 'democracy' appears in places throughout the texts, I maintain that it is mostly used in the sense that participation would lead to social and economic development, as opposed to a more concrete, political demand for democratisation as political participation. Indeed, political participation was the proverbial elephant in the room — while mentioned, its practicalities were never discussed in earnest. Such participation implied that citizens would share in the political decision making through consultation, but with little say in the overall implementation of the new social contract. Such participation was to assign responsibility (or duties) for the successful implementation of the social contract to society, but with little in terms of a shift of power between the state and its citizenry (or political rights) in the new social contract.

A central paradox in the *EHDR 2005* call for a new social contract is that this call was based on an unexplained mandate from all Egyptians. Rather than an agreement between citizens and the state, the report recommends venues for the state to instil in Egyptians 'values of participation, entrepreneurship, innovation and transparency', which would seem invaluable for the success of economic reform. Hence, according to the report, the Egyptian citizenry was simultaneously the agent pushing for change, and in need of state guidance to participate in it.

Established in 2008, and as per recommendations made in the *EHDR 2005*, the Social Contract Advisory, Monitoring and Coordination Centre was a joint project between the Egyptian government and the UNDP. The top-down tone and practice unfolds throughout the project's discussion:

> Egyptian society needs to have a common vision of reform and the state needs to use all possible venues to disseminate and engage the public in articulating this common vision, while at the same time, defining the roles and responsibilities of each partner. In other words, there is a need to first create a demand for reform (social advertising), based on the social contract, and then a need for a strategy of implementation.[53]

In the project's description above, the central agency of the state in implementing the social contract is abundantly clear. While the new social contract was a common vision, it was the state's role to engage the public in articulating this common vision, including in defining the rights and mainly the duties of both parties. Nevertheless, the state also had to be persuaded to push for reform. The Social Contract Advisory Centre tied the knot between citizens and the state in formulating a new social contract for Egypt.

The call made by the *EHDR 2005* and later EHDRs to end business as usual and enact a new social contract clearly walked a thin line between opting for more political participation and political stability. It is important to remember that the EHDRs were executed by the state itself, and they therefore reflected an internal state exchange. In the 'Preface' to the *EHDR 2005*, Osman Mohamed Osman, Egypt's minister for economic development and chairman of the board of the Institute of National Planning, writes: 'This report is therefore in harmony with government plans for the future of Egypt'.[54] Osman was intimating that the new social contract was in accordance with a state-driven thrust for change, but he was also implicitly (or unconsciously) referring to the political realm of possibility for such change, which, for obvious reasons, the authoritarian regime regarded as limited. The EHDRs no doubt reflected an internal debate within the state itself as to how far political reform should be taken.

The *EHDR 2008, Egypt's Social Contract: The Role of Civil Society*, paid further attention to political change through a call for a partial reversal of state–civil society relations. The state, now characterised as 'the old authoritarian and bureaucratic command regime', was to loosen its hold on civil society and allow it to flourish. This was not an easy process for the state. As the report says, 'the EHDR 2008 consistently draws attention to [the] fact that it is no simple matter for government to allow civil society to "take off" after a 50 year freeze, particularly given its national security concerns in these turbulent times'.[55] Nevertheless, the logic behind such a risky state action was that this transformation would benefit both the state and society under the new conditions of economic neoliberalisation, and therefore it had to happen.

Chapter One of the 2008 report explains that civil society organisations are vital partners in both the new social contract and in revitalising social solidarity in Egypt. This was no doubt in direct reference to a major state political concern that such organisations would challenge official state power. Here, the report sent a clear message that a call for more participation of civil society organisations in public life was to enhance rather than worsen the political status quo. It explains that the 'EHDR 2008 opens up a new vista for CSO [civil society organisation] engagement in national development. Its thrust is on the positive concepts and values found in Egypt's popular heritage regarding social solidarity'.[56] 'Positive concepts and values' here clearly indicates the non-oppositional stands of such organisations, as did the CSOs' commitment to social solidarity. According to the new social contract, while the old authoritarian and bureaucratic command regime would be loosened, CSOs were to loyally carry out their socio-economic role in development, with little say in politics.

The Social Contract Advisory, Monitoring and Coordination Centre mandate regarding how to promote citizens' and civil society organisations' participation emphasised an effort to facilitate closer cooperation of both with the state. Thus, regarding citizens, 'the Centre will help articulate a more engaging relationship between the state and the citizen ensuring better delivery of services and more engagement and participation from the citizen'. Regarding civil society organisations: 'The Centre will cooperate with CSOs/NGOs to ensure their active participation and engagement in the dialogue and monitoring of the social contract'.[57] As the Centre's mandate suggests, 'the task to reform is no longer a sole task for the government, but rather a shared task between government, the private sector, civil society and citizens'.[58] However, it is hard to see how this 'shared task' was to be accommodated within this overall state initiative, especially because many of those CSOs/NGOs were critical of the government and often supported the Islamic opposition, which was closely associated with the Muslim Brotherhood.

In the Preface to the *EHDR 2010 – Youth in Egypt: Building our Future –* Osman's message was even bolder:

> This report suggests that to complement such enabling conditions [for the youth], a number of prerequisite[s] must be addressed. Egypt's record of democracy and respect for human rights must match internationally accepted standards, corruption and deteriorating individual and community values must continue to be attended to, and religious intolerance eradicated. These are concerns that have been frequently articulated by young people in this report.[59]

In the statement above, the call to eliminate corruption, uphold human rights and augment democracy was among the demands that soon surfaced in Tahrir Square. This suggestion was now backed by 'internationally accepted standards', implicitly those set by the HDR. Significantly, the eradication of religious intolerance, ostensibly from the Islamic opposition, was supposed to balance greater political participation and reform in government services with political stability.

Despite the passage of time, changes in terminology and occasional changes in emphasis on various development goals, it is hard not to see similarities between the EHDR call for a new social contract, and that of the 1978–82 development plan. This is true of the overall economic reforms and structural adjustments suggested, as well as of the kind of politics called upon for the contracts' implementation.

The *EHDR 2005*'s plea for comprehensive planning to allow a complete departure from a 'business as usual scenario' was quite similar to an earlier call for action in the development plan:

> We have not considered it acceptable to use a national plan to build new structures on shaking foundations, adding more projects and investments to an unstable economy. Mere sincerity will not substitute for the serious attention which must be given to the existing social and economic problems which are felt today by every Egyptian, whatever his socio-economic level.[60]

Both the *EHDR 2005* and the 1978–82 development plan present a critical analysis of the contemporary situation and recognise the urgent need for comprehensive rather than piecemeal socio-economic change to solve Egyptian society's problems.

At the core of the comprehensive change embodied in the new social contract, both the EHDR and the development plan advocated the neoliberalisation of the economy. This included a greater role for a market-led as opposed to a state-led economy. Moreover, and of central importance, the new social contract included retrenchment in both state services and employment for all – notably for the effendi middle class – and the redirecting of state resources to the productivist welfare for those most in need. The EHDR and the plan supported citizen participation in public decision making and therefore also some decentralisation of the state's power. In both instances, however, democracy was circumscribed. It was supposed to enhance the economic reform and structural adjustment plans – not resist them – in order to facilitate social solidarity in a period of change. In a rather paradoxical fashion, this suggested top-down democratisation was meant to strengthen the current authoritarian regime rather than challenge it.

Both the plan and the EHDR project were recommendations for state action in which planners had to convince decision makers of the viability – economic, but also political – of the suggested reforms. Despite a semblance of citizen participation, choice and democracy, planners had to promote their envisioned comprehensive change in order to convince the public to accept it. Importantly, the call for a new social contract in the plan and the EHDR came during periods of rising social tension over the implementation of the old social contract – the plan in the aftermath of the Food Uprising, and the EHDR in a period of mounting dissatisfaction with the state that would lead to the January 2011 revolution. Hence, the planners' call for a new social contract was a clear indication of exacerbation over the insurmountable hardships of its implementation.

Planning as its own goal

In an article published in 1991, Alan Richards, a keen observer of Egypt's political economy, raised a well-known conundrum. Richards suggested that

> the government of Egypt . . . displayed a stubborn refusal to implement the kind of sweeping economic changes which most foreign and Egyptian economists believe are necessary to generate jobs and an acceptable standard of living for the rapidly growing population.[61]

Indeed, for more than three decades, there had been a planning consensus regarding the need for and the contours of a new social contract, but with little overall change in Egypt's political economy to facilitate it. Instead, new socio-economic policy and political reforms that would advance a new social contract in Egypt were postponed, diluted or layered side by side with the existing social contract, as detailed in Chapter Seven. It is therefore worth asking why – despite this broad consensus on what should be done, and the narrow success in implementing the planned reforms – planning itself did not dwindle.

To answer this question, we need to change our focus from planning outcomes and their evaluation to analysis of the planning process itself. In particular, who benefited from this planning process, how and in what ways? The discussion below uses the notion of 'rent' to answer these questions. Rent here stands for the creation of value – economic, social and political – through the process of planning. In this process, development plans acquired an intrinsic value, beyond the economic, social, and political value that their implementation was supposed to generate. Put differently, planning, rather than being a means to achieve a goal, became a goal in and of itself because it benefited the planners and the Egyptian state, with less attention being paid to achieved outcomes.

Since the 1970s, planning had been central to Egyptian negotiations for grants and loans with IFIs such as the IMF and the World Bank, as well as with international lenders and governments. Money obtained from IFIs was cheaper than borrowing on the free market, and Egypt also needed the IFIs' support to obtain better international credit, thereby reducing its expenditures when taking loans. The ability to present economic plans boosted Egypt's credentials as striving for economic reform and structural adjustment, often a prerequisite for financial support. IFIs, for their part, were happy to assist, on the condition that Egypt showed some readiness to push forward with their own (the IFIs') agenda for economic progress. Western governments were only too happy to take Egyptian planning as a sign of the country's moving toward the West, and later, of the Egyptian government's taking steps to stabilise the economy and through that, its politics. All sides involved were no less interested in the planning than in the actual implementation of the ERSA programme that it recommended.

In a rather paradoxical fashion, if economic planning in Egypt had worked, the role of local planners, IFIs and international development organisations would have been dissolved because said planning would have solved Egypt's economic hardships. Moreover, so would the leverage that Western governments had over the Egyptian government, and the latter's ability to exploit reform money to boost its own stability. None of the sides involved had any real interest in bringing about the prescribed change. Instead, Egypt's internationally recognised development plans created a façade of change that suited all sides, with relatively little actual change on the ground. ('Little' here refers to the considerable gaps between what these plans set out to do and what they actually achieved.) Instead of overcoming 'business as usual' in fixing the economy, society and politics, planning for reform had clearly become routinised or had itself turned into business as usual.

The timing of the publication of the various planning reports frequently suited the ad hoc needs of the Egyptian government in preparing for a new round of negotiations with IFIs and international lenders. Thus, the 1978–82 development plan was published just before Egypt entered a new round of talks with the IMF.[62] Moreover, one of the plan's recommendations, to establish a new industrial bank, supported Egypt's negotiations with the World Bank regarding the allocation of funds for that purpose.[63] In the 1991 World Bank report, a central recommendation for alleviating poverty in Egypt, one most coveted by the Egyptian government, was to establish an Emergency Social Fund 'to protect the low-income population groups directly affected during implementation of macroeconomic reforms'.[64] That same year, the Social Fund for Development (SFD) was established, clearly because of the World Bank's above recommendation, and it began operations in 1993.[65]

The EHDRs, ostensibly aiming to implement global best practices, went down well with international donors, lenders and foreign governments. Accordingly, the reports indirectly enhanced the Egyptian claim for financial assistance. Indeed, such a claim received significant support from a UNDP initiative meant to engage governments of developing states and donors in a '20:20' pledge, according to which local governments would invest 20 per cent of their national budgets in human development, and international donors would contribute 20 per cent of their aid budgets to human development. This initiative no doubt boosted political interest in the HDR project in Egypt; according the *EHDR 1995*, the 20:20 pledge would add a yearly sum of 300–400 million USD to Egypt's expenditures on human development.[66] While financial assistance during structural adjustments and various development projects was officially meant to promote economic reform in Egypt, further analysis suggests that these funds indeed supported those in alliance with the government no less than the process of change, as is expanded upon further in Chapter Seven.

Less discussed above but no less significant, planning and money allocated to various reform and adjustment projects was significant in terms of support for the operations of various Egyptian ministries, and a source of competition within the government of Egypt. Egypt's ministry of planning – once at the core of the state's command economy – was able to reinvent itself and benefit from leading the ERSA programme, that is, from reversing processes such as economic centralisation, which it had once been instrumental in propagating. From a political perspective, the announcement of new national planning initiatives also served as a way to publicly assess their political feasibility, based on the strength of public support for or opposition to them.

IFIs, international development institutions and foreign governments each had their own active interests that fueled the planning industry. The IMF and the World Bank had somewhat different agendas with regard to development, and occasional differences of opinion regarding priorities in bringing about economic reform and structural adjustment – the former was more preoccupied with overall national financial solvency, and the latter with financing projects that would facilitate the process. Still, and at the risk of stating the obvious, both of these Bretton Woods institutions had a keen interest in engaging with Egypt to push forward a global transformation based on a free-market economy. USAID was similarly ready to plan and implement ERSA programs that would enhance US policy in Egypt and, more broadly, the region. The actual implementation of economic reform was less significant than political stability. US development money and the government behind it (or other Western governments for that matter) would accept less economic reform in return for political stability, a fact of which the Egyptian government was all too aware. As suggested above, both the ILO, in its new initiative to promote planning based on basic needs, and the UNDP's EHDR project, which reasserted human development planning, readily found a partner in Egypt, as well as a field in which to conduct case-study-based research.

Egypt has had a long-standing tradition of obtaining expertise abroad, mainly from Western countries and through studies conducted by Western universities. This was true even during the heyday of Arab (and Egyptian) nationalism and under the economic regime of Arab socialism. In Egypt during the 1970s and afterward, high state officials, particularly ministers responsible for the Egyptian economy, invariably carried the pedigree of foreign education, most notably a PhD from abroad. Many had also accepted employment with foreign universities, and especially with the same IFIs with which Egypt often negotiated. Such experts (technocrats) – members of a global, upper-middle class – held lucrative positions in the bureaucracy and government, based on the professional knowledge they brought back to Egypt. Nevertheless, their expertise in the professional language of world institutions of development, as well as the international social capital they brought with them to their new positions, was no less important here. Egypt could not find better negotiators for reform in return for global financial aid. Elsewhere, I have studied the roll that glocal business mediators have played, since the 1970s, in reconnecting Egypt to the global economy, benefiting their own enterprises in the process.[67] As discussed throughout this chapter, one is tempted to assign a similar institutional function to economic experts turned state officials. This is not to imply that such experts put personal before national considerations, but to suggest that such engagement with global institutions, and with an Egyptian government keen on acquiring development money, carried its own reward.

Notes

1. Wizarat al-Shu'un al-Ijtima'iyya wa-l-'Amal, *al-Dustur al-Ijtima'i*.
2. 'Table of Contents', ibid.
3. Based on a keyword search in the compilation of Nasser's speeches in *ALMANHAL*.
4. Google Books Ngram Viewer, accessed 29 APril 2020, https://books.google.com/ngrams/graph?content=%22social+contract%22&year_start=1900&year_end=2008&corpus=15&smoothing=5&share=&direct_url=t1%3B%2C%22%20social%20contract%20%22%3B%2Cc0.
5. Ministry of Planning, Egypt, *The General Strategy for Economic and Social Development*, vol. 1 of *The Five-year Plan, 1978–1982* (Cairo, 1977).
6. Khalid Ikram, *The Political Economy of Reforms in Egypt: Issues and Policymaking Since 1952* (Cairo: AUC Press, 2018), 263.
7. Ministry of Planning, *General Strategy*, 16–17.
8. For a short biography of Abdel Razzak Abdel Meguid, written by his daughter, see Amina Abdel Razzak Abdel Meguid, 'Biography', accessed 30 April 2020, http://www.abdelrazzakabdelmeguid.com/biography.html.
9. Panayiotis C. Afxentiou, 'Basic Needs: A Survey of the Literature', *Canadian Journal of Development Studies / Revue canadienne d'études du développement* 11 no. 2 (1990): 241–57, https://doi.org/10.1080/02255189.1990.9669399.
10. Google Books Ngram Viewer, accessed 29 April 2020, https://books.google.com/ngrams/graph?content=%22basic+needs%22&year_start=1900&year_end=2019&corpus=15&smoothing=3&share=&direct_url=t1%3B%2C%22%20basic%20needs%20%22%3B%2Cc0.
11. Afxentiou, 'Basic Needs', 244.
12. Samir Radwan and Torkel Alfthan, 'Household Surveys for Basic Needs: Some Issues', *International Labour Review* 117, no. 2 (1978): 197–210.

13. Youssef Boutros-Ghali and Lance Taylor, 'Basic Needs Macroeconomics: Is It Manageable in the Case of Egypt?' *Journal of Policy Modeling* 2, no. 3 (1980): 409–36, https://doi.org/10.1016/0161-8938(80)90031-9. This research was supported by the World Bank and the Cairo University/Massachusetts Institute of Technology Technological Planning Program. International partnership in planning had been a constant feature of Egyptian planning. See the discussion of the first Five-Year Development Plan in Chapter Three and further discussion in this chapter. On basic needs in Egypt, see also Myrette Ahmed El-Sokkari, *Basic Needs, Inflation and the Poor of Egypt*, Cairo Papers 7 no. 2 (Cairo: AUC Press, June 1984).
14. For the biography of Youssef Butrus-Ghali, see 'Youssef Boutros Ghali', *Wikipedia*, accessed 30 April 2020, https://en.wikipedia.org/wiki/Youssef_Boutros_Ghali.
15. Ministry of Planning, *General Strategy*, 37.
16. Ibid., 38.
17. Ibid., 37–8.
18. Ibid., 38.
19. Ibid., 36.
20. Ibid., 93.
21. Khalid Ikram, 'Meeting the Social Contract in Egypt', *Finance and Development* 18, no. 3 (1981): 30–3.
22. Bent Hansen and Samir Radwan, *Employment Opportunities and Equity in a Changing Economy: Egypt in the 1980s, a Labour Market Approach*, Report of an Inter-agency Team Financed by the United Nations Development Programme and Organised by the International Labour Office, WEP Study (Geneva: International Labour Office, 1982), v.
23. See other reports in ibid., xiin1.
24. Ibid.
25. On Bent Hansen, see his obituary: George A. Akerlof, Pranab Bardhan, and Roger Craine, 'In Memoriam', University of California, accessed 30 April 2020, https://senate.universityofcalifornia.edu/_files/inmemoriam/html/benthansen.htm. For Samir Radwan, see 'Samir Radwan Curriculum Vitae', Arab Republic of Egypt Ministry of Finance, accessed 30 April 2020, http://www.mof.gov.eg/MOFGallerySource/English/PDF/Samir_Radwan%20CV-updated-2011.pdf.
26. For names of these economists and their papers, see Hansen and Radwan, *Employment Opportunities*, xiin2.
27. Ibid., xi.
28. Ibid., 16.

29. Ibid., 23–4.
30. Ibid., 19.
31. Ibid., 20.
32. Heba Handoussa and Gillian Potter, *Employment and Structural Adjustment: Egypt in the 1990s* (Cairo: AUC Press, 1991), Preface, n.p. Like the earlier, 1982, ILO report, this report was a result of a many of Egypt's most noted economists, both Egyptians and international academics.
33. Ibid., 19.
34. Ibid., 20.
35. Ibid., 19–20.
36. Ibid., 20.
37. World Bank, *Egypt: Alleviating Poverty during Structural Adjustment*, World Bank Country Study (Washington, DC: World Bank, 1991).
38. Ibid., v.
39. Ibid., xx.
40. Ibid., xx–xxi.
41. See the EHDRs, accessed 24 September 2020, http://hdr.undp.org/en/reports/national/EGY.
42. The analysis of the EHDR and its parent HDR projects is partly based on Relli Shechter, '"Choosing Our Future": Global Best Practices and Local Planning in the *Egypt Human Development Report*', special issue, *Journal of Levantine Studies* 10, no. 1 (Summer 2020), 45–67.
43. 'About Human Development', *United Nations Development Programme: Human Development Reports* (hereinafter *UNDPHDR*), accessed 30 April 2020, http://hdr.undp.org/en/humandev.
44. Mahbub ul Haq, 'The Advent of the Human Development Report', *Reflections on Human Development* (New York: Oxford University Press, 1995), 24–45.
45. *The Concept and Measurement of Human Development as Participatory Process*, Egypt Human Development Report (hereinafter *EHDR*) *1994*, UNDPHDR, accessed 30 April 2020, https://hdr.undp.org/content/concept-and-measurement-human-development-participatory-process.
46. *EHDR 1995*, ch. 1, accessed 18 April 2020, http://www.arab-hdr.org/publications/other/undp/hdr/1995/egypt-e.pdf.
47. Ibid., 13.
48. For critical analysis of participatory development, see Sylvia I. Bergh, 'Introduction: Researching the Effects of Neoliberal Reforms on Local Governance in the Southern Mediterranean', *Mediterranean Politics* 17, no. 3 (2012).

49. 'Preamble', *EHDR 2003*.
50. *EHDR 2005*, xi.
51. Ibid., 46.
52. Ibid., 1–2.
53. 'Government of Arab Republic of Egypt United Nations Development Programme, Project title: "Social Contract Advisory, Monitoring, and Coordination Center", Proposal ID: 00045653, Project ID: 00053972', 6, accessed 17 April 2020, https://www.undp.org/content/dam/egypt/docs/Poverty/03ProDocSocialContractCenter.pdf. The project's agreement was signed in the presence of Ahmed Nazif, then the prime minister of Egypt.
54. *EHDR 2005*, vii.
55. *EHDR 2008*, xi.
56. Ibid., 1.
57. 'Government of Arab Republic of Egypt United Nations Development Programme', 7.
58. Ibid., 5.
59. *EHDR 2010*, viii.
60. Ministry of Planning, *General Strategy*, 'Preamble', iii. Signed by Abdel Meguid, minister of planning.
61. Alan Richards, 'The Political Economy of Dilatory Reform: Egypt in the 1980s', *World Development* 19, no. 12 (1991): 1721.
62. 'Egypt Aided By I. M. F.'s Loan Accord', *New York Times*, 2 June 1978, accessed 2 June 2019, https://www.nytimes.com/1978/06/02/archives/egypt-aided-by-imfs-loan-accord-paris-meeting-scheduled.html.
63. World Bank, 'Report and Recommendation of the President to the Executive Directors on a Proposed Loan to the Development Industrial Bank with the Guarantee of the Arab Republic of Egypt for a Development Finance Company Project', 9 March 1978, accessed 2 May 2020, http://documents.worldbank.org/curated/pt/798001468234876265/text/multi-page.txt.
64. World Bank, *Egypt: Alleviating Poverty*, 124.
65. See, for a critical analysis of the SFD, El-Meehy, 'Rewriting the Social Contract'.
66. *EHDR 1995*, 11.
67. Relli Shechter, 'Glocal Mediators: Marketing in Egypt during the Open-Door Era (*infitah*)', *Enterprise and Society* 9, no. 4 (2008): 762–87.

7

THE PROBLEM WITH THE NEW SOCIAL CONTRACT

This chapter studies the political economy of attempts to implement the new social contract in the period between the mid-1980s – the end of the oil-boom – and the January 2011 Uprising. It questions why a seeming political consensus on the need to replace the old/effendi and broken social contract, and detailed planning for how to do so, barely materialised into a new social contract for Egypt. The old social contract, despite its many deficiencies and constant calls for change, turned out to be highly stable because the socio-economic and political costs of rewriting it proved too high for both the state and the newly established (post-oil-boom) middle-class society. State and citizens either had little incentive to strive for overarching change or distrusted the other side's willingness to follow through. It is in this context that grand ideas for economic transformation, human development and democratisation often failed to live up to their promise. Instead of a change from an old to a new social contract, elements of both were increasingly layered side by side.

The chapter first studies the public discourse on the decline of the middle class. Lamented since the 1970s, the socio-economic standing of the effendi middle class had over time eroded but not degraded completely, and a new middle class that would have benefited from and supported the reforms and that constituted an alternative political constituency had barely emerged. The chapter later highlights how the contours of an existing effendi social contract shaped both the partial implementation of the economic reform and structural adjustment (ERSA) programme and the partial political reform, or democratisation, in Egypt for over twenty years. Both represented different but intertwined aspects of the new social contract. The chapter also studies how informal economic and political practices subverted most of these reforms; such informal economic and political practices invariably supported a betwixt and between status quo in which the effendi social contract eroded but did not disappear, while the new social contract was partially implemented alongside the old.

'Farewell to the middle class'

References to the 'middle class' in Egyptian academic research and public discourse – the two are closely intertwined – first appeared when this social group was seemingly on the brink of its demise. A keyword search in the Centre d'études et de documentation économiques, juridiques et sociales (CEDEJ) archive of digitised Egyptian press for the period between the 1980s and 2008, the last year for which we have such records, gauges the interest in the topic. According to the timeline for 'middle class' on the CEDEJ website, its use peaked in 1998.[1] 'Adli Rumman, who conducted a quantitative analysis of research on the Egyptian middle class, also found growing scholarly interest in the middle class since the beginning of the 1990s.[2] In 1991 and 1992, *al-Hilal*, a highbrow scholarly magazine, launched a series of articles by some of Egypt's most prominent academics, who commented on the past and present situation of the middle class.[3] In 1998, a newly established magazine, *Ahwal Misriyya* (no. 1, published by *al-Ahram*'s Center for Political and Strategic Studies) similarly published a special issue on the middle class. As discussed below, the hardships of the middle class became a central focus of public concern.

During the 1970s, public commentators tacitly lamented the demise of the respectable, effendi middle class in Egypt, although as a term, 'middle class' was little used in the discussion of Egyptian society. However, after 1991, the introduction of a comprehensive ERSA programme led to a mounting outcry against the resulting deterioration in the economic condition of that class. Commentators hinted that the state was not doing enough to maintain the social contract that supported the middle class, and that hence, the state was relinquishing its moral economy. During the 1990s, and through the ERSA programme, the state seemed to have ended this social contract altogether. Public commentators argued that the state – once the mainstay of the middle class – had forsaken this class. This would indeed have been the case had only the officially stated goals of the ERSA been considered. Downsizing state employment, privatising the public sector and reducing the state budget – which meant cutting back on welfare expenditures and, most notably, on state subsidies – all harmed the middle class. According to the critics, the ERSA programme promoted globalisation, which had brought about this class's subjugation to world economic forces beyond Egypt's control – for example, through the flotation of the Egyptian pound – as well as Egypt's political subjugation to Western powers, particularly the United States.

The lively discussion in the semi-official press, such as *al-Ahram*, as well as in the opposition press, such as *al-Wafd*, was critical in tone. There was a broad consensus among scholars and press commentators that the Egyptian middle class was in crisis. What triggered so much interest, the first of its kind in Egyptian social analysis, was the ostensible disappearance of this class owing to contemporary economic hardships and state efforts at economic reform.

With such a public outcry over the demise of the Egyptian middle class came an attempt to define the middle class in socio-economic and political terms, as well as to evaluate its historical role in influencing and being influenced by the state and the economy. Egyptian scholars debated the exact definition and size of the 'middle class'. There was broad agreement that the term was rather vague and that this social group could be subcategorised, often into three groups: upper-, middle- and lower-middle class. There was also broad agreement among scholars regarding the making of Egypt's middle class and the reasons for its downfall.

According to the new historical meta-narrative, this class came into being under Muhammad Ali – the founder of modern Egypt – and his intertwined state-building and modernisation project in the early-to-mid-nineteenth century.[4] According to this narrative, Egypt's ruler required new civilian and military cadres to fulfil his vision, and he sent students to Europe, opened new schools in Egypt and employed graduates in state service. These initiatives were at the core of making the middle class in Egypt. According to most scholarship, despite its budding influence, Egypt's middle class – now often referred to as the 'new middle class' – had to await full independence after 1952 to reach its zenith.[5] It was then, scholars argued, that Nasser's regime encouraged the rapid expansion of this new middle class through new educational opportunities, notably in higher education, and the expansion of state employment of graduates. Interestingly, this narrative stood in partial contrast to the past Arab socialist regime's own glorification of, if not actual preference for, peasants and workers.

The analysis above emphasises that in both instances – under Muhammad Ali and later under Nasser – the middle class was a state creation. Such analysis often contrasted the Egyptian middle class with that of Europe, the latter having emerged as a result of economic transformation, in opposition to the old feudal regimes.[6] In Egypt the middle class's present and future fortunes were intimately related to the state and its economic and social development policies.

During the 1970s and 1980s, many who took part in the Egyptian public discourse implicitly lamented the demise of the established middle class (the respectable, educated, state-employed Egyptian) and the rise of and replacement by other, 'parasitic' social groups from below, from above and from the middle. The Open Door policy seemed to overturn the social contact that supported the middle class and the model of socio-economic development that underwrote its interests. Such lamentations – across the political and religious-secular divides – were implied because the term 'middle class' was not yet explicitly used.

During the 1990s, this critique continued. However, academic analysis belatedly acknowledged that the oil-boom had been a period of fast expansion for the middle class. According to Galal Amin, the 'middle class', as defined by income level, constituted 45 per cent of Egypt's population. Mahmoud Abdel-Fadil claimed that the middle class represented a somewhat smaller percentage (35%) of the nation.[7] Regardless of the exact number of middle-class Egyptians, the critique of their deteriorating economic condition remained associated with that of the nation as a whole. In particular, the educated, state-employed middle class had come to constitute the normative unit of analysis for the 'average' Egyptian in the public discourse on the dwindling welfare state.[8]

Similarly to the complaint made in an earlier critique, the assault on the middle class was understood to be the result of the newly introduced market economy, but this time it came in the guise of the ERSA programme (1991), which saw the further demise of the middle class. Indeed, the ERSA programme was a direct onslaught on middle-class employment and the state services that had long sustained this class. As a result, those commenting publicly agreed that the lower echelon of the middle class now lived close to the poverty line and often converged with the lower class or the poor. There was also general agreement that under the new state economic retrenchment, the middle class – long the mainstay of Egyptian society – was going through a process of pauperization and would soon disappear.

While the analysis of the middle-class crisis along the lines above was developing, Ramzi Zaki's well-received book *Farewell to the Middle Class*, published in 1997, captured the general public mood on how things had gone wrong for this class.[9] The book won an award for the best book on economics in 1999, presented by President Mubarak at the opening of the International Book Fair (2000). It received glowing reviews in the press, and the title was invariably used to capture the general mood of other public discussions on the middle class. Surprisingly, Zaki, a well-respected Egyptian economist who at that time worked in Kuwait, did not directly refer to the Egyptian middle class in his book. Rather, he discussed the hardships of middle classes in developing and developed nations around the globe; these classes struggled under the introduction of neoliberalism in many states. His critical conclusions regarding the global demise of the middle class struck a chord at home because he clearly, if implicitly, referred to Egypt's recent ERSA programme. Furthermore, Zaki tied this programme and its bleak consequences to the process of globalisation and its negative influence on developing nations, including Egypt.

According to Zaki, labour migration was a long, lingering hardship and high on the list of things that had gone wrong. Occurring under economic duress, labour migration compelled many to leave their families behind, and it often resulted in psychological hardship for the migrant and many family crises. Economic hardship further led many to take a second job in the informal economy, which was also often detrimental to people's emotional and physical health. Moreover, informal employment in the kind of menial jobs available brought about the de facto proletarianisation of the middle class. Married women had to search for jobs, and this search had exacerbated pressure on the existing labour market, pushing wages down. Poorer families had to remove children from school and send them out to work – to help with family earnings – which led to a rise in illiteracy and inhumane child employment. Rising costs for food and drink led to malnutrition and the spread, or sometimes return, of certain epidemics. The rise in the prices for medical treatment and medication further exacerbated health issues. According to Zaki, increased housing prices, the result of the commercialisation of this sector, coupled with a reduction in state subsidies, gave rise to residential overcrowding. Informal housing created inadequate infrastructure, such as a lack of running water or deficient sewage systems.[10]

To sum up Zaki's critique, the combined impact of globalisation and the neoliberalisation of the economy had a devastating impact on middle classes around the world. Disempowered middle classes went from being providers of welfare to becoming social groups badly in need of support. For many commentators discussing the dire straits of the Egyptian middle class in an age of intertwined economic reform and structural adjustment and globalisation, the Egyptian state was anything but helpful in its own middle class's time of need.

Zaki was also clear about who the winners and losers in this process were: the upper crust of the middle class and the economic elite gained much, while the core of the middle class grew poorer, experiencing pauperisation and proletarianisation. This in turn brought about the socio-political unrest associated with bread riots in many developing countries. Zaki did not immediately refer to this explicitly, but for him and many others, the bread riots demonstrated rising social opposition to current transitions, as well as the destruction of social solidarity in many countries. Under such circumstances, many in Egypt no doubt felt that 'farewell to the middle class' was an adequate, if pessimistic, description of the socio-economic transformation taking place.

The fault lines of economic reform

Much of Zaki's critique of what went wrong globally, and implicitly in Egypt, had already been prevalent in an earlier critique of how 'things went wrong' during the Open Door era. By the 1990s, there was broad, well-established social opposition in Egypt to the measures of economic neoliberalisation that would hurt the middle class, and Egypt's ruling elite were very much aware of this. As in the past, this opposition crossed political boundaries and was shared by left-leaning Egyptian intelligentsia and supporters of the Muslim Brotherhood alike. Many clearly felt that comprehensive economic reform would revoke a long-existing agreement between the state and society. This agreement was well rooted in the state's commitment to social justice as emanating from the effendi social contract of the past, a contract that now increasingly supported the struggling middle class.

Indeed, the critical association of the ERSA programme with the demise of the middle class made sense. If implemented, the ERSA programme would delink the long-lasting connection between education, particularly, higher education, and state employment. Furthermore, under the then current economic conditions in Egypt, structural adjustment in employment – the transition of educated employees from state employment to the private sector – would largely mean the proletarianisation of such employees. If not an actual change from white- to blue-collar jobs, employment in menial services, which was the sort of employment on offer by the mostly informal small and medium enterprises that constituted the majority of the private sector, would hardly be commensurate with their level of education. Nor would such jobs provide compensation commensurate with their middle-class status or their previous employment. For these reasons, many considered structural adjustment from respectable state employment to a private sector job to be a demotion, rather than a new economic opportunity, as the ERSA programme often suggested. Moreover, state employment was to be streamlined and become more disciplined, which spelled a greater squeeze on these state employees. Importantly, but tacit in much of the critique, social welfare in Egypt was diverted from supporting the middle class as a whole to supporting the poor – the lower-middle class and especially the lower class. Under the ERSA programme, the historical, effendi middle class would indeed have largely disappeared.

As it happened, the unfolding of the ERSA programme did not bring about the overall demise of the effendi middle class. It did not create large-scale opportunity for socio-economic mobility through a free-market initiative, as it had promised, nor did it unleash a new middle class that, having benefited from the economic transformation, would replace the old middle class as a new source of political support for the state. Instead, the ERSA programme was implemented so as to cause the least social disruption possible, to avoid a political backlash from the effendi middle class; though that class had remained the regime's main constituency, it had increasingly become the supporter of the government's main opposition – the Muslim Brotherhood. Not unlike other attempts at reform since the early 1970s, the programme reflected neither broad social agreement (a new social contract) regarding the change required, nor the necessary strong political will to implement it to the letter. In this state of affairs, and with the memory of the 1977 Food Uprising still very much alive, the government postponed the programme for as long as possible.[11] This situation continued even after the end of the oil-boom, which spelled a sharp decrease in state revenues and spiralling public debt. State evasion of comprehensive economic reform was also a strategic device to extract better conditions (or rent) for Egypt in its negotiations with IFIs.

By 1986, Egypt had entered an economic recession. The country further found itself in a crisis, owing to an increase in debt, compounded by debt service obligations.[12] Egypt re-entered the by now routine talks with the IMF and the World Bank in an attempt to refinance its mounting state debt in return for signing an economic plan that would stabilise and later bring structural change to the economy. Nevertheless, throughout the late-1980s there was little change in actual economic policy.

The 1991 ERSA programme was a combination of the economic dead-end described above and a new economic opportunity in the form of political rent, which Egypt received for supporting the coalition forces during the First Gulf War.[13] This rent boosted the economic reform and cushioned the structural adjustment through huge debt forgiveness and debt restructuring, as well as immediate financial help. Officially, and following global best practices of the day, the programme was supposed to set the economy on a new course, one recommended since the late 1970s but never truly implemented. Yet, the existing social contract shaped the implementation of the ERSA programme of the 1990s such that it neither constituted full-fledged reform nor resulted in the complete demise of the educated, state-employed middle class, its replacement by a market-based new middle class, or its proletarianization. The implementation of the ERSA programme mostly meant the dilution of the economic articles of the social contract, rather than its replacement, and the addition of new economic initiatives based on the new social contract beside the old. Here too, the Egyptian regime attempted a complicated juggling act in which the dilution of these economic articles would somehow also dilute the heritage of the revolutionary state, but without weakening the political support for Egypt's still thinly disguised military regime.

A central aspect of the ERSA was rigorous fiscal discipline, or a better balance between state earnings and state expenditures. This new fiscal discipline came in the aftermath of a decade in which the government of Egypt expanded its relative expenditures on social services in line with its ongoing commitment to the social contract. For the period between 1980/81 and 1989/90, this constituted an increase from 11 per cent to 17.8 per cent of the budget.[14] During this period, state expenditures on education increased from 5.1 per cent to 8.8 per cent of the state budget, with expenditures on higher education more than doubling. Expenditures on health increased only slightly, from 2 per cent to 2.8 per cent, and those on social affairs decreasing from 1.4 per cent to 1.1 per cent. In short, a familiar, pre-revolutionary bias promoting education, particularly higher education, over other state social expenditures persisted during the 1980s – regardless, as we shall see also under the ERSA programme, of the search for structural adjustment.

Hidden in the above-mentioned expenditures, but also a long-term trend in Egypt, was a bias toward financing state employment rather than providing social services, as was demonstrated in the share of ministries' budgets spent on 'salaries' in relation to the share spent on 'subsidies and supplies'.[15] During the period between 1980/81 and 1989/90, the state increased the portion of the budget used for compensation for state employees relative to that used for the provision of services to citizens. Thus, the functional distribution of the budget for salaries rose from 26.65 per cent to 67.45 per cent, and that of subsidies and supplies decreased from 72.75 per cent to 18.08 per cent. As in the past, there was a clear bias in the distribution of state services expressed in geographical gaps in state allocation, with urban dwellers benefiting more from state provision than rural dwellers, and Upper Egypt more than Lower Egypt. There was, therefore, a direct state preference for allocating funds to the middle class.

During the ERSA programme, the above, familiar lines of state distribution did not change much. Between 1990/91 and 1998/99 expenditures on education increased as a proportion of government spending from 10.2 per cent to 17 per cent. Moreover as a part of the GDP, expenditures on education grew from 4.8 per cent to 5.5 per cent.[16] An earlier state commitment to education did not diminish under the newly introduced fiscal austerity. As in the past, the state did not reform its free education policy, and education remained skewed toward university education, thereby benefiting the effendi middle class. Furthermore, expenditures on salaries within the education budget remained proportionally high in relation to other items, such as subsidies, supplies and investment. Concurrently, the supply of education continued to trail demand, and the quality of education was far from satisfactory. As in the past, this period saw a notable rise in alternative, private education, as well as complaints over the informal privatisation of the education system from within through, for example, private classes given by schoolteachers. The 'liberalisation' of the education system was mostly the result of a private search for market-based solutions to inadequate state education at all levels, including by Islamic for- and not-for-profit organisations, regardless of the increase in state expenditures on education.

Under the newly introduced fiscal discipline, state expenses on health were eroded, but not restructured. As with education, the state tacitly encouraged the migration of those who could afford it to private health alternatives. Here too, Islamic for- and not-for-profit organisations took on a central role in offering such alternatives. Despite broad agreement among professionals and significant public dissatisfaction, reform of the state health services barely materialised. The familiar gaps between rural and urban Egypt and Lower and Upper Egypt remained intact. Out-of-pocket payments by patients, a measure often recommended in international reports on state health reforms, rarely took shape for fear of public opposition.[17]

Before the start of the ERSA programme, the 1990s saw a further reduction in state expenditures on subsidies, which dropped from 5.2 to 1.6 per cent of the GDP.[18] This drop took shape against the background of significant public opposition. To avoid public outcry, the government took two indirect actions to reduce subsidies. First, it periodically restructured the subsidy system, gradually phasing out the number of subsidised items over time, as opposed to cancelling them immediately. Second, as Ilya Harik has suggested, the state weaned citizens off of dependence on subsidies by 'psychological conditioning', whereby the state consistently failed to deliver goods and services on time and in acceptable quality, thereby wearing down public expectations of state subsidies by attrition.[19] Indeed, this was true of other welfare articles as well, leading to the gradual erosion of the social contract. Furthermore, as with education and health, the state implicitly encouraged those who could afford do so to search for free-market food alternatives. At times, the new subsidy cuts were coupled with an increase in state repression. An unpopular ERSA programme came into effect during the early 1990s, when Egyptian public opinion was focused on a political-turned-security crisis – the result of the state's campaign against Islamic terrorism.[20] Finally, public anger over subsidy cuts was tacitly diverted toward the Western governments and IFIs that had purportedly forced the ERSA programme upon Egypt.

Economists agreed that the remaining food subsidies indeed targeted the poor.[21] The rough flour used in the making of the local-type (*baladi*) bread – the main subsidised commodity – was the primary, yet choiceless, option for those most in need. Nevertheless, and despite a system of rationing cards, the majority of Egyptians – including large segments of the middle and upper classes – still held cards, and food subsidies were by and large universal, as opposed to particularly targeting the poor. Measuring who the real poor were and targeting them more closely was expensive and difficult in administrative terms. Yet, a no less important explanation for why the state avoided a progressive subsidy system was that subsidies had long been informally considered part of a comprehensive public wage system in Egypt, and hence were part of the social contract that supported middle-class state employees. Indeed, to counter an adverse outcome for its employees, the government periodically increased their wages to compensate for subsidy cuts. The relative success of reducing food subsidies was very apparent in comparison to state subsidies for energy, which benefited middle- and upper-class society more than the poor, for whom subsidies lingered much longer.[22]

Beginning in the 1980s, and as with subsidies, the state attempted to limit state employment through attrition: what it could not achieve by decreasing wages, it did by increasing the waiting period for such jobs.[23] Differential waiting periods, with the more educated waiting less time for employment, suggest that state employment as the central article of the social contract had been eroded, the logic being that less-educated employees were more dispensable.

Moreover, because state employment had by then become significantly feminised, and nearly 80 per cent of graduate women were employed by the state, middle-class women were particularly vulnerable to the new policy, and unemployment rates for women were much higher than they were for men.[24] Despite these expanded waiting periods, the government decision that graduates who found employment in the private sector would be erased from the waiting lists for government jobs created an uproar in the Egyptian press, leading to mass resignations from private jobs.[25] White-collar state employment remained coveted because it continued to offer compensation and benefits unmatched in the private sector, regardless of an official state effort to invigorate the market economy in Egypt.

The state, for its part, continued to view state employees as an important political constituency. Throughout the 1990s, despite a marked increase in waiting periods, hiring of state employees in the civil service continued to expand at 4.8 per cent per year, twice the rate of the overall employment growth, and regardless of an overall decrease in compensation for such employees.[26] This trend took place in clear contradiction to the ERSA programme that was supposed to reduce state employment and facilitate job creation in the private sector.

The increase in the number of white-collar state employees in the civil service is especially bewildering in comparison to the downsizing of employment in the blue-collar public sector. As had happened since the early years of the Open Door policy, the public sector continued to be the main object of economic reform, for two reasons. First, as before, reform of the public sector – and under the ERSA programme also its partial privatisation – allowed the state to have the resources to retain its commitment to (partially) fulfil the social contract with the effendi middle class. Second, blue-collar state employees – despite being included in this social contract – supposedly constituted a lesser threat to the state. Additionally, privatisation benefited a new economic-turned-political elite.

Under the ERSA programme, slightly more than a third of designated public enterprises (314 in total) were sold, but the all-important (and white-collar) financial sector remained in government hands.[27] An official, Public Enterprise Office report estimated that between 1993 and 2000, the number of public sector employees dropped from just over 1,000,000 to under 600,000, with 220,000 transferring to the private sector when their place of employment was privatised; 110,000 choosing an early retirement package; and 150,000 whose jobs were discontinued owing to natural retirement or death.[28] The privatisation scheme and the public sector reform were far from popular with the public. Nevertheless, for the state they provided the least-harmful-case scenario for implementing the ERSA programme, in terms of public protest against the unfolding events. Because public sector labour unions, which could lobby or strike against the partial dismantling of the public sector, were headed by members of the ruling party leadership, they would not rise against their own. However, after 1998, and especially after July 2004, when the newly appointed 'government of businessmen' headed by Ahmad Nazif seemed set to expedite privatisation, there was a significant increase in labour protests in an attempt to prevent another wave of privatisation.[29]

In preparation for the economic hardships associated with the ERSA programme, and under the recommendation of a 1991 World Bank report, the government of Egypt established the internationally funded Social Fund for Development (SFD, which started operations in 1993). Initially an emergency fund, the SFD subsequently became an important, permanent fixture in Egypt's welfare scheme.[30] According to Asya El-Meehy's analysis, the SFD's initiatives served limited income groups, but such groups did not include the very poor. Moreover, the SFD promoted its programs to 'state-linked elements of the middle classes, or unemployed university graduates and civil servants, who can meet the government salary collateral requirement'.[31] Under the ERSA programme, and a recurrent trope in the implementation of this programme, the SFD was a new institution that supported those segments of the middle class most hurt by the retrenchment of the effendi social contract.

Egypt's public housing policy – in itself a seeming aberration in an age of economic reform and structural adjustment transformation promoting privatisation – reflected a state socio-economic bias similar to that of the SFD. In 1996 and again in 2005, two separate large-scale public housing projects that, on paper, were to secure low-income housing solutions for those most in need, turned out to largely benefit middle- and upper-class investors.[32] This was the result of housing loans that were predicated upon employment with the state, coupled with payments made in instalments and mortgage schemes whose cost de facto excluded those most in need. No less important, the distribution of SFD funds and state-housing projects reflected a clear bias toward clients of the regime and against opposition elements often associated with the Muslim Brotherhood, making it a loyalty-based alongside a class-based provision of state-services. This was also true for state regulation and help of nongovernmental organisations (NGOs). Thus, an officially dictated economic transformation was implemented, in part, with a clear attempt to sustain political support for the Egyptian regime.

In 1996, a new rent law was introduced, mandating gradual increases in rents over a period of five years, and later the final cancellation of rent control. Thus, a central article of the social contract seemed to succumb to the ERSA programme. In fact, this law was more of a response to a de facto process of liberalisation from below in a market that had already been mostly informal and, therefore, unregulated. A new rent law was long overdue but postponed for fear of urban middle- and upper-class renters' reactions. In comparison to the long-overdue urban rent law, a new rural tenancy law and its fast implementation represented less of a state political (and economic) concern for lower-class rural dwellers. This law raised land rents from 1992 to 1997. It stipulated free-market rents after 1997, when rents further spiked dramatically. Registering little in public opinion or in the Egyptian parliament, the new tenancy law caused a local resistance and violence in rural regions.[33] Such upheavals suggest that the new law was quite contentious for those bearing its brunt. Similarly to the partial privatisation of the public sectors, however, both small farmers who rented land and blue-collar labourers clearly exerted less influence on the middle-class dominated public discourse and the opposition to state action.

In the theory behind the ERSA programs, reduction of taxation is assumed to be part of an exchange between state- and market-provided services. Citizens would pay less in taxes when the state reduced the distribution of public services. Therefore, they would have more free income to compensate for the reduction in state provision of goods and services. In Egypt, these tax cuts did not take place. Instead, since the early 1990s, the state had introduced a new, indirect sales tax, which hardly represented the benefit of economic transformation for the majority of society, especially for the poor.

Not unlike in the case of subsidy cuts, the transition to a new system of direct taxation was officially postponed because it would seemingly require a new administrative capacity, which the state could not create fast enough. Moreover, the introduction of income tax – a more egalitarian (progressive) form of taxation – would only be introduced in the mid-2000s, and then only partially.[34] A substantial, if implicit, consideration in avoiding comprehensive tax reform was the omnipresence of the informal economy. Tax reform, especially the change from indirect to direct taxation, would have required the formalisation of the economy to determine who should pay and how much – a change that many across society opposed. This change in taxation would, no doubt, have brought a renewed call for citizen discretion regarding state spending, and hence, a more public voice in politics.

To conclude, in implementing the ERSA programme, the state took incremental and indirect steps to reduce social welfare and subsidies and to change the employment structure so as to avoid, as far as possible, antagonising its citizenry, particularly the effendi middle class. The way that the ERSA programme unfolded did not expose a new economic social contract – it revealed the gradual erosion of the old one. The ERSA programme did not spell farewell to the middle class. Rather, the educated, state-employed middle class went through a process of attrition and dilution of its economic status. In avoiding much of the ERSA programme, Egypt's ruling elite perhaps avoided even greater opposition to the programme, but they likewise did not reap the potential benefits of the programme's successful implementation. Most notably, they were unable to bring about social support from among those benefiting from the economic reform.

A swing of the political pendulum

Part One discusses the transformation from a liberal social contract to the effendi social contract, especially between the end of World War II and the 1952 revolution. Driving this transformation was a growing conviction in the effendi-led political discourse that Egypt required a stronger state to facilitate socio-economic development and greater social justice. Beginning in the early 1970s, Sadat's Corrective Revolution and later the Open Door policy similarly intertwined the economic and political reforms of the Nasserite/effendi social contract. In this intertwining, economic reform – a new economic social contract – deregulated Egypt's command economy. Concurrently, political reform – a new political social contract – allowed citizens a greater say in politics, and therefore, the folding back of the authoritarian regime.

Under President Mubarak, and as expressed in the public and political discourse, the two reforms (and social contract/s) continued to be intertwined. Yet, the public and political discourse also experienced a continuous pendulum swing between the two, which ended up stalling both. Bounded by constant emphasis on socio-political stability, Mubarak's political reform preserved the social structure as well as the power of those in authority. The political reform in Egypt contained fault lines of reform by attrition, dilution and institutional layering similar to those of Egypt's fractured ERSA programme. Under Sadat, and later under Mubarak, this back-and-forth political pendulum contradicted the hope that market liberalisation would lead to political liberalisation. It also contradicted a rentier state theory analysis that predicted that less state redistribution of resources to citizens would force the authoritarian state to allow more citizen political participation, and therefore democratisation.[35]

This section follows the swing between the political and the economic new social contract/s, based on the analysis of the timeline for the term 'social contract' in the CEDEJ archive. The timeline exposes the contours of state/official and public use of this term for the period between the 1980s and 2009.[36] During the mid-1980s, according to this timeline, the term 'social contract' reemerged in the press, picking up steam in 1987. 'Social contract' surfaced again and with much greater intensity during the mid-1990s, reaching an increased pace in 1999. During the years 2000–9, results for the term 'social contract' reveal a declining interest in this term in the press. The narrative below elaborates on this timeline in terms of the pendulum swing between political and economic reform, while putting the timeline in the context of unfolding events in Egypt.

Egypt's public and political discourse on the social contract did not often betray class issues, or the socio-economic or political conflicts emanating from such issues. Instead, both the Egyptian regime and its opposition invariably emphasised the need for social and political harmony as being central to any reform. In light of the previous discussion on the mounting public and political concerns regarding the future of the struggling middle class, which all sides considered the mainstay of society, it should be clear that the public and political discourses were not devoid of such concerns either. Rather, and while tacit in the discourse, the effendi middle class and its socio-economic and political concerns were, to a large extent, congruent with those of 'society' in many of these discussions.

In the aftermath of the 1977 Food Uprising, Sadat's new social contract harmonised existing politics, thereby stabilising the political status quo in a period when economic reform raised socio-political tensions. Under Mubarak's first years in power, the new social contract did the same. From 25–26 February 1986, conscripts from the Central Security Force revolted in Cairo against a rumoured extension of their compulsory service. Islamic militants soon joined in. In reaction the government imposed a general curfew and sent the army to restore order. In the aftermath of the events, Mubarak gave a long-awaited speech before the People's Assembly (8 March 1986).[37] In his speech, not unlike Sadat's speech in the aftermath of the 1977 Food Uprising, Mubarak commended the army and security forces for successfully putting down the revolts. He criminalised the revolts, as opposed to treating them as a political affair, and promised swift punishment for those responsible for public unrest and the destruction of property. In another similarity with Sadat's 1977 speech, Mubarak broadly defined democracy as the right of a 'responsible' opposition to express its opinion, without causing public unrest. He also reiterated a state response of forcefully putting down street protests and glorification of the army, and the speech further exposed a diluted version of democracy. Importantly, martial law, first introduced after Sadat's assassination, had been extended during the revolt and would remain in place well into the 2000s, to set the legal mechanism for future repressive steps to be taken as the government saw fit.

A few months later, on 12 November 1986, Mubarak gave another long speech, celebrating the joint opening session of the Egyptian People's Assembly and the Consultative Council. In his speech, directly referring to the notion of a new political social contract, Mubarak suggested:

> Instead of allowing our society to go astray and drown in dispute and imaginary battles from which there can emerge neither victor nor vanquished, we must

adhere to our unity, which is based on a *new social contract* [emphasis added]. Duties and rights, goals and objectives, the admissible and the inadmissible can all be defined. At the same time, such a contract can tolerate differing views and opinions and can accept the consensus of our nation.[38]

In this speech, though the duties and rights, goals and objectives, and the mechanisms for their implementation were not specified, President Mubarak presented the new social contract as a tool for participatory politics. Such politics were to avoid social and political frictions, and they were to harmonise society and state–society relations, despite these tensions. He implicitly revoked the rule of law ('duties and rights, goals and objectives, the admissible and the inadmissible can all be defined') as a central venue for harmonising Egyptian socio-politics through a new agreement between the state and its citizenry.

In response to Mubarak's speech, the semi-official *al-Ahram* (28 November 1986) published an extended discussion on how to implement the new social contract. In the discussion academics, state officials and representatives of the Socialist Labour Party debated various venues for facilitating the introduction of the new social contract to Egypt's political system.[39] In line with Mubarak's speech, commentators discussed how to best support the political freedom of individuals and legally established institutions. Accordingly, the new social contract was supposed to allow the media to express an unbiased ('objective') opinion on current affairs. It would further allow political organisations and trade unions to do the same, and to negotiate such affairs with state officials in the government and government organisations. The government, for its part, would be responsive to these representatives of the people. In putting forward this agenda, the discussion in *al-Ahram* facilitated a future conference with representatives of all parties to discuss a new agreement with the state. Here too, however, as in Mubarak's speech, political participation was circumscribed by the demand for a loyal opposition, and criticism, when brought up, was not to cross the implied boundaries set by those in authority.

During the 1990s, Egypt experienced continuous militant Islamic opposition to the state and embarked on a well-trumpeted 'war on terror' against those religious militants. No less a threat to Mubarak's regime was the rise of the Muslim Brotherhood as a political movement supported by a well-organised web of social organisations that often supported the struggling middle class. During this period, a mounting, widespread public outcry against the ERSA programme – across both the political spectrum and the religious–secular divide – further challenged the regime. Worldwide, the end of the Cold War enhanced a new push toward a global, Western-led system of governance that was based on the intertwining of the free-market economy and democracy. While the ERSA programme – a seeming move toward a free-market economy in Egypt – had already started, the regime faced a growing call for political reform.

'Social contract' as it appears in the CEDEJ collection, changed course – from an official state call for the creation of a loyal opposition to a public demand for political participation in politics. Importantly, this public demand for a new social contract used the same central argument as the regime's, but in reverse. According to the contemporary public discourse, political participation would harmonise society, but it would be the result of a social rather than a state initiative, hence the demand for more public participation in politics.

On 18 January 1995, in a lecture to the Book Fair in Cairo, Muhammad Hasanayn Haykal, a past Nasserist and a well-known journalist and political commentator, argued that 1995 could be the beginning of the twenty-first century in Egypt.[40] According to Haykal, Egypt was facing multiple economic and social hardships – from a slowdown of economic growth to expanding socio-economic gaps. The year 1995 could therefore be a new starting point because a change was clearly required, and a peaceful change was preferred to one of violence. (Here, Haykal implicitly referred to the ongoing struggle between the state and radical Islamist groups.) For Haykal, the year 1995 could constitute a new beginning because it was a year of multiple elections, including for the trade unions, the mid-term election to the Consultative Council and new general elections to the People's Assembly. According to him, if these elections could be kept free from state interference, they would constitute an important step toward the required change. Haykal added that those free elections should be conducted with two preconditions: they should retain social unity, but they should also retain the current political power. He called for the resolution of the crisis in a planned and organised fashion. In addition, he suggested that the president appoint a vice president or a presidential council to assist him with the rapid transformation ahead.

In tandem with the above, Haykal appealed for the establishment of a new social contract in Egypt. For him, this social contract did not have to be a comprehensive, new bill of rights putting forward the rights and duties of citizens. Rather, it should expand on venues that would allow support for the collective security, not least through further facilitating a freer public discourse. The new social contract should include a 'candid reference' – as Haykal put it – to human rights as defined by the UN, including the right to learn, the right to health, the right to work and the rights to democracy, culture and, as recently added, happiness. Haykal suggested that this new social contract should structure the required future political and constitutional changes. He added that the last (old) social contract had been established under a socialist state and had become irrelevant over time. The 1971 constitution had also become obsolete. A new social contract would lead the way to political and constitutional reform.

Haykal's speech, according to the oppositional and Nasserist *al-'Arabi*, caused a great stir and further debates.[41] In reality, Haykal's suggestions were not exactly radical and, in many respects, they echoed Mubarak's earlier call (quoted above) for a new social contract in the form of legalised public participation (consultation) in debates on state policies, but little actual participation in policy making.

In the mid-1990s, Haykal was not the only public intellectual calling for a new political social contract; such calls also came from among the Islamists. For example, Tariq al-Bishri, a senior jurist, historian and well-known public commentator, likewise called for a new social contract, which he termed a new 'national project'.[42] This new national project, according to al-Bishri, should reflect a better balance of power between the state and social forces and among those social forces themselves. This new balance would end the zero-sum mentality that characterised the Egyptian politics of the day, and it would therefore reharmonise politics. The national project would retain the concentration of power in the community so that it could achieve its goals. Shahrough Akhavi, who studied al-Bishri's call for a new social contract, suggests that al-Bishri remained silent as to how this might transpire.[43] While neither al-Bishri's new national project nor Haykal's new social contract were politically radical, they did carry a call for social participation in political decision making.

On 2 February 1995, President Mubarak was indirectly asked about Haykal's suggestions in an interview he gave to the newspaper *al-Hayat*.[44] (Haykal was not mentioned by name, but it was clear from the discussion that his lecture provided the immediate context for the journalist's questions.) Mubarak rejected the suggestion of adding a vice president or a presidential council to assist him in his work. He further refused the idea of formally introducing a new social contract, which he associated with the Nasserite National Charter, arguing that this new social contract was irrelevant. This was quite a surprising statement considering his own (1986) call for a new social contract, quoted above, and a contemporary state initiative to promote a new social contract globally and in Egypt, as discussed below.

Most likely, President Mubarak rejected the new social contract in the context of Haykal's other suggestions for political reform, notably his proposal for a new constitution. To this suggestion Mubarak responded:

> Our constitution stipulates democratic socialism, which we interpret in the way that suits our society. Namely, social justice and a tax system. A constitution cannot be made over [every] one, five, or ten years. The constitution should not be touched for generations and long periods of time.

From the quotation above, and again in contrast to Mubarak's own use of the term 'new social contract' to suggest greater political participation, he was plainly taken aback by Haykal's rather similar call. In the context of escalating public criticism of Egypt's ERSA programme, such political participation would no doubt have led to even more criticism. The suggestion for a new constitution – which implied the limitation of the presidential role – was also flatly rejected.

Mubarak further commented, 'amending the constitution is not my preoccupation. My real preoccupation is to raise the living standard and improve education. When the foundations are strong, I am not going to be alarmed by what some people say about constitutional amendments'. According to Mubarak, in a period of economic reform, political liberalisation had to wait. Haykal's suggestions for loyal opposition that amplified Mubarak's earlier vision of political liberalisation were put on hold. Mubarak clearly viewed such a political concession as a nuisance that would interfere with the 'real', economic task ahead. Moreover, Mubarak implicitly referred to the old/effendi social contract, whereby citizens' economic rights replaced political rights. Accordingly, he rejected constitutional reform, even though the current (1971) constitution still stipulated a socialist economy – a clear anachronism at the height of the state-led ERSA programme in Egypt, and in a post–Cold War world.[45]

Mubarak's objection to the new political social contract came at the same time that Egypt became actively involved in a global, UN-led call for a new economic social contract. In 1995, UN Secretary-General Butrus-Ghali, an Egyptian academic-turned-politician, presided over a new initiative to resolve global poverty in a World Summit for Social Development that convened in Copenhagen.[46] In a speech before the UN General Assembly, Amr Musa, Egypt's Foreign Minister, referred to this initiative as a new, international social contract. According to Musa, this new social contract was to promote cooperation and mutual respect on an international level and across states and cultures.[47] Globally, Egypt had committed itself to joining a new social contract, indeed, to be one of its leaders. Beginning in 1994, Egypt was also one of the first contributors to the UNDP's human development report. Notably, Egypt signed up for a new global economic social contract while Mubarak rejected the political social contract at home. This gap between the economic and political social contracts – in contradiction to the global best practices of the period, in which economic and political reform intertwined – would become a familiar feature of Egypt's political economy in the coming years.

During the second half of the 1990s, the new economic social contract, in tandem with the global trend, would become officially associated with alleviating poverty and cushioning the impact of the ERSA programme in Egypt. As outlined earlier in this chapter, this was a period during which public commentators lamented the demise of the Egyptian middle class under the ERSA programme. Furthermore, the late 1990s saw a rise in labour protests. There was mounting public concern over the ERSA programme's negative impact on society. The state, in turn, joined the new global initiative of searching for market-based as opposed to state-financed solutions to ongoing economic hardship, and therefore for an alternative moral economy, as such.

Contemporary press clips in the CEDEJ archives well reflect this state initiative to adapt the new social contract. For example, on 7 April 1997, in an op-ed in *al-Jumhuriyya*, Ahmad Hasan al-Bara'i (a Cairo University professor, and a future minister of workforce and migration) called – as did, he argued, many of his colleagues – for a new social contract that would reflect the changing economic realities in Egypt. Al-Bara'i explained that with the introduction to Egypt of a free-market economy and privatisation, businesses and labour unions should renegotiate suitable employment and working conditions for workers. On 19 January 1998, *al-Wafd* reported that Minister of Social Insurances and Social Affairs Mirfat al-Talawi had announced the importance of a new social contract between the state, the market and civil society as a tool to fight poverty through the facilitation of new, more egalitarian economic opportunities for the poor.

From the above comments and many more, it is apparent that the new economic social contract had become a welfare issue. That being the case, the state would also have to promote market-based welfare solutions for citizens. These solutions, from a larger role in philanthropy among private entrepreneurs to NGO provision of social services and employment, would also relieve the economic pressure on state budgets through the partial privatisation of the welfare state, and hence also the commodification of welfare services. Importantly, the ERSA programme, once at the core of the state's call for a new social contract, was no longer central, and was now taken for granted. Instead, the new social contract as put forward by the state was about the need for social reform – to underwrite (or cushion) the ongoing economic reform.

In October 1999, the state effort to 'welfarize' the new social contract culminated in a national conference sponsored by Susan Mubarak, the president's wife, which was to further explore the initiatives mentioned above.[48] Indeed, the conference officially engaged with social development, which by then, as reflected in the press, had become synonymous with the new social contract. Although President Mubarak had earlier called for a new social contract to help citizens in need, the fact that the conference had been delegated to the president's wife, thereby feminising it, made it clear that the search for this new social contract was now in the realm of social affairs, as opposed to that of politics.[49]

The official purpose of the conference was to facilitate a public discussion (in reality a discussion delegated to upper-middle-class experts) on how to bring about social development, as well as to indicate to citizens that the state was searching for ways to relieve economic hardship. This attempt at welfarisation of the new social contract in the contemporary public political discourse merged the goals of the old and new social contracts. In both, it was the paternalistic state that took charge of relieving the citizens' grievances. However, this paternalistic state had now increasingly given up on its own welfare institutions, and would seek a market-based solutions to such grievances instead.

By the mid-2000s, in addition to the state-initiated new welfare-based social contract that was to lead to social reform, the state once more engaged with an initiative for a new political reform that would offer a new political social contract. After July 2004, in opposition to the newly appointed 'government of businessmen' headed by Ahmad Nazif, and under the growing political influence of the president's son, Gamal Mubarak, there was an upsurge in public demand for political participation. The demand for a new constitution resurfaced as well. In August 2004, the call for comprehensive political reform found a voice in Kifaya, the broad Egyptian movement for change (which included Islamists), whose Declaration to the Nation was amplified by the sprawling new Arab media of the period.[50] The Egyptian government was also apprehensive about the rise of its main political challenger – the Muslim Brotherhood. In 2005, in a clear attempt to contain the opposition, the Egyptian government initiated its own political reform, offering freer parliamentary elections and, more so, the first elections to the presidency. In addition, the Egyptian constitution was to be reformed.

Analysis of both the elections and the reformed constitution has, unsurprisingly, led to the same conclusion – that the seeming introduction of democratisation (the election) and a reformed, formal social contract (the constitution) did not essentially change Egyptian politics. Lisa Blaydes has argued that to the extent that the elections allowed more political freedom of speech, hence formally venting protest, they also facilitated government reaction against potential opposition because they allowed the state to reckon who the protesters were and what kind of grievances they raised. Therefore, the election allowed the state to contain such openly made opposition.[51] Thus, the December 2005 parliamentary elections saw a significant increase in opposition representatives, especially from among the Muslim Brotherhood. However, the ruling National Democratic Party (NDP) still dominated the parliament. Similarly, the presidential elections during the same year exposed potential contenders but hardly brought a serious challenge to Mubarak's presidency. If anything, it enforced the formal legitimacy of Mubarak's regime, despite the low voter turnout.

In early 2007, the 1971 constitution was finally amended, yet not replaced. (Earlier, the amendment of article 76 of the 1971 constitution had enabled the 2005 presidential elections). In a clear contradiction to the official call for wider public participation in the making of the new constitution, the Egyptian government abruptly brought amendments to be discussed in a conference of the ruling NDP, and in parliament, before they were voted on in parliament – a vote boycotted by the opposition – and rushed to a public vote. Such government actions demonstrated that the amended constitution was not the result of a true or free engagement of the citizens with the state. Nathan Brown, Michele Dunne and Amr Hamzawy suggest that both the constitutional process and the constitutional amendments were semblances of political participation in party politics and provided a greater balance between the branches of government, while they limited actual political competition and kept power with the executive branch and the ruling party.[52]

Central in the amendment to the 1971 constitution was a rather dated acknowledgement of the economic transformation that Egypt had undergone over the previous thirty-five years. Thus, in the amended constitution, development of economic initiative and the protection of property rights replace a socialist economy as the basis of the national economy (article 4).[53] In the same article – squeezed in between two liberal economic principles – the national economy is also based on social justice. Accordingly, free market economic development would not bring about social and class friction. Taxation (article 38) is, in addition, to be based on social justice. Among his other duties, the president is to ensure, as in the past, social justice (article 73). Importantly, there was little change in the constitutional articles guaranteeing socio-economic rights to citizens – the existing social contract – regardless of this social contract's clear erosion over time.[54] In short, social justice would now include the past guarantee embodied in the old social contract for equality of opportunity alongside an attempt in the new social contract to facilitate social reform along with economic reform. In both cases, there was an ongoing emphasis on avoiding social tensions.

From the analysis above, beginning under Sadat and continuing under Mubarak, the pendulum swing from an emphasis on a new political social contract (political participation) to a new economic social contract (social development) hollowed out both of these reforms. Different economic and political aspects of the social contract/s were implemented incrementally, indicating the stickiness of the old/effendi social contract in the name of social and political stability, and therefore also the stickiness of state–middle class relations in Egypt, despite the erosion of state welfare over time.[55] The dual agenda of the new economic and political social contract allowed Egypt's ruling elite to use such ambiguity to keep the status quo: the comprehensiveness of the new social contract turned it into an impediment to overall economic or political change.

An informal status quo

The informal political economy had already emerged under Arab socialism in response to the state's command economy, as did contemporary networks of economic-political patronage.[56] Since the 1970s, in an age of oil-boom and Open Door policy, this informal political economy had deepened, as it had beginning in the 1990s under state policies of economic reform and structural adjustment. While various aspects of economic and political informality have been covered in the literature, the analysis below particularly emphasises two central attributes of this political economy that, despite shifting official state economic policy, showed great persistence: (a) the development of an informal political economy as a mirror image of the formal search for a new social contract over time, and (b) as a result, the de facto enhancement of the status quo via mechanisms of economic liberalisation and political participation.[57] This informal political economy, therefore, reinforced Egypt's self-made trap of avoiding a comprehensive transformation from the old social contract to a new social contract. It did so by sustaining an authoritarian regime, now under a thin veneer of democratisation, concurrently with its main social constituency – the educated, state-employed middle class – despite the growing erosion (crisis) of the latter.

Economic informality flourished in areas where the old, command economy ceased to function, but also in places where neither the formal market economy introduced by the Open Door policy nor the ERSA programme replaced it. Likewise, informal politics flourished under partial political reform, which certainly did not mean democratisation. In both cases, the informal economy and informal politics were officially unaccounted for and ignored. Yet, they were crucial in sustaining a political economy of betwixt and between – of a partially broken old social contract and partially fulfilled promises for a new social contract. An informal political economy facilitated new forms of socio-economic mobility into the middle class and middle-class reproduction without an overall change in socio-economic stratification. In short, an informal political economy facilitated the layering of the old and new social contracts side-by-side. Moreover, in many respects this political economy helped to sustain political stability despite constant public reference to multiple socio-economic crises.

Since the 1970s, the informal economy had come to embody the free-market economy in Egypt, allowing for unregulated and sometimes illegal economic initiatives, with little state taxation or state support. Moreover, the informal economy became ever more present in the gaps between what the state had pledged to citizens and what it actually delivered. This was true both for the provision of goods and services and for providing a living wage to state employees. Importantly, the informal economy in a sense privatised the economic activity of the state itself, allowing state employees to fend for themselves while officially working for the state. Notable examples here were private construction on state land, bribes (*baksheesh*) paid to state officials, state officials taking a second or even third job, and the resale of state-regulated and subsidised goods on the black market. All such practices were illegal but normative, and they spread across society and classes.

The literature on the informal economy has often engaged with the topic in terms of the survival strategies of the lower and the impoverished middle classes – for example, the operation of informal small and middle enterprises, informal housing and the moonlighting of state employees – that helped the average Egyptian stay economically afloat. This literature has also discussed informal state redistribution to these social groups. Studies on networks of privilege and crony capitalism in Egypt have referred to the intensifying involvement of an economic elite – including from the military – with the informal economy, which resulted in the siphoning of wealth to the superrich, causing a rise in economic inequality.[58] While different in purpose (and having different moral implications), these two aspects of the informal economy were the end result of similar processes of a political economy of informality and its systems of patronage. Both flourished because a formal – transparent and regulated – market economy had not really materialised in Egypt.

The state's economic policy had often been shaped by informality, outside of the new economic social contract. It kept a system of indirect taxation intact so as to allow for an informal economic status quo. Moreover, instead of a formal reform of taxation, the state used tax inflation – decreasing state financial commitments through printing money and other regulatory means – to finance chronic shortages in revenues with little public oversight of these actions.[59] In the examples of Egypt's economic policy above, there had been little state transparency or accountability, both of which should have emanated from the global best practices supposedly embodied in the new social contract.

NGOs' activity provided another aspect of informality in creating a fuzzy seamline between government and nongovernment provision of social services. By definition, 'non-governmental organisation' indicates a degree of independence from the state. However, in many cases, the NGOs' activity became a semi-formal venue for the state to supervise and support the allocation of social services, the latter of which had now been reduced under the ERSA programme. The state maintained firm regulation of the NGOs' activities and remained deeply involved in their operations. At times, NGOs were established by state officials and employed state employees. The state also financially supported some NGOs, while withdrawing such support from those NGOs affiliated with the opposition, especially the Muslim Brotherhood. NGOs, in turn, often employed members of the middle class and extended services to this social group in areas, such as education and health, where the state no longer did so.[60] In many respects, therefore, the spread of NGOs, including Islamic NGOS, informally underwrote an official state effort to balance its budget while still tacitly supporting the government's main constituency under the old/new social contract.

Informal political participation permeated formal politics on the municipal, regional and national levels. This political informality closely intertwined with the extension of the informal economy and the networks of patronage it had helped to establish. Of importance was the exchange between state economic assistance, including overlooking informal and illegal economic practices, in return for political support for politicians. Here, as in the informal economy, such practices had become normative across classes, although they manifested themselves through different venues. Moreover, informal politics had become deeply embedded in the processes of stilted democratisation in Egypt.

Since the late 1970s, the establishment of political parties had facilitated informal politics. Parties, particularly the ruling NDP, had turned into venues for access to state patronage, leading to the receipt of state resources. In 2004, the formation of the so-called 'government of businessmen' was the pinnacle of this process. Some of Egypt's largest entrepreneurs-turned-politicians now dominated key state ministries; their appointment seemed to many to be part of a larger effort to secure for Gamal Mubarak, the president's son, a future appointment to his father's position. President Mubarak was part of what Roger Owen has termed 'monarchical presidential regimes', in the Middle East.[61]

Elections became the focal point for the informal economic-political exchange. Blaydes, for example, identifies a two-tiered system of such exchange: before elections, lower-class voters received direct, personal allocations in the form of increased wages, and the regime also increased wages for middle-class state employees in return for their vote.[62] Before the 2005 presidential elections, President Mubarak pledged the public construction of 500,000 housing units for those in need, if he were to be elected.[63] Thus, under the informal exchanges, state provision had in practice switched from maintaining the old social contract and its related moral economy to safeguarding an authoritarian regime from the peril of democratisation under the new social contract, but used similar mechanisms of provision for the struggling effendi middle class.

The informal political economy discussed above was primarily intended to stabilise the social structure, especially the struggling middle class, which remained the central constituency of not only the regime but also the Muslim Brotherhood, the regime's main opposition. The analysis above emphasises how the main articles of the social contract had eroded and occasionally transformed from their original intent, but had never entirely disappeared. New economic and political institutions associated with economic and political reform, or a new social contract, were subverted to allow state provisioning, mainly of the middle class, in exchange for its political support or to avoid its opposition. Moreover, the state largely evaded key areas of required reform, most notably in education and state employment.

Egypt's educated, state-employed middle class had not disappeared, as critics of Egypt's neoliberalisation have lamented, despite being reduced in size and despite the diminishing returns and extended waiting period for state employment.[64] However, neither had a new middle class – in theory, the expected result of those preaching for economic reform – fully emerged. A partially broken old social contract and partially fulfilled promises for a new social contract barely sustained the former, yet failed to allow the transition to the latter. High unemployment rates among the educated, particularly the university educated – arguably Egypt's most acute socio-economic problem – strongly testified to such a situation.[65] The contours of this unemployment – more unemployed in rural as opposed to urban regions, and very high unemployment among educated women – further suggest a familiar bias in the broken, but yet-to-disappear social contract.

Notes

1. Egyptian Press Archive of CEDEJ, *Bibliotheca Alexandrina*, accessed 10 May 2020, http://cedej.bibalex.org/Results.aspx?SearchType=Advanced&lang=en&Title=%22%u0637%u0628%u0642%u0629+%u0648%u0633%u0637%u0649%22&Language=&Country=Egypt&Type=&Page=1&SearchReset=0. I used 'advanced search' in titles for 'middle class' (in Arabic) and for the country Egypt. In the timeline available on this webpage, the year 1998 showed fifteen results out of the total of seventy-four. 'Middle class' did not yield results for the period between 1970 and 1979. For the 1980s, the only two results were for the year 1989. For the 1990s the website yielded thirty-three results. For the period between 2000 and 2008, 36 results. Note that this search included a few entries less relevant to the discussion on the middle class in Egypt. Nevertheless, the timeline does indicate a growing public interest in the middle class during the late 1990s, which is my central argument here.
2. Howaida 'Adli Rumman, *al-Tabaqa al-Wusta fi Misr: Dirasa Tawthikiyya Tahliliyya* (Cairo, 2001), 10, table (no number). According to 'Adli Rumman's analysis, this debate peaked between 1990 and 1995 with 20 publications (35.7% of the total) and decreased slightly to 16 publications (28.6%) for the period between 1995 and 2001, the last year of the research.

3. *Al-Hilal*, August 1991–September 1992. The participants in this dialogue were Galal Amin, Mahmud ʿAwda, ʿAsim al-Dasuki, Mahmoud Abdel-Fadil, Yunan Labib Rizq, Ahmad ʿAbbas Salih, Ibrahim Fathi and Raʾuf ʿAbbas. As suggested from this list, and in ʿAdli Rummanʾs analysis (*al-Tabaqa al-Wusta fi Misr*, 11, table [no number]), it was mostly sociologists, economists and political scientists, in descending order, who joined the discussion first, followed by historians.

4. In addition to the sources cited in Rumman, see Muʾmin Kamal Shafiʿi, *al-Dawla wa-l-Tabaqa al-Wusta*; Yunan Labib Rizq, *Shuʾun wa-Shujun Taʾrikhiyya* (Cairo: Al-Hayʾa al-Misriyya al-ʿAmma li-l-Kitab, 2005), 11–96; and ʿAbd al-Basit ʿAbd al-Muʿti, *al-Tabaqa al-Wusta al-Misriyya: Min al-Taqsir ila al-Tahrir* (Cairo: Maktabat al-ʾUsra, al-Hayʾa al-Misriyya al-ʿAmma lil-Kitab, 2006). For the post–2011 Uprising period, see ʿAshri, *al-Tabaqa al-Wusta*; Ahmad Husayn Hasan, *al-Tabaqa al-Wusta wa-l-Taghayyur al-Ijtimaʿi fi Misr: Tahlil Susyutaʾrikhi (1975–2005)* (Cairo: Markaz al-Mahrusa li-l-Nashr wa-l-Khidmat al-Suhufiyya wa-l-Maʿlumat, 2016). For an attempt at gauging middle-class public discourse (if not political domination), see Muhammad Sayyid Ahmad, *Jadaliyat al-Tabaqa wa-l-Khitab fi al-Mujtamaʿ al-Misri* (Cairo, 2019). See also his *al-Khitab al-Siyasi li-l-Tabaqa al-Wusta al-Misriyya: Dirasa Tahliliyya li-Afkar baʿd Rumuz al-Tabaqa al-Wusta* (PhD diss., Jamiʿat al-Munya, 2005).

5. ʿAshri, *al-Tabaqa al-Wusta*. Yunan Labib Rizq, *Shuʾun wa-Shujun Taʾrikhiyya*, discusses the growing political role of the lower-middle class before the 1952 revolution, and the warm relations between the Free Officers and this class. However, he also later studied how the middle class was, itself, 'nationalised' under the revolution and through state action.

6. This was true for the studies cited in Rumman, *al-Tabaqa al-Wusta fi Misr* (see her analysis on pp. 20–1) as well as for later studies, for example, in Rizq, *Shuʾun wa-Shujun Taʾrikhiyya*.

7. Galal Amin, 'al-Tabaqa al-Wusta wa-Humum al-Mujtamaʿ al-Misri', *al-Hilal*, August 1991. Mahmoud Abdel-Fadil, 'al-Tabaqa al-Wusta wa-ʾAzmat al-Mujtamaʿ al-Misri', *al-Hilal*, January 1992.

8. For this argument in a different context see Marlon Barbehön and Michael Haus, 'Middle Class and Welfare State – Discursive Relations', *Critical Policy Studies* 9, no. 4 (2015): 473–84, https://doi.org/10.1080/19460171.2015.1009840.

9. Ramzi Zaki, *Wadaʿan li-l-Tabaqa al-Wusta: Taʾammulat fi al-Thawra al-Sinaʿiyya al-Thalitha wa-l-Libiraliyya al-Jadida* (Cairo: Dar al-Mustaqbal al-ʿArabi, 1997). During this period, and in addition to his highly productive academic work, Ramzi Zaki was a frequent contributor to the Egyptian press

across the range of political affiliation. Between 1993 and 1997, according the website of the CEDEJ archive, he published fourteen often-critical articles on Egyptian economic affairs in various press venues. See a list, 'Search Results', Egyptian Press Archive of CEDEJ, *Bibliotheca Alexandrina*, accessed 12 May 2020, http://cedej.bibalex.org/Results.aspx?SearchType=Simple&SearchField= All&SearchText=ramzi+zaki&lang=en&Page=1&SearchReset=0.

10. Zaki, *Wada'an li-l-Tabaqa al-Wusta*. See a summary of the above on pp. 141–3.
11. Ikram, *Egyptian Economy*, 60, 63.
12. Ikram, *Political Economy of Reforms*, 279–80.
13. Raymond A. Hinnebusch, 'The Politics of Economic Reform in Egypt', *Third World Quarterly* 14, no. 1 (1993): 159–71, https://doi.org/10.1080/01436599308420318.
14. Analysis here is based on World Bank, *Egypt: Alleviating Poverty*, 223, table J6. Less accounted for in the analysis above were per capita expenditures, which would suggest deteriorating qualities of services, despite a rise in overall state expenditures, and therefore, the further necessity for economic reform.
15. Ibid., 226–9, tables J12–J15.
16. *EHDR 1998/1999*, 76.
17. Mariz Tadros, 'State Welfare in Egypt since Adjustment: Hegemonic Control with a Minimalist Role', *Review of African Political Economy* 33, no. 108 (2006): 237–54. Alaa Shukrallah and Mohamed Hassan Khalil, 'Egypt in Crisis: Politics, Health Care Reform, and Social Mobilization for Health Rights', in *Public Health in the Arab World*, ed. Samer Jabbour, Rita Giacaman, and Marwan Khawaja (Cambridge: Cambridge University Press, 2012), 477–88.
18. Ikram, *Political Economy of Reforms*, 288.
19. Harik, *Economic Policy Reform in Egypt*, 107–8.
20. Samer Soliman, *The Autumn of Dictatorship: Fiscal Crisis and Political Change in Egypt under Mubarak* (Stanford, CA: Stanford University Press, 2011), 157–8.
21. Richard H. Adams Jr, 'Self-Targeted Subsidies: The Political and Distributional Impact of the Egyptian Food Subsidy System', *Economic Development and Cultural Change* 49, no. 1 (2000): 115–36, https://doi.org/10.1086/452493; Akhter U. Ahmed et al., *The Egyptian Food Subsidy System: Structure, Performance, and Options for Reform*, International Food Policy Research Institute (IFPRI) Research Report 119 (Washington, DC: IFPRI, 2001), accessed 24 September 2020, https://ideas.repec.org/p/fpr/resrep/119.html; and Gouda Abdel-Khalek and Karima Korayem, *Fiscal Policy Measures in Egypt: Public Debt and Food Subsidy* (Cairo: AUC Press, 2000).
22. Harik, *Economic Policy Reform in Egypt*, 92–5.

23. In 1984, the waiting period between graduation and appointment to state employment was already three-and-a-half years for university graduates and four years for vocational secondary and technical institute graduates. By 1987, this waiting period grew to five and six years, respectively. Later, hiring of graduates was suspended, but not formally abolished. Instead, the waiting time for a position was further extended. In 1995, the last cohorts of graduates who were offered appointments were the 1983 university graduates and the 1982 vocational secondary and technical institute graduates, with their waiting time having reached twelve and thirteen years, respectively. Assaad, 'The Effects of Public Sector Hiring', 90.
24. See ibid., 93 and 95, respectively, for the percentage of female employment in the public sector, and rates of female unemployment in relation to males.
25. World Bank, *Unlocking the Employment Potential in the Middle East and North Africa: Toward a New Social Contract* (Washington, DC: World Bank, 2004), 35, box 2.1, accessed 17 May 2020, https://openknowledge.worldbank.org/handle/10986/15011.
26. El-Meehy, 'Rewriting the Social Contract', 59. See Ikram, *Egyptian Economy*, 242, table 8.9, for different numbers but the same trend. For decreasing compensation for civil service employees, see Assaad, 'The Effects of Public Sector Hiring', 92.
27. Ikram, *Political Economy of Reforms*, 293.
28. Ikram, *Egyptian Economy*, 81.
29. Joel Beinin, 'Workers and Egypt's January 25 Revolution', *International Labor and Working-Class History* 80, no. 1 (2011): 190–2, https://doi.org/10.1017/S0147547911000123.
30. El-Meehy, 'Rewriting the Social Contract', 114.
31. Ibid., 117.
32. Yahia Shawkat, 'Mubarak's Promise: Social Justice and the National Housing Programme: Affordable Homes or Political Gain?', *Égypte/Monde Arabe* 11 (2014): 203–33; and David Sims, 'Affordable Housing Policies in Egypt after the 2011 Revolution: More of the Same?', in *The Political Economy of the New Egyptian Republic*, ed. Nicholas S. Hopkins, Cairo Papers vol. 33, no. 4 (Cairo: AUC Press, 2015), 174–93.
33. Ray Bush, 'Politics, Power and Poverty: Twenty Years of Agricultural Reform and Market Liberalisation in Egypt', *Third World Quarterly* 28, no. 8 (2007): 1599–615; Reem Saad, 'Egyptian Politics and the Tenancy Law', *Counter-Revolution in Egypt's Countryside: Land and Farmers in the Era of Economic Reform*, ed. Ray Bush (London: Zed Books, 2002), 103–25; and Joya, *The Roots of Revolt*, 195–228.

34. For a political economy analysis of taxation in Egypt, see Soliman, *Autumn of Dictatorship*, 109–18.
35. See a critical discussion of the rentier state theory in Egypt's political economy in ibid., 138–43.
36. Egyptian Press Archive of CEDEJ, *Bibliotheca Alexandrina*, accessed 24 September 2020, http://cedej.bibalex.org/Results.aspx?SearchType=Advanced&lang=en&Title=%d8%b9%d9%82%d8%af%20%d8%a7%d8%ac%d8%aa%d9%85%d8%a7%d8%b9%d9%8a&Language=%d8%b9%d8%b1%d8%a8%d9%8a&Country=Egypt&Type=Press. I used 'advanced search' in titles for 'social contract' in Arabic, for the country of Egypt, and for press articles, with 802 results for the entire period. When searched according to decade, there were no results for 1970–9. For the years 1980–9, the CEDEJ database showed forty results, among them fourteen for the year 1987. For 1990–9, 'social contract' showed 402 results, peaking in 1999 with 103 results. For the years 2000–9, 'social contract' produced 352 results; the timeline for this period demonstrates a constant decrease in the use of this term, from seventy-five in 2000 to thirty-four in 2009. Note that this search included a few entries less relevant to the discussion on the social contract in Egypt and that the total number of entries was slightly higher than those accounted for in the timeline above.

    I also compared this search with a similar keyword search for 'social justice' for this period; the two terms often intertwined in Egyptian political discourse, accessed 24 September 2020, http://cedej.bibalex.org/Results.aspx?SearchType=Advanced&lang=en&Title=%d8%b9%d8%af%d8%a7%d9%84%d8%a9%20%d8%a7%d8%ac%d8%aa%d9%85%d8%a7%d8%b9%d9%8a%d8%a9&Language=%d8%b9%d8%b1%d8%a8%d9%8a&Country=Egypt&Type=Press. Throughout this period, the two terms showed comparable timelines. For 'social justice' the overall results for the years 1970–2009 were 995. For the years 1970–9, the CEDEJ database showed nine results, among them eight for the year 1978. For 1980–9, fifty-one results, among them eleven for 1987. For the years 1990–9, 374 results, among them seventy-eight for 1999. For 2000–9, 429 results, among them ninety-six in 2000. As further suggested by these numbers, 'social justice' in the press showed an overall increase in use during 2000–9, while 'social contract' declined, a point well vindicated by the discussion in this chapter.
37. Robert Springborg, *Mubarak's Egypt: Fragmentation of the Political Order* (Boulder, CO: Westview Press, 1989), 25.
38. 'Mubarak Addresses Joint Legislative Session'. This speech has been translated in Foreign Broadcast Information Service (FBIS) NC 12 I 830 Cairo Domestic Service in Arabic, 0912GMT, 12 November 1986, n.p.

39. The recently established (1978) Socialist Labour Party was encouraged by Sadat to counter the political left. Raymond William Baker, *Sadat and After: Struggles for Egypt's Political Soul* (Cambridge, MA: Harvard University Press, 1990), 123.
40. Muhammad Hasanayn Haykal, 'Bab Misr ila al-Qarn al-Wahad wa-l-'Ishrin', in *Mubarak wa-Zamanuhu min al-Minassa ila al-Maydan*, 2nd ed. (Cairo: Dar al-Shuruq, 2013), 262–88.
41. Muhammad Sayyid Ahmad, 'Rushtatat Haykal fi Kunsultu al-Afkar: Farida Gh'iba Ismaha 'al-'Aqd al-Ijtima'i', *al-'Arabi*, 6 March 1995.
42. The analysis of al-Bishri's call for a new social contract follows Akhavi, 'Sunni Modernist Theories of Social Contract'.
43. Ibid., 38.
44. 'Mubarak on Regional Issues, Muslim Brotherhood'. This speech has been translated in FBIS, MW 11402112295 London *al-Hayat* in Arabic, 12 February 1995, p. 5. Mubarak's quotations below are from the same interview.
45. Bruce Rutherford has suggested that Mubarak had long advocated an argument according to which Egyptians and Egypt's stage of economic development were not yet ready for democratisation. See in his *Egypt after Mubarak: Liberalism, Islam, and Democracy in the Arab World*, new ed. (Princeton, NJ: Princeton University Press, 2017), 233. A strong political motivation for keeping the 1971 constitution was that it enhanced Mubarak's authoritarian regime by centralising the power with the president. See Nathalie Bernard-Maugiron, 'Strong Presidentialism: The Model of Mubarak's Egypt', in *Constitutionalism in Islamic Countries: Between Upheaval and Continuity*, ed. Rainer Grote and Tillman Röder (New York: Oxford University Press, 2012), 373–86.
46. See a report on this summit in *al-Ahram*, 1 January 1995.
47. 'Musa Addresses UN General Assembly', FBIS, NC2609122192 Cairo MENA in Arabic, 1530 GMT, 25 September 1992. Musa reiterated this call for a new social contract twice more in the same venue. See Musa Addresses UN on Regional, World Issues', FBIS, NC2809090593 Cairo Arab Republic of Egypt Radio Network in Arabic, 0413 GA1T, 28 September 1993; and 'Musa Addresses UN General Assembly Session', FBIS, NCOJ 10124494 Cairo Arab Republic of Egypt Radio Network in Arabic, 1742 GMT, 30 September 1994.
48. The discussion above is based on articles found in the CEDEJ archive, keyword search for 'social contract'. As frequently happened with such state initiatives, and as documented in the press clips, there was a buildup in press coverage leading to the conference. There had also been accompanying expert analysis of the topics to be discussed. See, for example, *al-Ahram al-Iqtisadi*, 11 October

1999, based on an earlier, TV programme hosted by Rif'at 'Assam, chief editor of *al-Ahram al-Iqtisadi*.
49. *Al-Ahram al-Iqtisadi*, 11 October 1999; and *al-Ahram*, 20 September 1999.
50. Yoram Meital, 'The Struggle over Political Order in Egypt: The 2005 Elections', *Middle East Journal* 60, no. 2 (2006): 267.
51. Lisa Blaydes, *Elections and Distributive Politics in Mubarak's Egypt* (Cambridge: Cambridge University Press, 2011), 64–76.
52. Nathan Brown, Michele Dunne, and Amr Hamzawy, *Egypt's Controversial Constitutional Amendments, 2007* (Washington, DC: Carnegie Endowment for International Peace, 2007), accessed 18 May 2020, https://carnegieendowment.org/files/egypt_constitution_webcommentary01.pdf.
53. For an article-by-article comparison of the 1971 and 2007 constitutional amendments, see 'The Constitution of the Arab Republic of Egypt, 1971 (as Amended to 2007)', Constitutionnet, accessed 18 May 2020, http://constitutionnet.org/sites/default/files/Egypt%20Constitution.pdf. The analysis here is further based on ibid.; Stilt, 'Constitutions in Authoritarian Regimes'; and Bernard-Maugiron, 'Strong Presidentialism'.
54. These articles are found in part two, 'Basic Foundation of Society', Chapter One 'Social and Moral Foundations' of the amended 2007 constitution.
55. The term 'stickiness' is borrowed from Selina Ho, *Thirsty Cities: Social Contracts and Public Goods Provision in China and India* (Cambridge: Cambridge University Press, 2019).
56. Springborg, *Family, Power, and Politics*.
57. In the vast literature on informal economic and political practices in Egypt, especially relevant to the discussion here are: Singerman, *Avenues of Participation*; Cilja Harders, 'A Revolution of Logics of Action? Renegotiating the Authoritarian Social Contract in Egypt', in *Euro-Mediterranean Relations after the Arab Spring: Persistence in Times of Change*, ed. Jakob Horst, Annette Jünemann, and Delf Rothe (London: Ashgate, 2013), 103–22; and Julia Elyachar, *Markets of Dispossession: NGOs, Economic Development, and the State in Cairo* (Durham, NC: Duke University Press, 2005), 66–95. See also (in a different context): Jaime Saavedra and Mariano Tommasi, 'Informality, the State and the Social Contract in Latin America: A Preliminary Exploration', *International Labour Review* 146, no. 3 (2007): 279–309.
58. Steven Heydemann, ed., *Networks of Privilege in the Middle East: The Politics of Economic Reform Revisited* (New York: Palgrave Macmillan, 2004). For a close ethnography of such networks in Egypt, see John Sfakianakis, 'The Whales of the

Nile: Networks, Businessmen, and Bureaucrats during the Era of Privatization in Egypt', in ibid.; and Hamouda Chekir and Ishac Diwan, 'Crony Capitalism in Egypt', *Journal of Globalization and Development* 5, no. 2 (2014): 177–211.
59. For tax inflation, see Soliman, *Autumn of Dictatorship*, 98–101.
60. For the migration of welfare from the state to NGOs, see Denis Joseph Sullivan, *Private Voluntary Organizations in Egypt: Islamic Development, Private Initiative, and State Control* (Gainesville: University Press of Florida, 1994); and Salwa Ismail, *Political Life in Cairo's New Quarters: Encountering the Everyday State* (Minneapolis: University of Minnesota Press, 2006). Ismail has termed this process 'the relocation of welfare', see the title of Chapter 4, *Political Life*, 66. For the middle class's involvement with Egyptian NGOs, see Maha M. Abdelrahman, *Civil Society Exposed: The Politics of NGOs in Egypt* (Cairo: AUC Press, 2004), 154–7; and Janine A. Clark, *Islam, Charity, and Activism: Middle-Class Networks and Social Welfare in Egypt, Jordan, and Yemen* (Bloomington: Indiana University Press, 2004), 42–81.
61. Roger Owen, *The Rise and Fall of Arab Presidents for Life* (Cambridge, MA: Harvard University Press, 2012).
62. Blaydes, *Elections and Distributive Politics*, 77–124.
63. Shawkat, 'Mubarak's Promise', 204.
64. According to *The Egypt Labor Market Panel Survey 2006*, between 1998 and 2006, government employment declined from 32 per cent to 25 per cent of the labour market. Ragui Assaad, 'Labor Supply, Employment, and Unemployment in the Egyptian Economy, 1988–2006', in *The Egyptian Labor Market Revisited*, ed. Ragui Assaad (Cairo: AUC Press, 2008), 35, figure 1.17.a.
65. Ibid, 29–32.

CONCLUSION
OLD SOCIAL CONTRACT, NEW SOCIAL CONTRACT

This book has set out to explore the puzzle of the social contract in Egypt – why did many of the tenets of the revolutionary social contract still hold strong decades after Nasser? Why has a new social contract still yet to materialise, despite the erosion of the older social contract? The analysis in this book has pushed against two central previous readings of the social contract in Egypt (and, more broadly, in the Middle East): that it has been mostly a top-down authoritarian bargain, and that it has been a populist bargain. Instead, offered here is a history of the social contract through an exploration of state–middle class relations and how those have shaped the social contract over time.

I have studied the trajectory of the social contract on three levels: the political discourse that brought about the making and remaking of the social contract; the relevant legislation, particularly the Egyptian constitutions in which the social contract was officially inscribed; and the actual implementation of the social contract through an analysis of state institutional capacity and state allocation of resources according to various articles of the social contract. Such cross-referencing has enabled the study of both the explicit and the implicit in Egypt's social contract, and often also the gaps between the two. The analysis demonstrates how the Egyptian social contract interacted with changing global trends in socio-economic development and governance. Such global trends, or global best practices, influenced the changing visions of the Egyptian social contract, but also its realms of possibility.

My analysis of the Egyptian social contract echoes Franz Fanon's critique of the post-colonial process in newly liberated states. I concur with Fanon that the political dominance of national middle classes created a gap between national liberation and the liberation of those most in need within the nation because this middle class followed its own self-interests rather than those of the masses.[1] I have studied how a self-centred effendi vision and practice of socio-economic development shaped that of the nation, and how an effendi social contract directed socio-economic development in Egypt over time. Politically, the effendi social contract stood at the core of authoritarianism in Egypt, as it largely impinged on the ability of a new social coalition to form and succeed in altering it. This was so mainly because state–society relations were based upon inverse relations between state-led socio-economic development and democratisation – Egyptians gave up on the former to obtain the latter – a situation that maintained a long-lasting deadlock on both economic and political reform in Egypt. This deadlock was particularly acute because any changes in the social contract would impact the state's main constituency – the state-educated, state-employed middle class.

After 1923, Egypt's constitutional monarchy launched a liberal social contract that was based on a global, nineteenth-century model of conservative social reform and political participation. Productivist welfare, mostly in the form of universal, compulsory (if far from satisfactory) elementary education, was supposed to provide the majority of Egyptians with limited tools to help themselves. Austere state economic management often delegated welfare services to civil society organisations and private or semiprivate benevolence – the distinction between private and state benevolence was not always clear. Both state and civil society welfare services centred on the urban regions, especially Cairo, where Egypt's upper- and effendi middle classes lived, as opposed to rural regions. The call for social reform – to alleviate poverty, ignorance and disease – was central to the elitist- and effendi-led national movement and identity. Regardless of all this, with Egypt still under semicolonial, British control, and the dominance of a land-owing elite but also an effendi middle class hesitant to initiate radical socio-economic change, there was a clear gap between the call for comprehensive social reform and its implementation.

Alongside an economically conservative-liberal social reform – and in an inverse logic to an austere state budget, including a reluctance to raise taxes – Egypt maintained a long-established tradition of socio-economic mobility based on elitist and modern state education leading to state employment. Indeed, a demand to expand both state education and state employment had been at the core of an elitist- and effendi-led national movement since the late nineteenth century. In the background, with Egyptians disadvantaged in terms of their ability to engage with the local market economy – the result of the capitulations and foreign domination in much of this economy – state employment remained the central venue of socio-economic mobility for the majority of educated Egyptians. During the 1920s, many an effendi had benefited from the concurrent expansion of higher education and the Egyptianising of state employment. However, expenditures on higher education and state employment for the effendi middle class capped state finance of welfare services for most Egyptians.

Egypt's liberal social contract was challenged not long after its introduction, especially after the late 1930s, by greater economic and political independence for the nation-state. A global movement toward statism from the left (socialism, communism), the right (fascism and Nazism), and the centre (liberal social democracy) further enhanced the appeal in Egypt of determined state action in the pursuit of socio-economic development. In such state-led development, an earlier call for conservative-liberal social reform had been integrated into and eclipsed by a new demand for social justice – equity and equality of opportunity – particularly for the effendi middle class. At the core of this change was the demographic growth of the effendi middle class, which led to ever-rising pressure on higher education and state employment and a squeeze on compensation for such employment. Close analysis of the contemporary call for social justice exposes a preference for matters related to the welfare of the effendi middle class over those of lower-class peasants and workers.

Between the aftermath of World War II and the 1952 Free Officers' revolution, a new, effendi social contract emerged in Egypt, in which the state took greater control of promoting social justice and economic nationalism, both of which were often associated with socialism. In all the above, an effendi middle class with a large constituency of state employees had a significant ideational and professional stake in statism. Spokespersons for the effendi middle class were often the ones who advocated the use of planning, administrative capacity and science and technology by the state for implementing socio-economic development. All such instruments of development were part of the effendi human capital (to use this notion somewhat anachronistically), or the effendi toolbox. The effendi middle class would also be the main beneficiary of augmented state services and employment. While the effendi middle class wanted to see a strong independent state spring into effendi-type action, this action was to be reformist (evolutionary) and securely set along class lines.

In the debate as to whether the Free Officers were a military junta or part of a new, modern middle class,[2] I largely take the second position, but with one reservation: Nasser and his colleagues constituted a new generation of effendis, not a new middle class. The Free Officers did not lack a coherent ideology when rising to power, as has been previously suggested in the research. Neither was their revolution a new beginning (a zero hour), as was emphasised by the regime itself, and later rehearsed in much of the available research. In short, I have argued that while not strictly the action of a class for itself (to paraphrase Karl Marx), the Free Officers' revolution carried a clear effendi vision and common tools for an intertwined thrust at socio-economic development carried out by a strong nation-state.

Historical contingency clearly influenced the outcomes of the 1952 revolution. Examples abound: the struggle for power among the revolutionaries, and against former allies such as the Muslim Brotherhood and the Egyptian left, enhanced Nasser's grip on power. Nasser's charismatic personality no doubt contributed to his success in capturing and keeping power. After 1956, the successful nationalisation of the Suez Canal Company; British, French and Jewish properties; and, later, Belgian property and that of some among the Egyptian upper class facilitated greater state command of the economy. Furthermore, Egyptianised segments of minority Christian and Jewish communities and Europeans – a sizeable part of the middle and upper class in Egypt – left. This vacated the social space that allowed for the rise of a new effendi elite or state bourgeoisie. The Cold War and the emergence of the Third World movement, in which Egypt took a central role, partially helped Egypt to sponsor state-led socio-economic development. Nevertheless, Nasserism's greatest success – and outright failure – was its enthusiastic embrace of the effendi social contract and its implementation.

Despite the seeming populism of Arab socialism, the effendi social contract under Nasser benefited middle society – a coalition of the urban middle class, the rural middle class and the upper crust of public sector workers. The majority of Egypt's citizens – peasants and workers, often in the informal economy – benefited less. At the core of the Nasserite/effendi social contract was the nexus between state-sponsored higher education and state employment. As in the past, but enhanced by official state corporatism, state employees further doubly benefited from the social contract as providers and, disproportionately, receivers of state services. Import substitute industrialisation – the main thrust at economic development – largely benefited middle-class citizens/consumers. The effendi social contract was for the most part an urban contract, since that was where the middle and upper classes lived. Urban regions, primarily Cairo, received a larger share of state investment in physical and human infrastructure, despite well-recognised gaps between urban and rural development in Egypt. A much-trumpeted land reform significantly benefited the rural middle class, and labour legislation mostly pertained to organised labour in the public sector. The effendi social contract as implemented under Nasser (and later) continued to channel socio-economic mobility in Egypt, as is suggested by the continuing waves of rural-to-urban migration. It was mainly in the cities – close to expanding state services, state education and state employment – that the lower class, especially the lower-middle class, sought socio-economic mobility. Egypt's economic and political elite were replaced by a new, effendi elite.

My analysis of Nasser's effendi state refutes some of the central premises of the so-called 'authoritarian bargain', or the simple, top-down exchange between citizens' economic and political rights, in which the state provided more of the first at the expense of the second. The liberal social contract under the constitutional monarchy was the first to introduce the principle of an agreement between citizens and the state as the basis for political legitimacy, a legitimacy based on the rights and duties of both sides, as articulated in the 1923 constitution. Indeed, since its inception, Egypt's political system had been challenged for not facing up to its responsibilities, the same responsibilities that the Free Officers set out to fulfil. Moreover, the Free Officers abrogated the 1923 constitution, but they immediately attempted to form a new one to replace it. Under Nasser, Egypt experienced several efforts at constitution making, ending with the interim 1964 constitution. This periodic change in constitutions, and the announcement of the National Charter, took place alongside or despite intensifying state repression in Egypt. Such adjustments suggest that the authoritarian bargain was, at the very least, conditional. If the state did not perform its end of the bargain – socio-economic development – it was supposed to return political rights to citizens. Importantly, this was to be an effendi bargain based on effendi vision and interests in development, as opposed to those of the entire citizenry or the people. Authoritarianism only enhanced the performance-based conditionality in which Nasser's regime demanded greater exclusivity of power in exchange for promising more to the effendi middle class.[3] To a large extent, therefore, Arab socialism as an ideology and practice was the heyday of the middle class in Egypt, if not a new middle class per se. The middling groups of workers and peasants benefited from it as well.

Along the same lines, but from a different perspective, the propensity for an authoritarian, performance-based bargain in Egypt did not start with Nasser. Under the constitutional monarchy, Egypt's political leadership – the palace and its cronies, but also their political rivals, and various extra-parliamentary effendi movements and parties – demonstrated a growing inclination toward authoritarianism. Freedom of speech and political participation were frequently limited, and the state regulated, curtailed and took charge of civil society organisations. In return the state progressively engaged in welfare provision and command of the economy.

Even before an authoritarian, military regime came to power, many who engaged in Egypt's effendi-led, public–political discourse called for state involvement in socio-economic development and blamed Egypt's political leadership for its lack. Mounting disappointment with the parliamentary system, its corruption, immorality, patronage and mostly its inability to bring swift relief to the economy and society, led to high hopes for the military intervention. Hence, the conditionality between state performance and authoritarianism became entrenched in politics before the revolution took place. Such conditionality secured support for the revolution and for future state commitment to socio-economic development or, when the latter did not work, to more citizen participation in politics. Escalating social unrest among workers and peasants further led to the 1952 revolution because it pushed many effendis to demand state interference to bring security back to Egyptian society, which has been another constant tenet of the citizen–state exchange ever since.

As recent Egyptian historiography attests, and as has been reflected for a long time in the nostalgia for that period, Nasser's Egypt was the heyday of the effendi middle class. Indeed, over time the main problem with Nasser's effendi social contract was its success in formalising effendi attributes of social reproduction – in enlarging a middle-class society in Egypt along effendi lines – a success that became unsustainable. This happened despite the generational diminishing returns for joining this social group, not least because alternatives to socio-economic mobility, notably through free economic initiative, barely existed, while state employees still benefited relatively more than others from state services.

Under Presidents Sadat and Mubarak, the central contours of the social contract remained the same, despite their erosion over time. Moreover, this social contract became the basis of a moral economy that was to support the lower echelons of Egypt's middle-class society, a consensual moral economy publicly shared by the state and its opposition, across both the political spectrum and the secular–religious divide. Especially under Mubarak, there was a growing tension between neoliberal reforms and contradictory steps that the state took to protect the state-educated, state-employed middle class – the regime's main constituency, but also its growing opposition.

State budgets continued to be biased toward higher, as opposed to elementary, education. Spending on education was higher than on health and welfare. Expenditures on state employment took much-needed funds from the infrastructure and services provided to the citizens most in need of such services. Universal state subsidies catered more to the established middle and upper classes than to the lower class, and to urban more than to rural regions. Taxation had been mostly regressive and universal, as opposed to being progressive and redistributive, and hence favoured better-off Egyptians over those of the lower class. Such a continuity in the social contract took place despite new economic opportunity in the form of a regional oil-boom, and regardless of rising public discontent over the implementation of the social contract and escalating concern over its sustainability.

The search for the means to finance the effendi social contract was at the core of the country's regional and international politics under Nasser, Sadat and Mubarak alike. Sadat's Open Door policy was logically closer to Nasser's 'third worldism' than was initially observed. Both Nasser and Sadat operated to maximise political rent based on Egypt's geostrategic position and seniority in the region – increasingly, by attempting to tap regional oil wealth. Nasser envisioned economic opportunity by means of postcolonial activism and reliance on the USSR, while Sadat identified a similar opportunity with the United States. Meanwhile Mubarak predicated a new ERSA programme on Western forgiveness and restructuring of debt in return for Egypt's participation in the coalition against Saddam Hussein during the First Gulf War.

For four decades or so, the persistence of Egypt's social contract, and the moral economy that enhanced that persistence, has supported the robustness of the country's authoritarian regime. The ruling elite and middle-class society did not really have an impetus to bring about an overall change to the political economy. Egypt's straddling of economic and political reforms meant that the country ended up with diluted versions of both.

Dependent on international rent, the state officially promoted an economic transformation based on a global best practice of neoliberalisation that, if fully implemented, would have rewritten the effendi social contract. Such a transformation would have decreased the role of the developing state in the economy through privatisation. It would also have reduced support for the effendi middle class by redirecting state provisioning toward new forms of productivist welfare – from vocational training to microloans – for the lower class (those most in need). As a result, state employment – long the mainstay of the middle class, and increasingly over time, of the lower middle class – would have been reduced and streamlined, bringing fewer employment opportunities and more regimented work to employees. An invigorated private sector was to absorb an employment surplus, but implicitly through the partial proletarianisation of the effendi middle class. The end result of this transformation would have been to facilitate fast economic growth that would somehow compensate for the rewriting of the economic articles of the existing social contract.

In return for the economic transformation above, and, to paraphrase Zaki's powerful words 'farewell to the effendi middle class', the state was to allow political freedom and citizen participation. These included increased freedom of speech and a greater say in managing the state, the right to organise on professional and political levels through the establishment of trade unions and parties and a more substantial role for civil society organisations in all such affairs. As discussed above, these were new venues for middle class reproduction, and were not infrequently organisational bases for political opposition, often by the Muslim Brotherhood. Thus, concurrent economic and political reforms, which were to undo the past nexus between the command economy and authoritarian politics, were at the root of the class-turned-political crisis. In many respects, both reforms became trapped as a result: the intertwined economic and political reforms could not progress as planned or promised, because they would have unsettled both the social and the political structures. Neither Egypt's political elite, nor their main constituency, the effendi middle class, were ready for any such abrupt change, and they did not trust the other side to reciprocate.

As narrated in Part Three, Sadat's Corrective Revolution, and later the Open Door policy, first introduced an official attempt to partially democratise in exchange for the partial liberalisation of the economy. Economic reform was to invigorate the state-led economy, particularly through industrialisation, in an attempt to safeguard the state funds required for financing state provisioning of effendi middle class citizens. Under oil-boom conditions, the number of the latter had significantly risen. Sadat expanded freedom of speech and political rights, but also abruptly reversed them at his own will, thus retaining the authoritarian character of the Egyptian regime. Citizens, for their part, as was clearly demonstrated in the 1977 Food Uprising, held the state responsible for various articles of the social contract – especially subsidies, whose share of an unsustainable state budget had considerably increased. Also, economic and political informality expanded under Sadat, whereas the formal economic and political reform of the social contract floundered. For the economy, informality largely stood for economic liberalisation from below – with little state interference, and therefore with tacit state encouragement. It also included the informal privatisation of the state itself, from moonlighting and corruption in public services to the growing role of the military in the civilian economy. Political reform and, notably, elections enhanced political patronage and vote buying, opening new routes for exchange between political participation and economic favour. In short, the expansion of middle-class society during this period also brought new measures for the informal incorporation of middle-class citizens within the existing political system, with little attempt to make comprehensive changes in Egypt's formal political economy.

In the 1980s, under Mubarak, the broken social contract remained as it was. Economic reform was largely stalled, despite mounting state debt, as was political reform, despite an official call for a new social contract. Past socio-economic channelling into the effendi middle class still prevailed, despite the creeping erosion of compensation in state employment and state services. The 1990s brought a haphazard neoliberal ERSA programme in response to a huge international (read Western) incentive. The public sector was partially privatised and public sector employment reduced, but the same did not apply to state employment in the bureaucracy. State services and subsidies continued to favour the middle class – albeit the lower echelon of this social stratum – as opposed to those most in need. Egypt's effendi middle class progressively became a struggling middle class, one living too close for comfort to a real or imagined poverty line.

Mubarak's regime demonstrated more tolerance of civil society, not least because the often religiously based NGOs increasingly provided employment and social services that the state did not, or better quality employment and services to the middle class than the state was able to. Hence, NGOs partly relieved the state of its economic responsibilities under the social contract. Also, the ERSA programme, and various glocal planning initiatives before and especially since the 1990s (the EHDRs), called upon the state to focus on the alleviation of poverty through schemes of productivist welfare, as opposed to facilitating socio-economic mobility into the effendi middle class. In many respects, this newly introduced initiative – and state retrenchment – was reminiscent of the conservative-liberal social reform of the first half of the twentieth century. It was introduced despite the fact that the state was still officially committed to broader tenets of social justice, and an effendi social justice as such: The abrupt implementation of the ERSA did not really open enough new economic opportunities to allow alternative venues for mobility into the middle class or for its reproduction. Thus, it forsook the first basic tenet of this social justice – equality of opportunity. The rise of crony capitalism forsook the second tenet – equity.

The state continually acknowledged the intertwining of economic and political reforms but often employed them as alternatives, and not in tandem. It used promises of public participation in politics, and applied a semblance of democratic principles of governance, such as party politics and elections, in exchange for state economic retrenchment. Stalling on bringing a new constitution to Egypt, a presidential election that only enforced Mubarak's presidency, and the grooming of Gamal Mubarak, the president's son, to take power after his father, hardly indicated the democratisation of Egypt. For Mubarak, like Sadat before him, the promise of political reform was the proverbial carrot in initiating economic reform, but state repression also loomed close by to replace this carrot with a stick. Gradualism, as often aspired to by Mubarak and the Egyptian government in implementing economic and political reforms, brought neither broad enough socio-economic change – and therefore a new social constituency to fully support the economic reform – nor the evolutionary end of authoritarianism in Egypt.

For thirty years Mubarak maintained the existing balance of diluted economic and political reforms in which the social contract had eroded but never entirely disappeared. One significant social result of this situation was that the effendi middle class became a diluted social category in itself.[4] It did not disappear, as Ramzi Zaki lamented in his *Farewell to the Middle Class*. However, higher education and state employment did stop delivering socio-economic mobility to the extent that it had been delivered under Nasser, and many a hope for ascent into the effendi middle class was dashed. Nor did a new social contract come into being to replace the old, which, had it happened, would have offered new hope for the middle class, and for the Egyptian citizenry more broadly. An elaborated informal political economy sustained the status quo by economically sustaining citizens as well as the existing political system.

The problem with the elusive new social contract – as both a public demand and a state promise – was that it continually failed to deliver what it seemingly contained. Indeed, the 2011 Uprising was a protest against the frustration associated with the top-down implementation of a new social contract that failed the moral economy of the old social contract while also failing to deliver a decent economic alternative or democratisation. Egypt did not undergo the kind of economic reform and structural adjustment that even partially allowed for the development of a new, open and transparent market economy. Neither did the authoritarian regime allow citizens to have full political rights or significant political participation.

Unsurprisingly, in its rather selective adaptation of the new social contract, the state focused first and foremost on economic reform, while citizens emphasised their political rights. Few of the economic and political reforms materialised as planned. Reform brought economic growth but also economic tribulation and inequality, and this was particularly true for the still largely educated, state-employed middle class. Especially glaring was the tremendous wealth of Egypt's new economic-turned-political elite, wealth that had been acquired through the spread of crony capitalism. Politically, more freedom of speech, including through new social media, facilitated political opposition and a call for democracy. Yet it also resulted in both an enlarged gap between this call and the possibility of bringing about gradual political change, and growing state repression. Arguably, the gap in expectations between the much promised but still unfulfilled new social contract created the coalition of discontent that sought to change politics and the system (*nizam*) during the 2011 Uprising. However, the protesters' demand for bread, freedom and social justice also reflected the past conundrum of the social contract in its entanglement of economic and political rights.[5]

Other social groups besides the effendi middle class – peasants and workers – played a significant role in the history of Egyptian politics. Their protests during the 1919 Revolution, before the 1952 revolution, during the 1977 Food Uprising and before and during the 2011 Uprising were a driving force in all these events. Nevertheless, throughout this book I have foregrounded the effendi middle class vision and interests that have shaped politics but also directed society – moulding it to conform with their vision and interests – not least through the establishment and longevity of the effendi social contract. Indeed, the disappearance of the term *effendiyya* in Nasser's effendi state and the emergence of the term 'middle class' in the public discourse of the 1990s, when this class seemed to have disappeared, suggest that class's centrality in Egyptian socio-politics over time. In the first instance, such vision and interests became hegemonic and hence invisible. In the second, the crisis of the effendi middle class was often equated with that of the entire society.

The analysis in this book has suggested that the question raised in the Introduction – how to promote a just and sustainable social contract in Egypt and other regional states – must largely be addressed by society. Regional authoritarian regimes will only be replaced by strong social coalitions whose joint hope for change and willingness to compromise – on both the vertical social contract with the state and the horizontal social contract between citizens – will allow for genuine change in politics. The 2011 Uprising in Egypt initially constituted such a coalition, but it ultimately failed under social constraints and a pushback by the military. Yet, for a brief moment in time, the uprising pointed in the right direction.

Notes

1. For a different interpretation that postpones Fanon's critique of the national middle class to the post-Nasserist era, see Salem, *Anticolonial Afterlives*, 159–205. As detailed in Part Two, the new effendis of the Nasser era had already established a state that significantly benefited their vision and interests.
2. See the Halpern-Perlmutter debate in *Comparative Studies in Society and History* – 10, no. 1; 11, no.1; 12, no. 1 – between 1967 and 1970.
3. 'Performance-based social contract' is taken from a typology of various social contracts found in Ho, *Thirsty Cities*, 240–2.
4. Galal A. Amin, *Egypt in the Era of Hosni Mubarak, 1981–2011* (Cairo: AUC Press, 2011), 85–100.
5. Noha Mellor, *The Egyptian Dream: Egyptian National Identity and Uprisings* (Edinburgh: Edinburgh University Press, 2016), 74–5, further suggests an inner middle-class debate and class friction between lower- and middle-class Egyptians over economic vs political rights.

BIBLIOGRAPHY

Abaza, Mona, *Changing Consumer Cultures of Modern Egypt: Cairo's Urban Reshaping* (Leiden: Brill, 2006).

'Abd al-Fatah, Muhammad Muhammad Tawfiq, Introduction to *al-Dustur al-Ijtima'i li-l-Jumhuriyya al-'Arabiyya al-Muttahida, ka-ma Wada'ahu al-Ra'is Jamal 'Abd al-Nasir*, by Wizarat al-Shu'un al-Ijtima'iyya wa-l-'Amal (Cairo: Wizarat al-Shu'un al-Ijtima'iyya wa-l-'Amal, 1961).

'Abd al-Mu'ti, 'Abd al-Basit, *al-Tabaqa al-Wusta al-Misriyya: Min al-Taqsir ila al-Tahrir* (Cairo: Maktabat al-'Usra, al-Hay'a al-Misriyya al-'Amma lil-Kitab, 2006).

'Abd al-Nasir, Huda Jamal, *al-Majmu' al-Kamila li-Khutub wa-Tasrihat al-Ra'is Jamal 'Abd al-Nasir, 1954–1970* (Cairo: Academic Bookshop, 2005–2009). Accessed 12 April 2020, https://platform.almanhal.com/Search/Result?q=&sf_31_0_3=Reign+of+Jamal+Abdul+Nasser+1954+-+1970&opsf_31_0=1.

'Abd al-Raziq, Husayn, *Misr fi 18 wa-19 Yanayir: Dirasa Siyasiyya Watha'iqiyya* (Beirut: Dar al-Kalima, 1979).

Abdalla, Ahmed, *The Student Movement and National Politics in Egypt, 1923–1973* (Cairo: AUC Press, 2008).

Abdel-Fadil, Mahmoud, *Development, Income Distribution, and Social Change in Rural Egypt, 1952–1970: A Study in the Political Economy of Agrarian Transition* (Cambridge: Cambridge University Press, 1975).

Abdel-Fadil, Mahmoud, 'Educational Expansion and Income Distribution in Egypt, 1952–1977', in *The Political Economy of Income Distribution in Egypt*, edited by Gouda Abdel-Khalek and Robert Tignor (New York: Holmes and Meier, 1982), pp. 351–76.

Abdel-Fadil, Mahmoud, *The Political Economy of Nasserism: A Study in Employment and Income Distribution Policies in Urban Egypt, 1952–72* (Cambridge: Cambridge University Press, 1980).

Abdel-Fadil, Mahmoud, 'al-Tabaqa al-Wusta wa-'Azmat al-Mujtama' al-Misri', *al-Hilal*, January 1992.

Abdel-Khalek, Gouda, and Karima Korayem, *Fiscal Policy Measures in Egypt: Public Debt and Food Subsidy* (Cairo: AUC Press, 2000).

Abdel-Malek, Anouar, *Egypt: Military Society: The Army Regime, the Left, and Social Change under Nasser* (New York: Random House, 1968).

Abdel Meguid, Amina Abdel Razzak, 'Biography'. Accessed 30 April 2020, http://www.abdelrazzakabdelmeguid.com/biography.html.

Abdelrahman, Maha M., *Civil Society Exposed: The Politics of NGOs in Egypt* (Cairo: AUC Press, 2004).

Abdulhaq, Najat, *Jewish and Greek Communities in Egypt: Entrepreneurship and Business Before Nasser* (London: I. B. Tauris, 2016).

Abou-El-Fadl, Reem, *Foreign Policy as Nation Making: Turkey and Egypt in the Cold War* (Cambridge: Cambridge University Press, 2018).

Abu Jaber, Kamel S., 'Salamah Musa: Precursor of Arab Socialism', *Middle East Journal* vol. 20, no. 2 (1966), pp. 196–206.

Abu-Laban, Baha, 'The National Character in the Egyptian Revolution', *Journal of Developing Areas* vol. 1, no. 2 (1967), pp. 179–98.

Abu-'Uksa, Wael, *Freedom in the Arab World: Concepts and Ideologies in Arabic Thought in the Nineteenth Century* (Cambridge: Cambridge University Press, 2016).

Abul-Magd, Zeinab, *Militarizing the Nation: The Army, Business, and Revolution in Egypt* (New York: Columbia University Press, 2017).

Adams, Richard H., Jr, *Development and Social Change in Rural Egypt* (Syracuse, NY: Syracuse University Press, 1986).

Adams, Richard H., Jr, 'Self-Targeted Subsidies: The Political and Distributional Impact of the Egyptian Food Subsidy System', *Economic Development and Cultural Change* vol. 49, no. 1 (2000), pp. 115–36. https://doi.org/10.1086/452493.

Afxentiou, Panayiotis C., 'Basic Needs: A Survey of the Literature', *Canadian Journal of Development Studies / Revue canadienne d'études du développement* vol. 11, no. 2 (1990), pp. 241–57. https://doi.org/10.1080/02255189.1990.9669399.

Agrama, Hussein Ali, *Questioning Secularism: Islam, Sovereignty, and the Rule of Law in Modern Egypt* (Chicago: University of Chicago Press, 2012).

Ahmad, Muhammad Sayyid, *Jadaliyat al-Tabaqa wa-l-Khitab fi al-Mujtama' al-Misri* (Cairo: 2019).

Ahmad, Muhammad Sayyid, 'al-Khitab al-Siyasi li-l-Tabaqa al-Wusta al-Misriyya: Dirasa Tahliliyya li-Afkar ba'd Rumuz al-Tabaqa al-Wusta', PhD diss., Jami'at al-Munya, 2005.

Ahmad, Muhammad Sayyid, 'Rushtatat Haykal fi Kunsultu al-Afkar: Farida Gh'iba Ismaha 'al-'Aqd al-Ijtima'i', *al-'Arabi*, 6 March 1995.

Ahmed, Akhter U., Howarth E. Bouis, Tamar Gutner, and Hans Löfgren, *The Egyptian Food Subsidy System: Structure, Performance, and Options for Reform*, International Food Policy Research Institute (IFPRI) Research Report 119 (Washington, DC: IFPRI, 2001). Accessed 24 September 2020, https://ideas.repec.org/p/fpr/resrep/119.html.

Akeel, H. A., and Clement M. Henry, 'The Class Origins of Egyptian Engineer-Technocrats', in *Commoners, Climbers and Notables: A Sampler on Social Ranking in the Middle East*, edited by C. A. O. Van Nieuwenhoijze (Leiden: Brill, 1977), pp. 279–92.

Akerlof, George A., Pranab Bardhan, and Roger Craine, 'In Memoriam', University of California. Accessed 30 April 2020, https://senate.universityofcalifornia.edu/_files/inmemoriam/html/benthansen.htm.

Akhavi, Shahrough, 'Sunni Modernist Theories of Social Contract in Contemporary Egypt', *International Journal of Middle East Studies* vol. 35, no. 1 (2003), pp. 23–49.

Ali, Sonia M., and Richard H. Adams Jr, 'The Egyptian Food Subsidy System: Operation and Effects on Income Distribution', *World Development* vol. 24, no. 11 (1996), pp. 1777–91.

Amin, Galal A., *Egypt in the Era of Hosni Mubarak, 1981–2011* (Cairo: AUC Press, 2011).

Amin, Galal A., 'al-Tabaqa al-Wusta wa-Humum al-Mujtama' al-Misri', *al-Hilal*, August 1991.

Ansari, Hamied, *Egypt, the Stalled Society* (Albany: State University of New York Press, 1986).

'Ashri, Mushira, *al-Tabaqa al-Wusta: Min Marhalat al-Izdihar ila Siyasat al-Ifqar* (Cairo: Misr al-'Arabiyya li-l-Nashr wa-l-Tawzi', 2014).

Assaad, Ragui, 'The Effects of Public Sector Hiring and Compensation Policies on the Egyptian Labor Market', *World Bank Economic Review* vol. 11, no. 1 (1997), pp. 85–118.

Assaad, Ragui, 'Labor Supply, Employment, and Unemployment in the Egyptian Economy, 1988–2006', in *The Egyptian Labor Market Revisited*, edited by Ragui Assaad (Cairo: AUC Press, 2008), pp. 1–52.

'Assam, Rif'at, 'Musawwighat al-'Aqd al-Ijtima'i al-Jadid'. Brought to print by Zainab Ibrahim. *al-Ahram al-Iqtisadi*, 11 October 1999.

Ayubi, Nazih N. M., *Bureaucracy and Politics in Contemporary Egypt* (London: Ithaca Press, 1980).

Baer, Gabriel, 'Egyptian Attitudes towards Land Reform, 1922–1955', in *The Middle East in Transition: Studies in Contemporary History*, edited by Walter Z. Laqueur (London: Routledge Library Editions, 2017), pp. 80–99.

Baker, Raymond William, *Egypt's Uncertain Revolution under Nasser and Sadat* (Cambridge, MA: Harvard University Press, 1978).

Baker, Raymond William, *Sadat and After: Struggles for Egypt's Political Soul* (Cambridge, MA: Harvard University Press, 1990).

Barawy, Rashed el-, *The Military Coup in Egypt: An Analytic Study* (Cairo: Renaissance Bookshop, 1952).

Barbehön, Marlon, and Michael Haus, 'Middle Class and Welfare State – Discursive Relations', *Critical Policy Studies* vol. 9, no. 4 (2015), pp. 473–84.

Baron, Beth, *The Orphan Scandal: Christian Missionaries and the Rise of the Muslim Brotherhood* (Palo Alto, CA: Stanford University Press, 2014).

Barrawi, Rashid al-, *Mashruʻat al-Sanawat al-Khams min al-Nahiyatan al-Nazariyya wa-l-Tabiqiyya* (Cairo: Maktabat al-Nahda al-Misriyya, 1948).

Barrawi, Rashid al-, and Muhammad Hamza ʻUlaysh, *al-Tatawwur al-Iqtisadi fi Misr fi al-ʻAsr al-Hadith*. 2nd ed (Cairo: Maktabat al-Nahda al-Misriyya, 1945).

Bechor, Guy, 'To Hold the Hand of the Weak: The Emergence of Contractual Justice in Egyptian Civil Law', *Islamic Law and Society* vol. 8, no. 2 (2001), pp. 179–200.

Beinin, Joel, 'Workers and Egypt's January 25 Revolution', *International Labor and Working-Class History* vol. 80, no. 1 (2011), pp. 189–96.

Beinin, Joel, *Workers and Peasants in the Modern Middle East* (Cambridge: Cambridge University Press, 2001).

Beinin, Joel, and Zachary Lockman, *Workers on the Nile: Nationalism, Communism, Islam, and the Egyptian Working Class, 1882–1954* (Princeton, NJ: Princeton University Press, 1987).

Belli, Mériam N., *An Incurable Past: Nasser's Egypt Then and Now* (Gainesville: University Press of Florida, 2013).

Berger, Morroe, *Bureaucracy and Society in Modern Egypt: A Study of the Higher Civil Service* (Princeton, NJ: Princeton University Press, 1957).

Berger, Morroe, *Islam in Egypt Today: Social and Political Aspects of Popular Religion* (Cambridge: University Press, 1970).

Berger, Morroe, *The Middle Class in the Arab World*, Princeton University Conference (Series) 9 (Princeton, NJ: Princeton University Conference, 1957).

Bergh, Sylvia I., 'Introduction: Researching the Effects of Neoliberal Reforms on Local Governance in the Southern Mediterranean', *Mediterranean Politics* vol. 17, no. 3 (2012), pp. 303–21.

Bernard-Maugiron, Nathalie, 'Strong Presidentialism: The Model of Mubarak's Egypt', in *Constitutionalism in Islamic Countries: Between Upheaval and Continuity*, edited by Rainer Grote and Tilmann Röder (New York: Oxford University Press, 2012), pp. 373–86.

Bianchi, Robert, *Unruly Corporatism: Associational Life in Twentieth-Century Egypt* (New York: Oxford University Press, 1989).

Bidewy, M. Fouad el., *The Development of Social Security in Egypt* (Cairo: Ministry of Social Affairs, 1953).

Bier, Laura, *Revolutionary Womanhood: Feminisms, Modernity, and the State in Nasser's Egypt* (Stanford, CA: Stanford University Press, 2011).

Binder, Leonard, *In a Moment of Enthusiasm: Political Power and the Second Stratum in Egypt* (Chicago: University of Chicago Press, 1978).

Blaydes, Lisa, *Elections and Distributive Politics in Mubarak's Egypt* (Cambridge: Cambridge University Press, 2011).

Boktor, Amir, *School and Society in the Valley of the Nile* (Cairo: Elias' Modern Press, 1936).

Botman, Selma, 'The Liberal Age, 1923–1952', in *The Cambridge History of Egypt*, vol. 2, *Modern Egypt, from 1517 to the End of the Twentieth Century*, edited by Martin W. Daly, 285–308 (Cambridge: Cambridge University Press, 1998).

Boutros-Ghali, Youssef, and Lance Taylor, 'Basic Needs Macroeconomics: Is It Manageable in the Case of Egypt', *Journal of Policy Modeling* vol. 2, no. 3 (1980), pp. 409–36.

Brown, Nathan J., 'Nasser's Legal Legacy: Accessibility, Accountability, and Authoritarianism', in *Rethinking Nasserism: Revolution and Historical Memory in Modern Egypt*, edited by Elie Podeh and Onn Winckler (Gainesville: University Press of Florida, 2004), pp. 127–43.

Brown, Nathan, Michele Dunne, and Amr Hamzawy, *Egypt's Controversial Constitutional Amendments, 2007* (Washington, DC: Carnegie Endowment for International Peace, 2007). Accessed 18 May 2020, https://carnegieendowment.org/files/egypt_constitution_webcommentary01.pdf.

Bush, Ray, 'Politics, Power and Poverty: Twenty Years of Agricultural Reform and Market Liberalisation in Egypt', *Third World Quarterly* vol. 28, no. 8 (2007), pp. 1599–615.

Chekir, Hamouda, and Ishac Diwan, 'Crony Capitalism in Egypt', *Journal of Globalization and Development* vol. 5, no. 2 (2014), pp. 177–211.

Citino, Nathan J., *Envisioning the Arab Future: Modernisation in U.S.-Arab Relations, 1945–1967* (Cambridge: Cambridge University Press, 2017).

Clark, Janine A., *Islam, Charity, and Activism: Middle-Class Networks and Social Welfare in Egypt, Jordan, and Yemen* (Bloomington: Indiana University Press, 2004).

Cole, Juan. R., *Colonialism and Revolution in the Middle East: Social and Cultural Origins of Egypt's 'Urabi Movement* (Cairo: AUC Press, 1999).

The Comprehensive Five-year Plan for the Economic and Social Development of the UAR, 1960–1965. Middle East Publications: The National Publications House Press, 1960.

'Constitution of the Arab Republic of Egypt', *Middle East Journal* vol. 26, no. 1 (1972), pp. 55–68.

'The Constitution of the Arab Republic of Egypt', 1971 (as Amended to 2007)'. *Constitutionnet*. Accessed 18 May 2020, http://constitutionnet.org/sites/default/files/Egypt%20Constitution.pdf.

Cooper, Mark N., *The Transformation of Egypt* (Baltimore, MD: Johns Hopkins University Press, 1982).

Cuno, Kenneth M., *The Pasha's Peasants: Land, Society, and Economy in Lower Egypt, 1740–1858* (Cambridge: Cambridge University Press, 1992).

Darling, Linda T., *A History of Social Justice and Political Power in the Middle East: The Circle of Justice from Mesopotamia to Globalization* (New York: Routledge, 2013).

Deeb, Marius, 'Labour and Politics in Egypt, 1919–1939', *International Journal of Middle East Studies* vol. 10, no. 2 (1979), pp. 187–203.

Deeb, Marius, *Party Politics in Egypt: The Wafd & Its Rivals, 1919–1939* (London: Ithaca Press, 1979).

Devarajan, Shantayanan, and Elena Ianchovichina, 'A Broken Social Contract, Not High Inequality, Led to the Arab Spring', *Review of Income and Wealth* vol. 64 (2018), pp. S5–S25.

De Vries, Jan, 'The Industrial Revolution and the Industrious Revolution', *Journal of Economic History* vol. 54, no. 2 (1994), pp. 249–70.

Diwan, Ishac, 'Understanding Revolution in the Middle East: The Central Role of the Middle Class', *Middle East Development Journal* vol. 5, no. 1 (2013), pp. 1350004-1–30.

'Egypt Aided By I.M.F.'s Loan Accord', *New York Times*, 2 June 1978. Accessed 2 June 2019, https://www.nytimes.com/1978/06/02/archives/egypt-aided-by-imfs-loan-accord-paris-meeting-scheduled.html.

Elyachar, Julia, *Markets of Dispossession: NGOs, Economic Development, and the State in Cairo*, Durham, NC: Duke University Press, 2005.

Ener, Mine, *Managing Egypt's Poor and the Politics of Benevolence, 1800–1952* (Princeton, NJ: Princeton University Press, 2003).

Erlich, Haggai, *Students and University in 20th Century Egyptian Politics* (London: F. Cass, 1989).

Faksh, Mahmud A., 'Education and Elite Recruitment: An Analysis of Egypt's Post-1952 Political Elite', *Comparative Education Review* vol. 20, no. 2 (1976), pp. 140–50.

Fanon, Frantz, *The Wretched of the Earth* (New York: Grove Press, 1968).

Foda, Omar D., *Egypt's Beer: Stella, Identity, and the Modern State* (Austin: University of Texas Press, 2019).

Francis, René, *Social Welfare in Egypt* (Cairo: Impr. Misr, 1950).

Gasper, Michael Ezekiel, *The Power of Representation: Publics, Peasants, and Islam in Egypt* (Stanford, CA: Stanford University Press, 2009).

Ginat, Rami, *Egypt's Incomplete Revolution* (London: Routledge, 1997).

Ginat, Rami, *A History of Egyptian Communism: Jews and Their Compatriots in Quest of Revolution* (Boulder, CO: Lynne Rienner Publishers, 2011).

Goldberg, Ellis, 'Peasants in Revolt – Egypt 1919', *International Journal of Middle East Studies* vol. 24, no. 2 (1992), pp. 261–80.

Gordon, Joel, 'The False Hopes of 1950: The Wafd's Last Hurrah and the Demise of Egypt's Old Order', *International Journal of Middle East Studies* vol. 21, no. 2 (1989), pp. 193–214.

Gordon, Joel, *Nasser's Blessed Movement: Egypt's Free Officers and the July Revolution* (New York: Oxford University Press, 1992).

'Government of Arab Republic of Egypt United Nations Development Programme', Project title: 'Social Contract Advisory, Monitoring, and Coordination Center', Proposal ID: 00045653, Project ID: 00053972'. Accessed 17 April 2020, https://info.undp.org/docs/pdc/Documents/EGY/00045653_Pov_Pro%20doc_Social%20Contract%20Center.pdf.

Gran, Peter, 'Asyut in Modern Times: The Problem of Invisibility', *International Journal of Middle East Studies* vol. 53, no.1 (2021), pp. 113–17.

Great Britain, Special Mission to Egypt, and Alfred Milner Milner, *Report of the Special Mission to Egypt* (London: H. M. Stationery off., 1921).

Halpern, Manfred, 'Egypt and the New Middle Class: Reaffirmations and New Explorations', *Comparative Studies in Society and History* vol. 11, no. 1 (January 1969), pp. 97–108.

Halpern, Manfred, *The Politics of Social Change in the Middle East and North Africa* (Princeton, NJ: Princeton University Press, 1963).

Halpern, Manfred, 'The Problem of Becoming Conscious of a Salaried New Middle Class', *Comparative Studies in Society and History* vol. 11, no. 1 (January 1969), pp. 27–30.

Hammad, Hanan, 'Daily Encounters That Make History: History from Below and Archival Collaboration', *International Journal of Middle East Studies* vol. 53, no. 1 (2021), pp. 139–43.

Hammad, Hanan, *Industrial Sexuality: Gender, Urbanization, and Social Transformation in Egypt* (Austin: University of Texas Press, 2016).

Hammond, Andrew, 'Cairo Communique: Egypt's Deep-Sixed 1954 Constitution a Reminder of What Might Have Been', *Washington Report on Middle East Affairs* vol. 21, no. 7 (2002), p. 55. 21 July 2009. Accessed 9 September 2020, https://www.wrmea.org/002-september-october/egypt-s-deep-sixed-1954-constitution-a-reminder-of-what-might-have-been.html.

Handoussa, Heba, and Gillian Potter, *Employment and Structural Adjustment: Egypt in the 1990s* (Cairo: AUC Press, 1991).

Hanna, Milad, *al-Iskan wa-al-Misyada: al-Mushkila wa-al-Hall* (Cairo: Dar al-Mustaqbal al-'Arabi, 1988).

Hanna, Milad, *Uridu Maskinan: Mushkila la-ha Hall* (Cairo: Ruz a-Yusuf, 1978).

Hanna, Sami A., and George H. Gardner, *Arab Socialism: A Documentary Survey* (Leiden: Brill, 1969).

Hansen, Bent, *Egypt and Turkey* (Oxford: Oxford University Press for the World Bank, 1991).

Hansen, Bent, and Girgis A. Marzouk, *Development and Economic Policy in the UAR (Egypt)* (Amsterdam: North-Holland, 1965).

Hansen, Bent, and Samir Radwan, *Employment Opportunities and Equity in a Changing Economy: Egypt in the 1980s, a Labour Market Approach*. Report of an Inter-agency Team Financed by the United Nations Development Programme and Organised by the International Labour Office, WEP Study (Geneva: International Labour Office, 1982).

Harders, Cilja, 'The Informal Social Pact: The State and the Urban Poor in Cairo', in *Politics from Above, Politics from Below: The Middle East in the Age of Economic Reform*, edited by Eberhard Kienle (London: Al-Saqi Publications, 2003), pp. 191–213.

Harders, Cilja, 'A Revolution of Logics of Action? Renegotiating the Authoritarian Social Contract in Egypt', in *Euro-Mediterranean Relations after the Arab Spring: Persistence in Times of Change*, edited by Jakob Horst, Annette Jünemann and Delf Rothe (London: Ashgate, 2013), pp. 103–22.

Harik, Ilya, *Economic Policy Reform in Egypt* (Gainesville: University Press of Florida, 1997).

Hasan, Ahmad Husayn, *al-Tabaqa al-Wusta wa-al-Taghayyur al-Ijtima'i fi Misr: Tahlil Susyuta'rikhi (1975–2005)* (Cairo: Markaz al-Mahrusa li-l-Nashr wa-l-Khidmat al-Suhufiyya wa-l-Ma'lumat, 2016).

Hatem, Mervat F., 'Economic and Political Liberation in Egypt and the Demise of State Feminism', *International Journal of Middle East Studies* vol. 24, no. 2 (1992), pp. 231–51.

Hatem, Mervat F., 'The Nineteenth Century Discursive Roots of the Continuing Debate on the Social-Sexual Contract in Today's Egypt', *Hawwa* vol. 2, no. 1 (2004), pp. 64–88.

Hatem, Mervat F., 'The Pitfalls of the Nationalist Discourses on Citizenship in Egypt', in *Gender and Citizenship in the Middle East*, edited by Suad Joseph (Syracuse, NY: Syracuse University Press, 2000), pp. 33–57.

Haykal, Muhammad Hasanayn, 'Bab Misr ila al-Qarn al-Wahad wa-l-'Ishrin,' in *Mubarak wa-Zamanuhu min al-Minassa ila al-Maydan*, 2nd ed (Cairo: Dar al-Shuruq, 2013), pp. 262–88.

Heydemann, Steven, ed. *Networks of Privilege in the Middle East: The Politics of Economic Reform Revisited* (New York: Palgrave Macmillan, 2004).

Heydemann, Steven, 'Social Pacts and the Persistence of Authoritarianism in the Middle East', in *Debating Arab Authoritarianism: Dynamics and Durability in Nondemocratic Regimes*, edited by Oliver Schlumberger (Stanford, CA: Stanford University Press, 2007), pp. 21–38.

Heyworth-Dunne, James, *An Introduction to the History of Education in Modern Egypt* (London: Frank Cass, 1968).

Hill, Peter, *Utopia and Civilisation in the Arab Nahda* (Cambridge: Cambridge University Press, 2020).

Hinnebusch, Raymond A., *Egyptian Politics under Sadat: The Post-Populist Development of an Authoritarian-Modernizing State* (Cambridge: Cambridge University Press, 1985).

Hinnebusch, Raymond A., 'The Politics of Economic Reform in Egypt', *Third World Quarterly* vol. 14, no. 1 (1993), pp. 159–71.

Ho, Selina, *Thirsty Cities: Social Contracts and Public Goods Provision in China and India* (Cambridge: Cambridge University Press, 2019).

Hobbes, Thomas, *Leviathan*, edited by Noel Malcolm (Oxford: Clarendon Press, 2014).

Holliday, Ian, 'Productivist Welfare Capitalism: Social Policy in East Asia', *Political Studies* vol. 48, no. 4 (2000), pp. 706–23.

Hourani, Albert, *Arabic Thought in the Liberal Age, 1798–1939* (London: Oxford University Press, 1967).

Huber, Valeska, 'Introduction: Global Histories of Social Planning', *Journal of Contemporary History* vol. 52, no. 1 (2017), pp. 3–15.

Hussein, Mahmoud, *Class Conflict in Egypt, 1945–1970* (New York: Monthly Review Press, 1973).

Huwaydi, Fahmi, 'Prime Minister Discusses Commodity Shortages, Popular Complaints', *al-Ahram*, 7 February 1975, pp. 3, 8. Translated in 'Middle East and North Africa: Global Perspectives, 1958–1994'. Readex (Naples, FL: Readex, 2015).

Ibrahim, Saad Eddin, 'Social Mobility and Income Distribution in Egypt, 1952–1977', in *The Political Economy of Income Distribution in Egypt*, edited by Gouda Abdel-Khalek and Robert Tignor (New York: Holmes and Meier, 1982), pp. 375–434.

Ikeda, Misako, 'Toward the Democratization of Public Education: The Debate in Late Parliamentary Egypt, 1943–52', in *Re-Envisioning Egypt 1919–1952*, edited by Arthur Goldschmidt and Amy J. Johnson (Cairo: AUC Press, 2005), pp. 218–48.

Ikram, Khalid, *The Egyptian Economy, 1952–2000: Performance, Policies, and Issues* (London: Routledge, 2006).

Ikram, Khalid, *The Political Economy of Reforms in Egypt: Issues and Policymaking Since 1952* (Cairo: AUC Press, 2018).

'Isa, Salah, *Dustur fi Sunduq al-Qumama: Qissat Mashru' Dustur 1954: Dirasa wa-Wathiqa* (Cairo: Markaz al-Qahira li-Dirasat Huquq al-Insan, 2001).

Ismail, Salwa, *Political Life in Cairo's New Quarters: Encountering the Everyday State* (Minneapolis: University of Minnesota Press, 2006).

Issawi, Charles Philip, *Egypt: An Economic and Social Analysis* (London: Oxford University Press, 1947).

Issawi, Charles Philip, *Egypt at Mid-Century: An Economic Survey* (London: Oxford University Press, 1954).

Issawi, Charles Philip, *Egypt in Revolution: An Economic Analysis* (London: Oxford University Press, 1963).

Iwan, James L., 'From Social Welfare to Local Government: The United Arab Republic (Egypt)', *Middle East Journal* vol. 22, no. 3 (1968), pp. 265–77.

Jawwadi, Muhammad Muhammad, *al-Bunyan al-Wizari fi Misr: Faharis Ta'rikhiyya wa-Kammiyya wa-Tafsiliyya li-Insha' wa-Ilgha' wa-Idmaj al-Wizarat wa-l-Qita'at al-Wizariyya, mundhu 1878 wa-Dirasa li-Tawzi' al-Mas'uliyat al-Wizariyya wa-l-Wuzara' alladhina Ta'aqabu 'ala kul Wizara, 1952–1996* (Cairo: Dar al-Shuruq, 1996).

Johnson, Amy J., *Reconstructing Rural Egypt: Ahmed Hussein and the History of Egyptian Development* (Syracuse, NY: Syracuse University Press, 2004).

Joseph, Suad, 'The Kin Contract and Citizenship in the Middle East', in *Women and Citizenship*, edited by Marilyn Friedman (Oxford: Oxford University Press, 2005), pp. 149–96.

Joya, Angela, *The Roots of Revolt: A Political Economy of Egypt from Nasser to Mubarak* (Cambridge: Cambridge University Press, 2020).

Kamrava, Mehran, 'The Rise and Fall of Ruling Bargains in the Middle East', in *Beyond the Arab Spring: The Evolving Ruling Bargain in the Middle East*, edited by Mehran Kamrava (New York: Oxford University Press, 2014), pp. 17–45.

Kandil, Hazem, *The Power Triangle: Military, Security, and Politics in Regime Change* (New York: Oxford University Press, 2016).

Kandil, Hazem, 'Why Did the Egyptian Middle Class March to Tahrir Square?', *Mediterranean Politics* vol. 17, no. 2 (2012), pp. 197–215.

Karanasou, Floresca, 'Egyptianisation: The 1947 Company Law and the Foreign Communities in Egypt', PhD diss., Oxford University, 1993.

Kedourie, Elie, 'The Genesis of the Egyptian Constitution of 1923', in *Political and Social Change in Modern Egypt: Historical Studies from the Ottoman Conquest to the United Arab Republic*, edited by P. M. Holt (London: Oxford University Press, 1968), pp. 347–61.

Kerr, Malcolm H., *The Arab Cold War 1958–1967: A Study of Ideology in Politics*, 2nd ed (London: Oxford University Press, 1967).

Kerr, Malcolm H., 'The Emergence of a Socialist Ideology in Egypt', *Middle East Journal* vol. 16, no. 2 (1962), pp. 127–44.

Khalil, Najwa Husayn, *al-Mujtama' al-Misri qabla al-Thawra fi al-Sihafa al-Misriyya, 1945–1952* (Cairo: Al-Hay'a al-Misriyya al-'Amma li-l-Kitab, 1995).

Khouri-Dagher, Nadia, 'The State, Urban Households, and Management of Daily Life: Food and Social Order in Cairo', in *Development, Change, and Gender in Cairo: A View from the Household*, edited by Diane Singerman and Homa Hoodfar (Bloomington: Indiana University Press, 1996), pp. 110–33.

Khuri, Yusuf Q., *al-Dasatir fi al-'Alam al-'Arabi: Nusus wa-Ta'dilat: 1839–1987* (Beirut: Dar al-Hamra', 1989).

Lahita, Muhammad Fahmi, *Ta'rikh Fu'ad al-Awwal al-Iqtisadi: Misr fi Tariq al-Tawjih al-Kamil*, vol. 3, *al-'Adala al-Ijtima'iyya: Misr wa-Mustawa Ma'ishat al-Misriyyin* (Cairo: Maktabat al-Nahda al-Misriyya, 1946).

Lia, Brynjar, *The Society of the Muslim Brothers in Egypt: The Rise of an Islamic Mass Movement, 1928–1942* (Reading: Ithaca Press, 1998).

Locke, John, *Second Treatise of Government* and *A Letter Concerning Toleration*, edited by Mark Goldie (Oxford: Oxford University Press, 2016).

Loewe, Markus, Tina Zintl, and Annabelle Houdret, 'The Social Contract as a Tool of Analysis: Introduction to the Special Issue on 'Framing the Evolution of New Social Contracts in Middle Eastern and North African Countries', *World Development* vol. 145 (2020), pp. 1–16.

Mabro, Robert, *The Egyptian Economy, 1952–1972* (Oxford: Clarendon Press, 1974).

Maghraoui, Abdeslam, *Liberalism without Democracy: Nationhood and Citizenship in Egypt, 1922–1936* (Durham, NC: Duke University Press, 2006).

Meehy, Asya El, 'Rewriting the Social Contract: The Social Fund and Egypt's Politics of Retrenchment', PhD diss., University of Toronto, 2009.

Meijer, Roel, 'Citizenship, Social Pacts, Authoritarian Bargains, and the Arab Uprisings', in *The Crisis of Citizenship in the Arab World*, edited by Roel Meijer and Nils Butenschøn (Leiden: Brill, 2017), pp. 67–104.

Meijer, Roel, 'Liberal Reform: The Case of the Society of the National Renaissance', in *Entre reforme sociale et mouvement national: identité et modernisation en Egypte, 1882–1962: actes du colloque "Réforme Social en Egypte" qui s'est tenu du 10 au 13 décembre 1992 à l'Institut français d'archéologie orientale Le Caire*, edited by Alain Roussillon, 129–62 (Cairo: CEDEJ, 1995).

Meijer, Roel, *The Quest for Modernity: Secular Liberal and Left-Wing Thought in Egypt, 1945–1958* (New York: Routledge Curzon, 2002).

Meital, Yoram, *Revolutionary Justice: Special Courts and the Formation of Republican Egypt* (New York: Oxford University Press, 2017).

Meital, Yoram, 'The Struggle over Political Order in Egypt: The 2005 Elections', *Middle East Journal* vol. 60, no. 2 (2006), pp. 257–79.

Mellor, Noha, *The Egyptian Dream: Egyptian National Identity and Uprisings*, Edinburgh: Edinburgh University Press, 2016.

Ministry of Education, Egypt, *Report of the Elementary Education Commission and Draft Law to Make Better Provision for the Extension of Elementary Education* (Cairo: Govt. Press, 1921).

Ministry of Planning, Egypt, *The General Strategy for Economic and Social Development*, vol. 1 of *The Five-year Plan, 1978–1982* (Cairo, 1977).

Misako Ikeda, 'Sociopolitical Debates in Late Parliamentary Egypt, 1944–1952', PhD diss., Harvard University, 1998.

Mitchell, Richard P., *The Society of the Muslim Brothers* (New York: Oxford University Press, 1993).

'Mubarak Addresses Joint Legislative Session', Foreign Broadcast Information Service (FBIS), NC 12 I 830 Cairo Domestic Service in Arabic, 0912GMT. 12 November 1986. n.p.

'Mubarak on Regional Issues, Muslim Brotherhood', Foreign Broadcast Information Service (FBIS), MW 11402112295 London *al-Hayat* in Arabic, 12 February 1995, p. 5.

'Musa Addresses UN General Assembly', Foreign Broadcast Information Service (FBIS), NC2609122192 Cairo MENA in Arabic, 1530 GMT, 25 September 1992.

'Musa Addresses UN General Assembly Session', Foreign Broadcast Information Service (FBIS), NCOJ 10124494 Cairo Arab Republic of Egypt Radio Network in Arabic, 1742 GMT, 30 September 1994.

'Musa Addresses UN on Regional, World Issues', Foreign Broadcast Information Service (FBIS), NC2809090593 Cairo Arab Republic of Egypt Radio Network in Arabic, 0413 GA1T, 28 September 1993.

'The New Egyptian Constitution', *Middle East Journal* vol. 10, no. 3 (1956), pp. 300–6.

The 1923 Constitution, Bibliotheca Alexandrina. Accessed 17 April 2020. http://modernegypt.bibalex.org/NewDocumentViewer.aspx?DocumentID=DC_20256&keyword.

O'Brien, Patrick, *The Revolution in Egypt's Economic System: From Private Enterprise to Socialism, 1952–1965* (London: Oxford University Press, 1966).

Offer, Avner, 'The Market Turn: From Social Democracy to Market Liberalism', *Economic History Review* vol. 70 (2017), pp. 1051–71.

Owen, Roger, *Lord Cromer: Victorian Imperialist, Edwardian Proconsul* (Oxford: Oxford University Press, 2004).

Owen, Roger, *The Rise and Fall of Arab Presidents for Life* (Cambridge, MA: Harvard University Press, 2012).

Perlmutter, Amos, 'Egypt and the Myth of the New Middle Class: A Comparative Analysis', *Comparative Studies in Society and History* vol. 10, no. 1 (October 1967), pp. 46–65.

Perlmutter, Amos, 'The Myth of the Myth of the New Middle Class: Some Lessons in Social and Political Theory', *Comparative Studies in Society and History* vol. 12, no. 1 (January 1970), pp. 14–26.

Podeh, Elie, and Onn Winckler, ed., *Rethinking Nasserism: Revolution and Historical Memory in Modern Egypt* (Gainesville: University Press of Florida, 2004).

Pollard, Lisa, 'Egyptian by Association: Charitable States and Service Societies, Circa 1850–1945', *International Journal of Middle East Studies* vol. 46, no. 2 (2014), pp. 239–57.

Pollard, Lisa, *Nurturing the Nation: The Family Politics of Modernizing, Colonizing and Liberating Egypt, 1805–1923* (Berkeley: University of California Press, 2005).

Posusney, Marsha Pripstein, 'Irrational Workers: The Moral Economy of Labor Protest in Egypt', *World Politics* vol. 46, no. 1 (1993), pp. 83–120.

Radwan, Samir, 'Samir Radwan Curriculum Vitae', Arab Republic of Egypt Ministry of Finance. Accessed 30 April 2020, http://www.mof.gov.eg/MOFGallerySource/English/PDF/Samir_Radwan%20CV-updated-2011.pdf.

Radwan, Samir, and Torkel Alfthan, 'Household Surveys for Basic Needs: Some Issues', *International Labour Review* vol. 117, no. 2 (1978), pp. 197–210.

Reid, Donald M., *Cairo University and the Making of Modern Egypt* (Cairo: AUC Press, 1991).

Rejwan, Nissim, *Nasserist Ideology: Its Exponents and Critics* (New York: Wiley, 1974).

Richards, Alan, 'The Political Economy of Dilatory Reform: Egypt in the 1980s', *World Development* vol. 19, no. 12 (1991), pp. 1721–30.

Rizq, Yunan Labib, *Shu'un wa-Shujun Ta'rikhiyya* (Cairo: Al-Hay'a al-Misriyya al-'Amma li-l-Kitab, 2005).

Rousseau, Jean-Jacques, *Rousseau: The Social Contract and Other Later Political Writings*, 2nd ed (Cambridge: Cambridge University Press, 2018).

Roussillon, Alain, 'La modernité disputée: réforme sociale et politique en Égypte', in *Entre réforme sociale et mouvement national: identité et modernisation en Egypte, 1882–1962*', edited by Alain Roussillon (Cairo: CEDEJ, 1995), pp. 9–35.

'Royal Decree No. 42 of 1923 on Building a Constitutional System for the Egyptian State'. *Constitutionnet*. Accessed 17 April 2020, http://constitutionnet.org/sites/default/files/1923_-_egyptian_constitution_english_1.pdf.

Rumman, Howaida 'Adli, *al-Tabaqa al-Wusta fi Misr: Dirasa Tawthikiyya Tahliliyya* (Cairo, 2001).

Russell, Mona, 'Competing, Overlapping, and Contradictory Agendas: Egyptian Education Under British Occupation, 1882–1922', *Comparative Studies of South Asia, Africa and the Middle East* vol. 21, no. 1–2 (2001), pp. 50–60.

Russell, Mona, *Creating the New Egyptian Woman: Consumerism, Education, and National Identity, 1863–1922* (New York: Palgrave Macmillan, 2004).

Rutherford, Bruce, *Egypt after Mubarak: Liberalism, Islam, and Democracy in the Arab World*. new edn. (Princeton, NJ: Princeton University Press, 2017).

Ryzova, Lucie, *The Age of the Efendiyya: Passages to Modernity in National-Colonial Egypt* (Oxford: Oxford University Press, 2014).

Saad, Reem, 'Egyptian Politics and the Tenancy Law', in *Counter-Revolution in Egypt's Countryside: Land and Farmers in the Era of Economic Reform*, edited by Ray Bush (London: Zed Books, 2002), pp. 103–25.

Saavedra, Jaime, and Mariano Tommasi, 'Informality, the State and the Social Contract in Latin America: A Preliminary Exploration', *International Labour Review* vol. 146, no. 3 (2007), pp. 279–309.

Sadat, Anwar El, 'Khitab al-Ra'is Muhammad Anwar al-Sadat ila al-Umma', *Bibliotheca Alexandrina*. Accessed 29 April 2020, http://modernegypt.bibalex.org/NewText Viewer.aspx?TextID=SP_568#.

Sadat, Anwar El, *The October Working Paper* (Cairo: Ministry of Information, State Information Service, 1974).

Safati, Ahmad al-, 'Hisad al-Sinin wa-l-Nahj al-Tanmawi al-Jadid', *Misr al-Muʿasira* vol. 77, no. 404 (April 1986), pp. 5–22.

Salem, Sara, *Anticolonial Afterlives in Egypt the Politics of Hegemony* (Cambridge: Cambridge University Press, 2020).

Sayyid-Marsot, Afaf Lutfi, *Egypt's Liberal Experiment, 1922–1936* (Berkeley: University of California Press, 1977).

Schewe, Eric, 'How War Shaped Egypt's National Bread Loaf', *Comparative Studies of South Asia, Africa and the Middle East* vol. 37, no. 1 (2017), pp. 49–63.

Schölch, Alexander, *Egypt for the Egyptians! The Socio-political Crisis in Egypt, 1878–1882* (London: Ithaca Press, 1981).

Selim, Gehan, 'Instituting Order: The Limitations of Nasser's Post-Colonial Planning Visions for Cairo in the Case of the Indigenous Quarter of Bulaq (1952–1970)', *Planning Perspectives* vol. 29, no. 1 (2014), pp. 67–89.

Sfakianakis, John, 'The Whales of the Nile: Networks, Businessmen, and Bureaucrats during the Era of Privatization in Egypt', in *Networks of Privilege in the Middle East: The Politics of Economic Reform Revisited*, edited by Steven Heydemann (New York: Palgrave Macmillan, 2004), pp. 77–100.

Shafiʿi, Muʾmin Kamal, *al-Dawla wa-l-Tabaqa al-Wusta fi Misr: Tahlil Susyuluji li-Dawr al-Dawla fi Idarat al-Siraʿ al-Ijtimaʿi* (Cairo: Dar Qabaʾ li-l-Tibaʿa wa-l-Nashr wa-l-Tawziʿ, 2001).

Shakry, Omnia El, 'Cairo as Capital of Socialist Revolution', in *Cairo Cosmopolitan: Politics, Culture, and Urban Space in the New Globalized Middle East*, edited by Diane Singerman and Paul Amar (Cairo: AUC Press, 2006), pp. 73–98.

Shakry, Omnia El, *The Great Social Laboratory: Subjects of Knowledge in Colonial and Postcolonial Egypt* (Stanford, CA: Stanford University Press, 2007).

Shamir, Shimon, ed., *Egypt from Monarchy to Republic: A Reassessment of Revolution and Change* (Boulder, CO: Westview Press, 1995).

Sharif, Muhammad al-, *ʿAla Hamish al-Dustur* (Cairo: Matbaʿat al-Iʿtimad, 1938).

Shawkat, Yahia, 'Mubarak's Promise: Social Justice and the National Housing Programme: Affordable Homes or Political Gain?', *Égypte/Monde Arabe* vol. 11 (2014), pp. 203–33.

Shechter, Relli, '"Choosing Our Future": Global Best Practices and Local Planning in the *Egypt Human Development Report*', Special Issue, *Journal of Levantine Studies* vol. 10, no. 1 (Summer 2020), pp. 45–67.

Shechter, Relli, 'Glocal Mediators: Marketing in Egypt during the Open-Door Era (*infitah*)', *Enterprise and Society* vol. 9, no. 4 (2008), pp. 762–87.

Shechter, Relli, 'Market Welfare in the Early-Modern Ottoman Economy – A Historiographic Overview with Many Questions', *Journal of the Economic and Social History of the Orient* vol. 48, no. 2 (2005), pp. 253–67.

Shechter, Relli, 'The 1923 Egyptian Constitution – Vision and Ambivalence in the Future of Education in Egypt', *History of Education* vol. 48, no. 5 (2019), pp. 630–45.

Shechter, Relli, *The Rise of the Egyptian Middle Class: Socio-Economic Mobility and Public Discontent from Nasser to Sadat* (Cambridge: Cambridge University Press, 2019).

Shepard, William E., *Sayyid Qutb and Islamic Activism: A Translation and Critical Analysis of Social Justice in Islam* (Leiden: Brill, 1996).

Shukrallah, Alaa, and Mohamed Hassan Khalil, 'Egypt in Crisis: Politics, Health Care Reform, and Social Mobilization for Health Rights', in *Public Health in the Arab World*, edited by Samer Jabbour, Rita Giacaman, and Marwan Khawaja (Cambridge: Cambridge University Press, 2012), pp. 447–88.

Sims, David, 'Affordable Housing Policies in Egypt after the 2011 Revolution: More of the Same?', in *The Political Economy of the New Egyptian Republic*, edited by Nicholas S. Hopkins, Cairo Papers vol. 33, no. 4 (Cairo: AUC Press, 2015), pp. 174–93.

Singerman, Diane, *Avenues of Participation: Family, Politics, and Networks in Urban Quarters of Cairo* (Princeton, NJ: Princeton University Press, 1995).

Sokkari, Myrette Ahmed El-, *Basic Needs, Inflation and the Poor of Egypt*, Cairo Papers 7, no. 2 (Cairo: AUC Press, June 1984).

Soliman, Samer, *The Autumn of Dictatorship: Fiscal Crisis and Political Change in Egypt under Mubarak* (Stanford, CA: Stanford University Press, 2011).

Springborg, Robert, *Family, Power, and Politics in Egypt: Sayed Bey Marei – His Clan, Clients, and Cohorts* (Philadelphia: University of Pennsylvania Press, 1982).

Springborg, Robert, *Mubarak's Egypt: Fragmentation of the Political Order* (Boulder, CO: Westview Press, 1989).

Starrett, Gregory, *Putting Islam to Work: Education, Politics, and Religious Transformation in Egypt* (Berkeley: University of California Press, 1998).

Stilt, Kristen, 'Constitutions in Authoritarian Regimes: The Egyptian Constitution of 1971', in *Constitutions in Authoritarian Regimes*, edited by Tom Ginsburg and Alberto Simpser (Cambridge: Cambridge University Press, 2014), pp. 111–38.

Sullivan, Denis Joseph, *Private Voluntary Organizations in Egypt: Islamic Development, Private Initiative, and State Control* (Gainesville: University Press of Florida, 1994).

Tadros, Mariz, 'State Welfare in Egypt since Adjustment: Hegemonic Control with a Minimalist Role', *Review of African Political Economy* vol. 33, no. 108 (2006), pp. 237–54.

Thompson, Elizabeth, *Justice Interrupted the Struggle for Constitutional Government in the Middle East* (Cambridge, MA: Harvard University Press, 2013).

Tignor, Robert L., *Anwar al-Sadat: Transforming the Middle East* (Oxford: Oxford University Press, 2016).

Tignor, Robert L., 'Equity in Egypt's Recent Past: 1945–1952', in *The Political Economy of Income Distribution in Egypt*, edited by Gouda Abdel-Khalek and Robert Tignor (New York: Holmes and Meier, 1982), pp. 20–54.

Tignor, Robert L., *Modernisation and British Colonial Rule in Egypt, 1882–1914* (Princeton, NJ: Princeton University Press, 1966).

Tignor, Robert L., 'Nationalism, Economic Planning, and Development Projects in Interwar Egypt', *International Journal of African Historical Studies* vol. 10, no. 2 (1977), pp. 185–208.

Ul Haq, Mahbub, *Reflections on Human Development* (New York: Oxford University Press, 1995).

United Arab Republic, Lajnat Kutub Siyasiyya, *al-Thawra al-Ijtima'iyya: Qawanin Yulya al-Majida* (Cairo: Lajnat Kutub Siyasiyya, 1961).

United Nations Development Programme: Human Development Reports, 'About Human Development'. Accessed 30 April 2020, http://hdr.undp.org/en/humandev.

United Nations Development Programme: Human Development Reports, *The Concept and Measurement of Human Development as Participatory Process, Egypt Human Development Report 1994*. Accessed 30 April 2020, http://www.mof.gov.eg/MOFGallerySource/English/PDF/Samir_Radwan%20CV-updated-2011.pdf.

United Nations Development Programme: Human Development Reports, *Egypt Human Development Report 1995*. Accessed 18 April 2020, http://www.arab-hdr.org/publications/other/undp/hdr/1995/egypt-e.pdf.

United Nations Development Programme: Human Development Reports, *Egypt Human Development Report 1998/1999*. Accessed 24 September 24 2020, http://hdr.undp.org/en/reports/national/EGY.

United Nations Development Programme: Human Development Reports. *Egypt Human Development Report 2005*. Accessed 24 September 2020, https://hdr.undp.org/reports/national/EGY.

United Nations Development Programme: Human Development Reports, *Egypt Human Development Report 2008*. Accessed 24 September 2020, http://hdr.undp.org/en/reports/national/EGY.

United Nations Development Programme: Human Development Reports, *Egypt Human Development Report 2010*, Accessed 24 September 2020, http://hdr.undp.org/en/reports/national/EGY.

Utvik, Bjorn Olav, *Islamist Economics in Egypt: The Pious Road to Development* (Boulder, CO: Lynne Rienner Publishers, 2006).

Vatikiotis, Panayiotis J., *The Egyptian Army in Politics: Pattern for New Nations?* (Bloomington: Indiana University Press, 1961).

Vatikiotis, Panayiotis J., *Nasser and His Generation* (New York: St. Martin's Press, 1978).

Vitalis, Robert, *When Capitalists Collide: Business Conflict and the End of Empire in Egypt* (Berkeley: University of California Press, 1995).

Vitalis, Robert, and Steven Heydemann, 'War, Keynesianism and Colonialism: Explaining State-Market Relations in the Postwar Middle East', in *War, Institutions and Social Change in the Middle East*, edited by Steven Heydemann (Berkeley: University of California Press, 2000), pp. 100–45.

Volait, Mercedes, 'Réforme sociale et habitat populaire: acteurs et formes (1848–1964)', in *Entre réforme sociale et mouvement national: Identité et modernisation en Egypte, 1882–1962*, edited by Alain Roussillon (Cairo: CEDEJ, 1995), pp. 379–409.

Volait, Mercedes, 'Town Planning Schemes for Cairo Conceived by Egyptian Planners in the Liberal Experiment Period', in *Middle Eastern Cities, 1900–1950: Public Places and Public Spheres in Transformation*, edited by Hans Chr. Korsholm Nielsen and Jakob Skovgaard-Petersen (Aarhus: Aarhus University Press, 2001), pp. 44–71.

Wahba, Mourad Magdi, 'The Meaning of Ishtirakiyah: Arab Perceptions of Socialism in the Nineteenth Century', *Alif: Journal of Comparative Poetics*, no. 10 (1990), pp. 42–55.

Wahba, Mourad Magdi, *The Role of the State in the Egyptian Economy: 1945–1981* (London: Ithaca Press, 1994).

Waterbury, John, *The Egypt of Nasser and Sadat: The Political Economy of Two Regimes* (Princeton, NJ: Princeton University Press, 1983).

Waterbury, John, 'Patterns of Urban Growth and Income Distribution in Egypt', in *The Political Economy of Income Distribution in Egypt*, edited by Gouda Abdel-Khalek and Robert Tignor (New York: Holmes and Meier, 1982), pp. 307–50.

Waterbury, John, 'The "Soft State" and the "Open Door": Egypt's Experience with Economic Liberalisation, 1974–1984', *Comparative Politics* vol. 18, no. 1 (1985), pp. 65–83.

Wickham, Carrie Rosefsky, *Mobilizing Islam: Religion, Activism, and Political Change in Egypt* (New York: Columbia University Press, 2002).
Wikipedia, 'Youssef Boutros Ghali'. Accessed 30 April 2020, https://en.wikipedia.org/wiki/Youssef_Boutros_Ghali.
World Bank, *Egypt: Alleviating Poverty during Structural Adjustment*, World Bank Country Study (Washington, DC: World Bank, 1991).
World Bank, *Report and Recommendation of the President to the Executive Directors on a Proposed Loan to the Development Industrial Bank with the Guarantee of the Arab Republic of Egypt for a Development Finance Company Project*, 9 March 1978. Accessed 2 May 2020, http://documents.worldbank.org/curated/pt/798001468234876265/text/multi-page.txt.
World Bank, *Unlocking the Employment Potential in the Middle East and North Africa: Toward a New Social Contract* (Washington, DC: World Bank, 2004). Accessed 17 May 2020, https://openknowledge.worldbank.org/handle/10986/15011.
Yousef, Hoda A., 'Losing the Future? Constructing Educational Need in Egypt, 1820s to 1920s', *History of Education* vol. 46, no. 5 (2017), pp. 561–77.
Yousef, Hoda A., 'Seeking the Educational Cure: Egypt and European Education, 1805–1920s', *European Education* vol. 44, no. 4 (2012), pp. 51–66.
Zaki, Ramzi, *Wada'an li-l-Tabaqa al-Wusta: Ta'ammulat fi al-Thawra al-Sina'iyya al-Thalitha wa-l-Libiraliyya al-Jadida* (Cairo: Dar al-Mustaqbal al-'Arabi, 1997).
Zeghal, Malika, 'Religion and Politics in Egypt: The Ulema of al-Azhar, Radical Islam, and the State (1952–94)', *International Journal of Middle East Studies* vol. 31, no. 3 (1999), pp. 371–99.
Zhang, Sarah, 'The Pitfalls of Using Google Ngram to Study Language', *Wired*, 18 December 2015. Accessed 29 April 2020, https://www.wired.com/2015/10/pitfalls-of-studying-language-with-google-ngram/.

Databases

ALMANHAL, https://www.almanhal.com.
Bibliotheca Alexandrina, Egyptian Press Archive of CEDEJ, http://cedej.bibalex.org/.
Bibliotheca Alexandrina, Memory of Modern Egypt, https://www.bibalex.org/en/Project/Details?DocumentID=1299&Keywords=modern%20egypt.
Constitutionnet, https://constitutionnet.org/.
Google Books Ngram Viewer, https://books.google.com/ngrams.
'Middle East and North Africa: Global Perspectives, 1958–1994', https://www.readex.com/products/middle-east-and-north-africa-global-perspectives-1958-1994.

INDEX

'Abd al-Fatah, Muhammad Muhammad Tawfiq, 175–6
Abdel-Fadil, Mahmoud, 211
Abdel-Malek, Anouar, 124, 136
Abdel Meguid, Abdel Razzak, 177, 178, 190
'adala ijtima'iyya see social justice
agricultural cooperatives, 132
al-Ahram, 161, 162, 210, 225
Ahwal Misriyya, 209
Akhavi, Shahrough, 227
al-'Arabi, 227
al-Azhar University, 110–11, 128
American University in Cairo (AUC), *Employment and Structural Adjustment: Egypt in the 1990s*, 187–8
Amin, Galal, 211
Anglo-Egyptian Treaty of Alliance (1936), 38, 54, 58
'aqd ijtima'i see social contract
armed forces, 101, 123, 125, 157, 224
authoritarianism, 2, 7–8, 13, 56, 91, 138, 246, 252, 253
  authoritarian pact, 4–5, 6, 249, 250
Awad, Louis, 107, 127
Ayubi, Nazih, 130

Baer, Gabriel, 78
Balta-Liman, Treaty of, 9, 39
al-Banna, Hasan, 63
al-Bara'i, Ahmad Hasan, 229–30
al-Barrawi, Rashid, 78, 121–2, 124
basic needs concept, 179–80
Berger, Morroe, 43–4, 71
Bibliotheca Alexandrina, 18
al-Bishri, Tariq, 227
Blaydes, Lisa, 231, 236
Boghdady, A., 104
Brown, Nathan, 232
bureaucratisation, 105–14
Butrus-Ghali, Butrus, 229
Butrus-Ghali, Mirrit, 57, 76, 78
Butrus-Ghali, Youssef, 180

capitalism, 55, 122, 124, 256
CEDEJ website, 209, 223, 226, 229
Central Agency for Public Mobilization and Statistics (CAPMAS), 189
Central Security Force, 224
children, 28, 29, 212–13
citizenship, 52
  agency, 7–8
  choice, 194

citizenship *(cont.)*
   political participation, 6, 7, 10, 39,
      193–4, 195–6, 198, 223, 225, 231,
      232, 252–3, 254–5
   socio-economic rights and duties, 16
civil society organizations (CSOs), 106, 109,
   197–8, 246, 250, 252–3
class delineation, 11
Commission on the Expansion of
   Commerce and Industry, 35, 40, 60
Commission on the Reorganisation of the
   Public Health Services, 35
Company Law (1947), 60, 79–80
Constitutional Commission, 41
constitutions, 16, 126, 231
   1923 constitution, 25, 35, 36–7, 38–9,
      40–3, 92–3, 95, 96, 249
   1954 draft constitution, 92–3, 94–7, 102
   1956 constitution, 92, 93–6, 97, 98, 102
   1964 constitution, 97, 100–2, 105, 126,
      137, 249
   1971 constitution, 145, 146–9, 153,
      154, 227, 232
   layering, 148–9
   pashas' constitution, 92–7
   reform, 228–9
   and the social contract, 35–46, 249–50
   social justice, 52, 232
consumerism, 170
Corrective Revolution, 145, 146–54, 160,
   177, 222, 253
corruption, 126, 168, 169
Cromer, Lord, 31, 32
cronyism, 126, 168–9, 234, 256

Darling, Linda, 51–2
decolonialisation, 23, 53
democratisation, 7, 195–6, 199, 208–9,
   231–2, 253, 255
Department of the Fellah, 74
Development Plan 1978–82, 1, 175, 176–8,
   180–5, 201–2
disease epidemics, 68
Dunn, Michele, 232

Economic Agency, 125
economic management, 15, 17, 35
   economic reform and structural
      adjustment programme (ERSA), 7,
      145, 202, 203, 208–10, 211–12,
      214–17, 219–22, 226, 229, 233–4,
      252, 254
   Egyptianisation of, 60
   fiscal discipline, 216–17
   foreign expertise, 203–4
   free market economy, 9, 33–4, 38–9, 40,
      135, 179, 180, 194, 203, 214, 226,
      230, 232
   opposition to reform, 213–14
   recession, 215
   state budget and public debt, 76–7, 114,
      139, 162, 179, 215, 216, 230, 246–7,
      251, 253
   state role in, 55–7, 58, 60–1, 66, 67, 88,
      93, 95–6, 99, 102–5, 148, 179–80,
      247, 250, 252
Edict of Gulhane (1839), 35
education, 25, 35, 103, 106–7, 121, 155,
   186, 246
   1923 constitution, 40–3, 93
   1954 draft constitution, 93, 94
   1956 constitution, 93–4
   1964 constitution, 102
   1971 constitution, 149
   and class mobility, 156–7, 158
   as a cure for social ills, 45, 64, 65, 66, 74
   Egyptianisation of, 66
   equality issues, 127–8, 132
   free education principle, 41, 65, 102,
      127, 156
   growth of, 42, 70–1, 127
   higher education, 8, 11, 17, 25, 29, 32,
      33, 41, 42, 45–8, 46, 70–1, 107, 125,
      126, 127–9, 155–7, 182
   and illiteracy, 71–2, 128, 149, 152
   importance of, 28
   legislation, 72
   lower-middle class, 128–9
   in the October Paper, 152–3, 156

parental earnings and education levels, 128
public demand for, 30
reform, 30–3, 65–6, 127, 152–3, 182, 193
religious education, 110–11
rights to, 93, 102
school attendance, 128
and state employment, 30–5, 247
state spending on, 33, 42, 45, 71, 107, 216–17, 251
of women, 28, 29, 42, 72, 155
effendi middle class, 3–4, 6, 25, 67, 179, 180, 189, 190, 192, 251, 246
centrality in making and breaking the social contract, 13–14
class tensions, 11–12
decline of, 209–13
development of, 8–11
disappearance of, 12–13
effendi status, expansion and dilution of, 126–31
new effendis, 120–6
and the oil boom, 155
and productivist welfare, 25–30
recruitment for state management, 124–6
state bourgeoisie concept, 123–4, 135, 147–8
as a state creation, 210–11
state discipline of, 130–1
see also social contract
effendiyya, 120–1, 138, 256
Egypt
British rule of, 9–10, 27, 28, 30–4, 35, 36, 37–8
government ministries, 58–60, 66, 105–14
martial law, 61, 87, 224
monarchy, 36, 37–8, 52, 54, 87, 138, 246, 250
national movement, 32, 34, 36, 45–6
Egypt Human Development Report project (EHDR), 17, 175, 185, 188, 190–200, 203, 229

EHDR 1994, 191
EHDR 1995, 192, 202
EHDR 1996, 192
EHDR 1997, 193
EHDR 1998/9, 193–4
EHDR 2003, 194
EHDR 2005, 194–6, 197, 199
EHDR 2008, 197–8
EHDR 2010, 198–9
elections, 226, 231, 236, 254–5
Elementary Education Commission, 33, 35
employment, 25, 57–8, 155, 252
and the 1923 constitution, 43, 44
balance between state earnings and expenditure, 216
blue-collar state employees, 219
demand for state employment, 33, 129, 158
and education, 30–5, 157
Egyptianisation of state employment, 43, 67, 247
Employment and Structural Adjustment: Egypt in the 1990s (AUC), 187–8
Employment Opportunities and Equity in a Changing Economy: Egypt in the 1980s (ILO), 185–6
'Employment Strategy: Egypt in the 1990s' (conference), 186–7
equality issues, 34–5, 73, 97
evaluation of state employees, 181
expenditure on state employment, 72–3, 216
of graduates, 129, 130, 157, 158, 181–2, 184, 240n23
imbalances, 185–6
legislation, 72
privatisation, 219–20
qualifications, 71, 130
reasons for joining state employment, 44
rights to work/work conditions, 94, 96, 97, 101, 102
socio-economic background, importance of, 129–30
and standard of living, 67, 148, 155, 160

employment *(cont.)*
  state employment attrition policy, 218–20, 252
  state employment expansion, 157
  strikes, 69, 134, 220
  structural adjustment, 214
  structural duality of, 134–5
  survey of, 1954, 43–5
  trade unions, 148–9, 220, 226, 252
  transitions required, 187–8, 252
  wages, 72, 79–80, 108, 148, 158, 181, 216, 217
  women, 44, 94, 96, 157, 158, 170, 212, 219
  working conditions, 40, 68–9, 79, 133–5
  workplace efficiency, 148
  youth, 94
Ener, Mine, 29
energy, 159, 173n29, 218
ERSA programme *see* economic management

Fanon, Frantz, 13, 246
Farouk, King, 54
fat cats (*qitat samina*), 168–9
First Five Year Development Plan (1960–5), 91, 102–5, 126
fitna notion, 164
food supply, 66, 111, 117–18n54, 158–9, 213, 218
  Food Uprising 1977, 6, 161–5, 176–7, 215, 253
Fouad, King, 54, 55
Free Officers' revolution 1952, 3, 5, 12, 13, 54, 61, 70, 78, 81, 87–8, 92, 98, 99, 146, 154, 248, 249, 250
  and emergence of the new effendis, 120–6
  and mass exodus of foreigners, 122
  reasons for, 91–2, 119
  and state management recruitment, 124–6
free trade, 151

Gasper, Michael, 26
gender aspects, 14, 26, 28
  education, 42, 72
Ginat, Rami, 98
global best practices, 14–16, 17, 36, 53, 88, 98, 229, 245
globalisation, 210, 212, 213
Google Books Ngram Viewer, 15, 17, 176, 179
governance, 15, 17
government of businessmen, 220, 231, 236
gradualism, 255

Hafiz, Suleiman, 96
Halpern, Manfred, 120, 123
Hamzawy, Amr, 232
Handoussa, Heba, 185, 187–8, 194
Hansen, Bent, 100, 185
ul-Haq, Mahbub , 191
Harik, Ilya, 217–18
al-Hayat, 228
Haykal, Muhammad Hasanayn, 226–7, 228
health, 35, 40, 45, 102, 149, 213
  expenditure on, 75–6, 107, 109, 216, 217
  state role in, 68
Heydemann, Steven, 40
Higher Council for Social Reform, 57
Hijazi, ʿAbd al-ʿAziz Mohamed, 161, 162
al-Hilal, 209
al-Hilali, Nagib, 65
housing, 35, 40, 67, 76, 111–13, 155, 159–60, 213, 220–1, 236
Human Development Index (HDI), 191
human rights, 227
Hussein, Ahmed, 75
Hussein, Taha, 65
Huwaydi, Fahmi, 161

Ikram, Khalid, 177, 184
illiteracy, 71–2, 128, 149, 152
import substitute industrialisation (ISI) model, 69, 79, 113, 180, 249

individualism, 55
industrialisation, 68–9, 79, 103, 113, 151, 253
industrious revolution concept, 166
infitah see Open Door policy
inflation, 66, 67, 158, 159, 235
informal economy, 166, 168, 212
  informal political economy, 233–7, 253
Institute of National Planning (INP), 190
international financial institutions (IFIs), 165, 188, 201, 203
International Labour Organization (ILO), 179, 180, 203
  Employment Opportunities and Equity in a Changing Economy: Egypt in the 1980s, 185–6
International Monetary Fund (IMF), 162, 163, 181, 201–2, 203, 215
intifada haramiyya (Uprising of Thieves), 164
investment, 151–2, 167, 168
'Isa, Salah, 92
Islam/Islamists, 14, 51, 143–4, 170, 227
Issawi, Charles, 72, 75, 76

Johnson, Amy, 74
Joseph, Suad, 64
July 1961 laws, 97–8, 100
al-Jumhuriyya, 229–30

Khalid, Khalid Mohammed, 136
Khalil, Najwa Husayn, 61–2, 66, 79, 121
Khouri-Dagher, Nadia, 163
Kifaya, 231

labour, 69, 133–4
Lahita, Muhammad Fahmi, 53–5
land reform, 77–9, 95, 96, 97, 131–3, 249
landownership/property ownership, 94–5, 96, 97, 98, 101, 147–8
Law 32 (1964), 108–9
Law 49 (1945), 59, 108
Law 157 (1960), 110

Law 247 (1953), 110
Law Setting the Wages for Graduates' Diplomas, 72
liberalism, 3, 15, 18–19, 35, 37
  liberal social contract, 25–50
  productivist welfare, 25–30
lower classes, 14, 119, 131–9, 249, 256
  labour regulation and workers' protection, 69, 70
  peasant question, 26–7, 28, 45, 53, 62, 70
  political activism, 68–9
  poverty alleviation, 131–3, 188–90, 193–4, 202, 230
  representation on the NCPF, 135–7
  social mobility, 165–71
  urban poor, 27–8
  working conditions, 40, 68–9, 79, 133–5

Mabro, Robert, 105
Maghraoui, Abdeslam, 37
Mahir, Ali, 54, 57, 106
marriage, 170
media
  freedom of, 64, 161, 256
  interviews with government ministers, 161–2
  nationalisation of, 98
  social question/social crisis, mentions of, 61–3, 66–70, 79
El-Meehy, Asya, 220–1
Meijer, Roel, 80
middle-class *see* effendi middle class
Middle East Supply Centre (MESC), 56, 66
middle society, 119–20
migration, 68, 69, 78, 112, 133, 153, 166–8, 212, 249
Military Technical Faculty, 125
Milner report, 34–5, 43
Ministry for Social Affairs and Employment, *The Social Constitution of the United Arab Republic*, 175–6

Ministry of Awqaf, 110
Ministry of Commerce and Industry, 58, 66, 111
Ministry of National Economy, 59
Ministry of Planning, 202
Ministry of Public Health, 58
Ministry of Social Affairs (MOSA), 58–60, 63, 73–5, 78, 79, 108–9
Ministry of Supply, 59, 66, 111
Ministry of Village and Rural Affairs, 59
Mitchel, Timothy, 76
moral economy, 6–7, 20n6, 80, 89, 94, 130, 139, 144, 154, 157, 251, 255
mosques, 110
Mubarak, Gamal, 231, 236, 255
Mubarak, Hosni, 6, 16, 169, 212, 223, 251, 252, 254–5
  election pledges, 236
  interviews, 228–9
  new social contract, rejection of, 228–9
  rejection of constitutional reform, 228–9
  speeches, 224–5
Mubarak, Susan, 230
Muhammad 'Ali, 8, 30, 39, 54–5, 210
Musa, Amr, 229
Muslim Brotherhood, 11, 12, 13, 55, 57, 58, 63, 66, 87, 125, 136, 143–4, 161, 163, 198, 214, 215, 221, 235, 236, 248, 253
  and land reform, 77–8
  as a threat, 225–6, 231
muthaqqafin (cultured), 156

Naguib, Muhammad, 96
al-Nahhas, Mustafa, 59, 80
Nasser, Gamal Abdel, 3, 6, 12, 16, 19, 56, 61, 81, 121, 146, 176, 210–11
  compared with Sadat, 150–1, 251–2
  and emergence of the new effendis, 120–6
  Nasserism as a populist regime, 137–9
  national goals of the regime, 97–8
  political power struggles, 96–7
  and the social contract 1952–70, 87–90, 248–51
  speeches, 97, 98, 107
National Charter, 16, 91, 97, 98, 99–100, 104–5, 107, 126, 131, 135, 136, 137, 150–1, 228, 249
National Congress of Popular Forces (NCPF), 135–7
National Democratic Party (NDP), 177, 231–2, 236
nationalisation, 88, 97, 98–9, 101, 248
Nazif, Ahmad, 220, 231
neoliberalism, 15, 16, 144, 176, 192, 194, 195, 197, 199, 212, 213, 237, 251, 254
New Civil Code, 96
Non-Aligned Movement, 98
non-governmental organisations (NGOs), 99, 105, 131, 170, 198, 221, 230, 235, 254

O'Brien, Patrick, 103–4
October Working Paper (1974), 16, 145, 149–54, 156, 160, 177
oil boom, 145, 154–60, 171, 211, 215, 251, 253
Open Door policy, 145, 146, 149–53, 161, 163, 165, 171, 177, 211, 213, 222, 233–4, 251–2, 253
Osman, Osman Mohamed, 185, 190, 197, 198
Ottoman Empire, 9–10, 35–6, 39
  circle of justice, 51–2
Owen, Roger, 236

pensions, 94, 102, 108, 149
Perlmutter, Amos, 123
Permanent Council for National Production, 102
Permanent Council for public Welfare Services (PCPWS), 108
philanthropic organisations, 27–30, 73, 230, 246
  regulation of, 59–60, 108–9

Pollard, Lisa, 26, 27
population, 62, 64, 71, 112
prices, 66, 67
property rights and ownership *see* landownership/property ownership

Qaisunni, Abdel Aziz, 163
qitat samina see fat cats

Radwan, Samir, 180, 185
religion, 11, 14, 26, 28, 106, 164, 170
  intolerance, 198
  state role in, 110–11, 143–4
remittances, 153, 154, 167, 168, 169
rent control, 35, 40, 67, 111–12, 159–60, 221
research methodology and sources, 16–19
Revolution 1919, 35, 52, 122
Richards, Alan, 200
rule of law, 39, 41–2, 225
Rumman, Howaida 'Adli, 209
rural affairs, 63–4, 68, 74, 103, 131–3
  health service provision, 107–8
  rural middle class, growth of, 169–70
Rural Social Centres (RSCs), 74, 79
Ryzova, Lucie, 26, 120, 122

Sadat, Muhammad Anwar, 6, 16, 111, 125, 145, 146, 224
  compared with Nasser, 150–1, 251–2
  Corrective Revolution, 145, 146–54, 160, 177, 222, 253
  October Working Paper (1974), 16, 145, 149–54, 156, 160, 177
  Open Door policy, 145, 146, 149–53, 161, 163, 165, 171, 177, 211, 213, 233–4, 251–2, 253
  purge of Nasserites, 146–7
  speeches, 163–5
Salem, Sara, 91
al-Sanhuri, 'Abd al-Razzaq, 65, 96–7
self-help, 25, 28–9, 43, 75, 179, 189, 193, 246

Sen, Amartya, 191
Sidqi Commission *see* Commission on the Expansion of Commerce and Industry
Sidqi, Ismail, 56, 57
social contract, 248–9
  breaking down of the effendi social contract, 145–74
  and constitutions, 35–46, 52
  effendi role in, 13–14
  effendi social contract, 3–4, 6, 13, 18–19, 51–86, 246, 248–9
  as history, 1–22
  liberalism, 25–50
  in Nasser's effendi state 1952–70, 87–90, 248–51
  new social contract, birth of, 175–200
  new social contract, problems of, 208–44
  planning process, 200–4
  search for a new social contract, 1970–2011, 143–4
  social origins of, 7–14
  swing between the political and economic new social contract/s, 222–33
  as a term, 3, 176, 223, 226
  welfarisation of, 230–1
Social Contract Advisory, Monitoring and Coordination Centre, 196, 198, 1
social freedom, 99
Social Fund for Development (SFD), 202, 220
social insurance, 74, 75, 102, 149
social justice, 3, 5, 6, 23, 53, 88, 130, 138, 184, 232, 247, 254
  circle of justice, 51–2
  hierarchy of, 61–70
  implementation, 70–81
  and social solidarity, 147
  and socialism, 53–61
  state role in, 64
social mobility, 11, 156–7, 158, 165–71, 234, 255
social question, 52–3, 61–2

social reform, 23, 25, 35, 230–1, 232
  politicisation of, 58
  productivist welfare, 25–30, 74, 183–4, 246, 254
  in rural areas, 63–4
  social engineering, 56–7, 76, 119
social solidarity, 147
socialism, 53–61, 119, 138, 247
  Arab socialism, 6, 55, 88, 97–105, 124, 125, 132, 135, 146, 147, 154, 250
  governmental socialism, 55
  socialist conduct principle, 147–8
Socialist Labour Party, 225
Society of the National Renaissance, 57
state finances, 39–40
statism, 56, 57–8, 59, 67, 81, 247–8
  bureaucratisation and regulation, 105–14
strikes, 69, 134, 220
subsidies, 67, 111, 131, 132, 133, 139, 146, 154, 158–9, 160, 162, 163, 165, 180–1, 190, 213, 216, 251, 253
  reduction of, and system restructuring, 217–18
Suez Canal, 88, 154, 248

al-Talawi, Mirfat, 230
taxation, 30, 39, 39–40, 45, 51, 77, 95, 97, 113, 147, 165, 221–2, 232, 235, 251
Taylor, Lance, 180
Thompson, Elizabeth, 52
trade unions, 148–9, 220, 226, 252

'Ubayd, Makram, 60
'Ulaysh, Hamzah, 78
umma, 26

United Arab Republic (UAR), 97, 98, 100
United Nations Development Programme (UNDP), 1, 185, 191, 196
upper-class, 119, 122–3, 138, 168–9
Uprising of 2011, 1, 4, 14, 255–6, 257
'Urabi Revolt (1879–82), 10, 36, 52
USAID, 203

Vries, Jan de, 166

al-Wafd, 210, 230
Wafd Party, 36, 38, 57, 59, 61, 64, 78, 80–1, 87, 112
Wahba, Mourad, 149–50
Waterbury, John, 114
wealth redistribution, 79, 80, 99
women, 26, 64, 136–7, 166
  education, 28, 29, 42, 72, 155
  employment, 44, 94, 96, 157, 158, 170, 212, 219
  October Working Paper statements, 153–4
  representation on the NCPF, 136–7
World Bank, 201, 202, 203, 215, 220
  Egypt: Alleviating Poverty during Structural Adjustment, 188–90

Young Egypt Party, 55, 57
Youssef, Hoda, 30
youth, 154, 198
  employment, 94

Zaghlul, Saad, 36
Zaki, Ramzi, 212–13, 238–9n9, 252, 255